Real People, Real Problems, Real Solutions

AF739695

Real People, Real Problems, Real Solutions offers a clear introduction to psychoanalytic practice from a Kleinian perspective and shows how the modern Kleinian works with the most taxing of their patients.

Illustrated by extensive case material, this book:

- Discusses Freud's original theoretical concepts and examines Klein's contributions to the field of psychoanalysis, clarifying and comparing the two approaches in the clinical setting.
- Identifies and explores who makes up the psychoanalyst's most challenging case load. Clinical material and dynamic theory help provide an understanding of the more difficult patients – often borderline, narcissistic, or psychotic in nature – who seek treatment for their distress, and demonstrate how the Kleinian psychoanalytic approach is helpful to these individuals.
- Reviews the current state of traditional methods of training at psychoanalytic institutes, which are shown to be in need of renewal and critical restructuring, especially for those who encounter difficult and taxing patients on a regular basis.

Through its integrated blending of clinical and theoretical findings *Real People, Real Problems, Real Solutions* shows how the average psychoanalyst and psychotherapist face many difficult patients in a typical day's work. This honest examination of challenging clinical problems will be a refreshing read for all practicing and training psychoanalysts and psychotherapists.

Robert Waska has worked in the field of psychology for the last 25 years. Certified as a psychoanalyst and psychoanalytic psychotherapist from the Institute of Psychoanalytic Studies, Dr Waska maintains a full-time practice in San Francisco and Marin County.

Real People, Real Problems, Real Solutions

The Kleinian psychoanalytic approach with difficult patients

Robert Waska

Routledge
Taylor & Francis Group
LONDON AND NEW YORK

First published 2005 by Routledge
2 Park Square, Milton Park, Abingdon, Oxfordshire OX14 4RN

Simultaneously published in the USA and Canada by Routledge
711 Third Avenue, New York, NY 10017

Routledge is an imprint of the Taylor & Francis Group, an informa business

Copyright © 2005 Robert Waska

Typeset in Times by Garfield Morgan, Rhayader, Powys
Cover design by Hybert Design
Cover image: 'Red' by Elizabeth Walton

All rights reserved. No part of this book may be reprinted or reproduced or utilized in any form or by any electronic, mechanical, or other means, now known or hereafter invented, including photocopying and recording, or in any information storage or retrieval system, without permission in writing from the publishers.

British Library Cataloguing in Publication Data
A catalogue record for this book is available from the British Library

Library of Congress Cataloging-in-Publication Data
Waska, Robert T.
Real people, real problems, real solutions : the Kleinian psychoanalytic approach with difficult patients / Robert Waska.– 1st ed.
p. cm.
Includes bibliographical references and index.
ISBN 978-1-58391-718-3 (hbk)
ISBN 978-1-138-01196-0 (pbk)
1. Klein, Melanie. 2. Psychoanalysis—Practice. 3. Psychotherapist and patient. 4. Analysands. I. Title.

RC506.W375 2005
616.89'17–dc22

2004016627

Contents

Acknowledgments

Over time, I have more and more gratitude for my wonderful wife. She continues to be a constant inspiration, support, and gentle critic for my ideas and writing style.

My patients make this book possible. It is through my daily contact with them and their lives that my ideas flow. I believe clinical material must be the foundation of any comprehensive psychoanalytic writing. My creativity and desire to understand the mysteries of the mind are fueled by the analyst–patient relationship. I thank all my patients for the insight they provide. I have altered, disguised, and censored all clinical material to protect their privacy.

Acknowledgment is due to the professional journals that have allowed the reprint of certain material. I thank the *American Journal of Psychoanalysis* for permission to reprint material in Chapter 7, *Psychodynamic Counselling* for permission to reprint material in Chapter 8, *Psychoanalytic Social Work* for permission to reprint material in Chapter 9, the *Journal of Contemporary Psychotherapy* for permission to reprint material in Chapter 10, *Psychodynamic Practice* for permission to reprint material in Chapter 12, and *Issues in Psychoanalytic Psychology* for permission to reprint material in Chapter 13.

Introduction

This book begins with a summary of the psychoanalytic method, first with the Freudian approach and then with an overview of the Kleinian stance. Levenson (1983) describes how the many different schools within psychoanalysis all share a common principle. The analyst sifts through the patient's symptoms, associations, and transference reactions to put some sort of order to the patient's experience. This is relayed to the patient in the form of a transference interpretation. When successful, this brings on new material that is then again reordered within an object-relational context.

Chapter 1 introduces the reader to the basic ingredients of the Freudian approach and how this perspective helps the patient to understand and process their internal experiences. The core techniques that guide the Freudian analyst are examined.

Chapter 2 offers a brief historical background of Melanie Klein and the psychoanalytic movement she fostered. Her views on the mind are outlined and compared to Freud's theories. Contemporary Kleinian approaches to psychoanalysis are explored, including the Kleinian understanding of the ego and the object.

Chapter 3 provides the reader with an understanding of the role of the contemporary Kleinian psychoanalyst. While many essential cornerstones of classical theory and clinical technique remain unchanged, the Modern Kleinian is an analyst who now emphasizes certain methods over others. Recent literature is reviewed to show the details of what makes up today's Kleinian practitioner.

Chapter 4 discusses the utility of the psychoanalytic perspective as an instrument of theory building, a method of diagnosis, and a manner of treatment. Psychological treatments that are infused by the psychoanalytic method have a deeper and richer quality. These offer more for patients who need more, due to their shattered inner lives. These difficult and complex patients are explored from both a Freudian and then a Kleinian perspective. Case material is used to look at the internal states of mind these individuals struggle with and the types of often chaotic, dynamic situations they establish in the analytic setting.

Because of these less than ideal therapeutic circumstances, many treatments never seem to get off the ground. They end almost as quickly as they begin. Diagnostically, these patients are often borderline, narcissistic, or psychotic. While it is easy to dismiss these cases as failed, aborted, or unanalyzable, they are valuable to study. In private practice settings, the psychoanalyst is used to these brief, disjointed, and inconsistent experiences with patients who test the analyst's ability to organize, understand, and transform the elements of their pathology. In Chapter 5, case material is used to illustrate these vexing situations that usually combine a lack of frequency, acting out of internal conflicts and phantasies in an intense and complicated manner, and an abortive termination after a short stay in treatment.

In Chapter 6, psychoanalytic treatment is examined as a process in which the analyst helps a patient understand unconscious feelings and phantasies by using interpretation. The greatest block to this process is the patient's acting out the transference within and outside the clinical setting. This acting out is sometimes in physical action, but often occurs as strong projections and projective identification mechanisms. Many patients begin a psychoanalytic treatment only to quickly destroy the process via this type of acting out. While frequency, use of couch, method of termination, and other methodology are helpful to consider, analysis of the transference and the resistance (acting out) to the analysis of the transference remain the cornerstones. Melanie Klein's contributions are reviewed and case examples of acting out are provided.

For a variety of reasons, psychoanalytic training is done in a vacuum. Chapter 7 looks at how psychoanalytic training often teaches a theory and a way of practicing that does not always translate well to day-to-day private practice work. The clinical realities of psychoanalytic practice prove the psychoanalytic method to be one that provides help to a wider audience than classical psychoanalytic training programs might suggest. The psychoanalytic approach offers the analyst many special opportunities to work with and be helpful to a wide variety of patients. Analysts who accept the limitations as well as the wide application and broad benefits of the psychoanalytic approach may have a more fulfilling experience than their training experiences might foster. At the same time, the analyst's level of therapeutic skill, the patient's diagnosis, and many multiple external factors create different limitations in the practice and outcome of psychoanalytic work.

So, in Chapter 7, extensive case material is used to show the broad range of patients who are helped by the psychoanalytic method. The clinical material also shows the less than perfect, but often good enough outcomes of these difficult cases with often severely disturbed patients.

Chapter 8 takes a detailed look at the mental structure commonly found in patients who challenge us the most. From a Kleinian viewpoint, the intra-psychic and interpersonal aspects of the paranoid-schizoid patient (Klein, 1946) are explored. The issue of early external trauma is discussed and compared with the optimal conditions one would hope for with infantile development. An extensive case report of a psychotic patient is used to show the benefits of using the analytic method with a very difficult patient who was unable to break out of severe persectory fears and phantasies.

As discussed in the previous chapters, there are many brief, demanding, aborted cases that no one ever writes about. The typical psychoanalyst or psychoanalytic psychotherapist, however, has many of these short-lived, intense encounters with more severely disturbed patients. These cases add to our knowledge about the mind and its functions, and should not be ignored as non-analytic or non-instructive. In addition, it is unrealistic to think we can always help a very anxious and troubled person to enter the treatment process with immediate success. It is more instructive to apply the analytic method, offer the patient what we can, and have both analyst and patient learn as much as they can in the time they are able to stay together. In Chapter 9, case material is used to bring technical concepts and theory to life. The reader becomes more familiar with the Kleinian approach to working analytically with these difficult patients.

Whether focusing on transference or extra-transference material, the Kleinian analyst interprets the patient's internal phantasies and anxieties regarding the self and its important objects. This analytic stance tends to relieve the patient's immediate anxiety and set the stage for potential self-reflection and the start of basic working-through processes.

As candidates, and later as practicing analysts, we filter the idea of what patients, analysts, and the analytic process should look like through our own ego-ideal. The literature often leans toward a theoretical ideal and further distorts the picture. Finally, we are often confused by the quest for the perfect patient who meets the criteria for analyzability outlined by our training institute, our supervisors, our teachers, and our own demanding superegos. Chapter 10 examines several cases of clinical work that fall far short of any ideal. However, these realistic snapshots of day-to-day clinical work are too important to be simply ignored as failed cases with unanalyzable patients. Often, even the briefest of clinical encounters enriches the analyst's understanding of human functioning; it occasionally benefits the patient as well. If the analyst uses the analytic stance with all of his patients, a useful discourse may take place with some of them. These cases are not so-called standard or complete analytic treatments, but the results are often valuable to the practitioner and potentially helpful to the patient.

Therefore, Chapter 11 continues to consider the many patients who enter into treatment and remain for only a brief time. While the analyst may wish to conduct a long-term intensive treatment with multiple weekly visits and a focus on the transference, dreams, and free associations, some patients make that wish impossible. These patients define the nature of the analytic process by their acting out, their financial hardships, their external chaos, and by particular self-object phantasies, often persecutory in nature. Some of these encounters prove beneficial and others seem to end with things merely *status quo*.

Using case material, several such treatments are explored and the psychoanalytic method is shown to be beneficial to some degree in many such cases. While brief and often chaotic encounters with difficult patients are common in private practice settings, not much is written about them (Waska, 2003). This lack of attention in the literature seems to say that these cases are not really analytic since they don't follow the regular rules. The analytic method is too powerful to be discarded due to lack of allegiance to certain formulaic rules or environmental criteria. Even in less than optimal settings with irregular or atypical cases, the analyst can help the patient toward better internal integration to some degree. This is the analytic goal with cases that stretch the norm of a traditional framework.

Chapter 12 deals with the public image of whom and what a psychoanalyst is and how they provide help to patients. This image is cloudy, confusing, and often negative. The distortion of what the average analyst does in his or her private practice is complicated by the professional literature. The literature often provides an idealized picture of someone practicing "pure" psychoanalysis with pre-qualified patients, screened as "analyzable," while modifications, countertransference problems, or seemingly unreachable patients are avoided. This creates a false image of what analysts really do in the clinical situation and maintains a distant and difficult-to-grasp idea for the public. If the field of psychoanalysis is to sustain itself, which is not the case in current times, it will have to be more honest and open with the public and within its own professional circles about what it really means to be a practicing psychoanalyst. These matters are discussed and several cases from an average day in the life of an analyst are provided to begin shedding light on this timely issue.

In Chapter 13, the clinical reality of day-to-day practice for the psychoanalyst in private practice continues to be examined. The discrepancies between what psychoanalysts actually do, what kind of patients they really see, and the true nature of how they practice is compared to the type of training psychoanalytic institutes provide. Considering the resulting disjuncture, several ideas are proposed for improvement. The overall negative public view of psychoanalysis is discussed and the way the profession creates an idealistic, unrealistic caricature is explored. Finally, two case examples are presented to show the difference between actual psychoanalytic treatments in the real world and the more rigid and idealistic visions of psychoanalysis offered in training programs.

Part I

The approach

Chapter 1

An overview of the psychoanalytic method

The Freudian model

The psychoanalyst works in a way distinct from other professions. Friends may give advice and suggestions. Social workers help modify the patient's environment, social system, and day-to-day stresses. Crisis counselors use behavioral interventions and direct suggestion. Pastors offer direction according to spiritual laws and religious doctrine. Counselors give practical ideas for the problems of daily living, emphasizing logic and common sense. They act as a sort of coach, professional friend, or mentor. Psychiatrists and physicians prescribe medications to help raise or lower certain moods and alleviate certain symptoms. The psychoanalyst will use these approaches when necessary. Most of the time, however, the techniques and goals are quite different.

Psychoanalytic therapy, as based on the theories of Sigmund Freud and his followers, is a profoundly different approach from other helping fields. Freud introduced a theory and technique from which all other psychotherapeutic approaches have evolved (Meier, 1989). Freud's premise of a dynamic unconscious and the importance of personality development as shaped by early parenting experiences is now taken for granted in many therapeutic approaches.

Psychoanalytic therapy is characterized by the study of the patient's interpersonal and intra-psychic relationship to the analyst as well as other persons, the patient's daydreams and night dreams, and their efforts to "tell all" or free associate. The analyst uses these criteria as a way to understand the patient's internal thoughts and feelings about himself and others. Psychoanalytic theory holds that all behavior and symptoms have deeper meanings which are initially unconscious. The patient's thoughts, feelings, and daydreams, however illogical or distorted, are carefully studied as an avenue into the unconscious mind's motivations. Just as a dream is analyzed rather than ignored, symptoms are examined rather than quickly eliminated. To the skilled medical physician, symptoms are clues to the deeper functioning of the human body. So too for the psychoanalyst when confronted with psychiatric symptoms.

The psychoanalyst helps the patient explore their unconscious ideas about the important people in their life and their desires and feelings toward them. Warded-off fears, anxieties, and aspirations are slowly understood and worked with. The relationship between the analyst and patient is used as a primary vehicle to understand how the patient's mind works.

Aggressive and loving feelings are directed not just at people in the patient's current circle of friends and family, but at internal images of these persons. These images are distorted by strong feelings and thoughts. Therefore, therapy is never a linear, one-to-one type of process. It is the examination of changing, dramatic, and contradictory versions of the self and important others.

The psychoanalytic approach tries to understand the impact of the past on the present and how that impact recycles throughout the patient's current life. Again, this is not just blaming parents for how they raised their children. The psychoanalyst realizes that child and parent impact each other and the child's internal phantasies shape their early history and memory just as much as external reality does.

The patient's deepest wishes, anxieties, and defenses against anxiety are looked at with the tool of transference/countertransference analysis. Interpretation is the primary vehicle in this process.

Transference refers to the rigid and repetitious manner in which the patient relates to the analyst and others, based on unconscious fears and desires. Countertransference is the way the analyst feels in response to this. Interpretation is what the analyst says to the patient about this. The analyst tries to organize and verbally translate the disguised and distorted feelings and thoughts that make up the transference. The analyst asks the patient to tell everything that he is thinking and feeling, to be as open as possible. The idea is to censor nothing. Every topic has the same value. This is an impossible request because the mind naturally censors itself. Therefore, how the patient deals with the request to tell all offers important information. The analyst observes and explores how the patient struggles with censoring certain topics while elaborating others.

The over-arching theoretical principal in psychoanalytic therapy is the concept of the dynamic unconscious and how it determines much of a person's actions and reactions. The major clinical principle is to help the patient engage with this internal world in order to work through basic conflicts and anxieties. Teyber (1988) has clarified the therapist's task as helping patients make the difficult transition from believing others are the source of their problems to seeing themselves as responsible. It follows that this shift brings the source of resolution from others to oneself (from external to internal). In the early stages of treatment, the patient often says, "it is their fault and they have to change!" This projection must be slowly understood and owned as a part of the self to be worked through.

This blaming of others is particularly true for more regressed or primitive patients functioning within the paranoid–schizoid position (Klein, 1946).

The paranoid–schizoid position is a more simplistic internal experience where projection is favored and all problems are externalized. On the other hand, higher functioning patients in the depressive position (Klein, 1935) tend to rely on introjection and come to treatment with strong feelings of guilt, self-blame, and the inability to acknowledge intense feelings toward others.

Out of countertransference discomfort, the analyst can easily fall into helping the patient externalize their problems. The more the patient and analyst blame others, the more the therapy feels like it is "us" against "them." This is much more comfortable than to have complicated, strong feelings permeate the therapeutic relationship. Indeed, this is why many psychotherapists avoid the transference. To fully engage the transference is to bring all of the patient's focus inwards, which often means the therapist is now blamed. When therapist and patient collude to avoid the transference, the treatment can seem more like a friendly chat where a friend gives advice. In this situation, therapists try to educate, reassure, explain, and even self-disclose. Talking about how the therapist deals with his life is a wonderful way to distract the patient from exploring and understanding how they experience and react to themselves and others, including the therapist.

The mind is composed of conflicting drives of love and hate, life and death, libido and aggression (Ursano and Sonnenberg, 1991). These conflicts create internal distress and external symptoms. Psychoanalytic therapy attempts to access these unconscious conflicts and help the patient see how they contribute to these problems, maintaining their own suffering. In this way, the patient begins to feel like a free agent, more independent, and capable of finding solutions to their complex lives.

By working through internal conflicts involving need, love, fear, and hate, which are externalized onto people, places, and things, a gradual integration takes place. Rather than being unable to make a decision or having to deny one's true feelings, these ideas and feelings become more of a helpful spectrum of reactions to reality. These various feelings can serve as a map or creative strategy of how to understand oneself better and to assess one's environment, instead of a signal to flee or fight. In other words, the less one distorts reality, the more one can deal with reality.

Counseling, compared to psychoanalytic therapy, often focuses solely on the interpersonal aspects of the patient's external life (how they are with their boss, family, and friends). Then, the counselor will try to use suggestion or manipulation to achieve a behavioral change in those interpersonal patterns.

Psychoanalytic therapy also focuses on, among other things, the patient's interpersonal patterns with the therapist and others. However, this information is used as a clue or pathway to the patient's intra-psychic organization. It is through the analysis of the intra-psychic material that lasting interpersonal change comes about.

Psychoanalytic therapy is best conducted frequently. A minimum of one or two sessions a week is needed for the process to occur. Otherwise, most of the conversation becomes a task of "catch up" about external events. Ideally, the patient is seen three to five times a week, but many successful treatments are carried out in a one to two sessions a week model.

Bibring (1954) outlined five basic techniques the analyst can engage in: suggestive, abreactive, manipulative, clarifying, and interpretive. The basic goal of psychoanalytic therapy is insight into unconscious conflicts and is achieved through the use of clarification and interpretation. All psychological therapies use all five techniques. However, psychoanalytic therapy places an emphasis on clarification and interpretation.

Suggestion is the imposition of certain beliefs onto the patient. By the use of authority and subtle or not-so-subtle direction, the therapist tells the patient what to do. This technique is modeled on hypnosis and does not allow for the patient's autonomy to be part of the cure. Telling the patient to bring in dreams or to stop fighting with his wife or to stop drinking are all part of the therapist's use of his power of authority to shape the patient's thinking and actions.

Abreaction refers to the use of emotional discharge as a therapeutic measure. Based on Freud's first model of the mind, the topographic model, the method is to get the patient to expel all pent-up emotions. It is used in "de-briefing" exercises and patients refer to it as "getting a load off their chest." The venting of emotions and ridding of dammed-up feelings is usually part of any therapy process, but is often used by itself in counseling treatments as the chief tool and goal. Finding an outlet for buried feelings and thoughts is important, but by itself usually offers only temporary relief.

Manipulation is similar in some ways to suggestion. It includes ways of trying to run the patient's life by advice, guidance and so forth. Reframing the patient's idea of something negative into something positive ("losing your job may be an opportunity to pursue what you really love") is a manipulation of perspective. Also, subtle encouragement of the psychological process of splitting is a common result of manipulation. This happens when the counselor or therapist positions the treatment as something good that stands against something else that is deemed bad. Counseling a battered woman on how to escape her abusive husband is a use of suggestion and manipulation in that the therapist tells the patient what to do and positions themselves as good and wise and the husband as bad and wrong. In the process, the patient's autonomy is forfeited and the abusive relationship is re-enacted in the treatment setting. Certainly there are times when it is appropriate and necessary to tell the patient what to do, but these life and death situations rarely arise.

The following is an example of manipulation and splitting contributing to an acting out of pathology rather than an analysis of it. I started to see a patient who had grown up in a family where she felt extremely controlled and infantilized by her mother. She grew up and married a man who controlled her and treated her as if she had no common sense. At one point, she was so upset over being bullied that she sought out a therapist. She went to this therapist for several years. From the patient's account, this therapist told her how to act, how to behave with her husband, and urged her to go back to school. The therapist would call the patient at home and "check up" on her each week to see if she was all right and if she was following through with the advice. My patient felt that this was very helpful and that it showed care. After our second appointment, my patient called and said she had bumped into this old therapist and told her that she was seeing me. The therapist told her that she could stop seeing me, resume treatment with her, and she would be charged a modest fee that she could "owe" and pay back later. My patient said this invitation was too good to pass up. I chose to not say anything because I felt I would be fighting a losing battle and would become a part of the splitting. I would end up criticizing the "bad" therapist and advocating she stay with me, the "good" therapist. This patient's "therapy" was really an acting out of a controlling and bossy mother/therapist with a submissive and bullied daughter/patient. They sided together as one good object to fight off the offensive bad husband object. Unfortunately, this is an all too common situation.

This patient never paid my bill either. I felt this was her defiant revenge in which she felt she would not give in to the object or share part of herself. In fact, by her actions, she demanded I give to her for free.

Finally, there are more outright manipulations of the patient and his environment such as hospitalization and medication. In general, manipulation is used with the idea that there can be positive therapeutic change by influencing the patient's experience. This emotional retraining or re-parenting is the central tenet in many non-analytic therapies. Generally, some schools of counseling or therapy advocate direct manipulation and use such ideas as "fostering the positive therapeutic alliance," while others avoid any use of manipulation and instead try to analyze both the positive and negative aspects of the transference. Freudian and Kleinian approaches advocate the full exploration of all positive and negative feelings, thoughts, and phantasies.

While suggestion, abreaction, and manipulation do not provide the patient with any degree of self-understanding or deep insight into the nature of the self, clarification and interpretation do.

As discussed above, the interactive counselor uses suggestion to manipulate the patient. This may or may not be deliberate and at times is unavoidable. Some analytic procedures are railroaded into counseling by the patient's resistance and defensive style. If a patient is prone to intense acting out, suggestion is sometimes helpful. If it can then be discussed and analyzed, the treatment may still be considered psychoanalytic. In this sense, parameters (Eissler, 1953) are part of every treatment, but remain a part of the treatment in only some situations. Sometimes I am called upon by the patient to be such a regular referee or policeman in their lives that we never have the time to dig deeper. When the patient keeps showing up with black eyes, new police warrants, or drunk, suggestion begins to move the treatment away from being psychoanalytic. This is not to say that now there has been some type of permanent contamination and that the treatment can never be shifted back into a more analytic process. Indeed, transference is such a fundamental part of the human experience that it can rarely be "ruined" by outside circumstances. However, without a certain degree of stability in the relationship and without a chance to investigate the acting out, the treatment can be forced into becoming an interactive counseling at best or else corrupted into premature closure.

The regular use of suggestion and the deliberate avoidance of the transference can certainly kill off any chance of achieving a psychoanalytic process. However, there are times when these two manipulations can actually be necessary in creating or maintaining a psychoanalytic treatment. When a young psychotic man told me he was about to move out of the country with a woman he had just met to marry her and give her the ten children she demanded, I asked him to tell me about it. When he told me he had purchased the airline tickets, I told him it was a bad idea and that he needed to return them immediately so we could have a chance to understand what was going on. In his case, he literally would have left treatment to pursue a self-destructive course of events. Based on his history of having done such things in the past, I used suggestion to save the treatment.

When a borderline patient continued beating his wife and breaking her car windows, I told him he must stop immediately. The first patient, the young psychotic man, stayed and we finished a treatment together that was very much an exploration of his phantasies about his internal objects. My telling him what to do or not do become part of our quest to understand how he invited me and others to lead him around and dominate him. With the second borderline patient, the treatment remained an interactive counseling in which I became an auxiliary ego support.

In clarification, the therapist or analyst helps the patient clarify his feelings, fears, and deeper thoughts. The therapist restates what the patient says in a clearer and more precise manner. This helps the patient view and reflect on what he is feeling and encourages him to elaborate on it further. When the patient says he is "uptight" and wants to "bust loose and get out of town," the therapist clarifies it by noting how he is probably feeling anxious and worried about something and wants to avoid it.

With interpretation, the main focus is on the patient's unconscious life. Instead of staying exclusively with what the patient has said, the therapist makes a hypothetical leap to explain the patient's material in the form of unconscious fears, wishes, and phantasies. This proposal or explanation is tried on for size by the patient and their reaction helps demonstrate the validity of the interpretation. Clarification prepares the way for the interpretation and helps in understanding the patient's reaction to the interpretation. This back and forth dynamic of using the techniques of clarification and interpretation constitutes the art of "working through."

Interpretations are usually statements about the transference. In other words, the therapist interprets the patient's deeper phantasies and fears about their relationship to the therapist and to other important people in their lives. After clarifying that the patient's "uptight" feelings of wanting to "bust loose" are probably feelings of deeper anxiety, the therapist might make the interpretation, "I think you are anxious because I suggested we start meeting more often." The therapist would then listen closely to the patient's response for any evidence to judge the accuracy of the interpretation.

Suggestion, abreaction, and manipulation exist in all psychotherapies. In psychoanalytic therapy, these techniques are used very sparingly and for the sole purpose of advancing the process of clarification and interpretation. Clarification is the analytic springboard to interpretation and works in collaboration with it as the basis for the analytic treatment process. Interpretation is the chief vehicle by which the analyst helps the patient see their unconscious object relations at work in transference and extra-transference situations.

Psychoanalytic therapy relies primarily on the tool of interpretation. It is used to analyze the patient's transference, defenses, and anxieties.

Freud's idea of what constituted interpretation changed as his theory of the mind evolved. When Freud was still influenced by the practice of hypnosis, interpretation constituted telling the patient about their repressed memories of seduction. Later, he realized these memories were not always literal mental records of past traumas, but unconscious phantasies that were repressed. Thus, interpretations became the vehicle of helping the patient realize his repressed sexual phantasies. With time, this included the element of repressed aggressive wishes. After Freud elaborated the structural model of the mind, interpretations became a method of exploring the patient's resistance and transference. The analyst now interpreted defenses that protected libidinal and aggressive wishes and associated fears.

Interpretations are those explanations given to the patient that move the patient to a greater knowledge of their inner life. Freudian interpretations encompass various goals. Transference interpretations focus on the therapeutic relationship as the best area to understand the patient's conflicts. Extra-transference interpretations explore manifestations of those conflicts in areas other than the patient–analyst pair. Reconstructions piece together data gathered in the analysis to build historical possibilities that would explain the patient's current dilemma. Character interpretations are used to help the patient explore long-standing ways of viewing and relating to the world. Resistance interpretations show the patient where they suddenly shift direction, change affect, divert attention, or turn away from their associations. Freudian interpretations tend to examine what is most at the surface of the mind and what is affectively prominent.

Laplanche and Pontalis (1973) outline interpretation as:

> (a) [The] procedure which, by means of analytic investigation, brings out the latent meaning in what the subject says and does. Interpretation reveals the modes of the defensive conflict and its ultimate aim is to identify the wish that is expressed by every product of the unconscious. (b) In the context of the treatment, the interpretation is what is conveyed to the subject in order to make him reach this latent meaning, according to rules dictated by the way the treatment is being run and the way it is evolving.
>
> (pp. 227–228)

They note that Freud first outlined his approach to interpretations as they applied to dreams:

> Starting from the account given by the dreamer (the manifest content), the interpretation, according to Freud, uncovers the meaning of the dream as it is formulated in the latent content to which the free associations lead us. The ultimate goal of the interpretation is the unconscious wish, and the phantasy in which this wish is embodied. Naturally the term "interpretation" is not reserved for the dream – that major product of the unconscious; it is also applied to its other products (parapraxes, symptoms, etc.) and, more generally, to whatever part of the speech and behavior of the subject bears the stamp of the defensive conflict.
>
> (pp. 227–228)

Interpretation is the analyst's main occupation in relation to the patient, whose main occupation is the attempt at free association. The patient provides information via memories, fantasies, wishes, fears, and actions that the analyst translates into words that go beyond the patient's conscious awareness. The patient eventually shifts their psychic relationship with the analyst to meet unconscious expectations and to relive old experiences. This establishes the transference neurosis, which interpretation is designed to explore, translate, and work through.

Moore and Fine (1990) write:

> Genetic interpretations connect present feelings, thoughts, conflicts, and behaviors with their historical antecedents, often dating back to early childhood. Reconstruction is part of the process of genetic

> interpretation, consisting of the piecing together of information about psychologically significant early experiences. This information is gathered from dreams, free association, transference distortions, and other sources of analytic data. Dynamic interpretations clarify conflicting mental trends that result in particular behaviors, feelings, and other mental activities. Transference interpretations reveal and explain distortions in the therapeutic relationship that are based upon the displacement onto the figure of the analyst of feelings, attitudes, and behaviors originally experienced with significant past figures, usually parents and siblings. Anagogic interpretation, usually involving dream material, uncovers and clarifies abstract ideas that, due to the difficulty of directly representing them in mental images, are represented in allegorical form.
>
> (pp. 103–104)

Campbell (1989) adds his own description of Freudian interpretation:

> [interpretation is] the description or formulation of the meaning or significance of a patient's productions and, particularly, the translation into a form meaningful for the patient of his resistance and symbols and character defenses . . . Interpretation has multiple functions, including providing the patient with insight and understanding; increasing the patient's awareness of his mental life; making unconscious aspects of experience conscious; undoing repression; constructing or reconstructing memories of critical and possibly pathogenic early experiences.
>
> (pp. 380–381)

Chapter 2

Melanie Klein and the Kleinian approach

At the age of twenty-eight, a woman named Melanie Klein read Freud's book on dreams. This led her into a lifelong fascination with the theory and technique of psychoanalysis. Klein went into analysis with Sandor Ferenczi and with his encouragement she started treating young children. This was revolutionary because no one had ever analyzed children younger than seven years of age.

Klein wrote her first paper in 1919, on the psychological development of children. She went into her second personal analysis with Karl Abraham in Berlin. There, in 1921, she began to treat adults as well as children. In 1927, Klein moved to England where she continued to write books, teach, and practice psychoanalysis until her death in 1962. She always based her interpretive technique on the transference. She consistently linked the here-and-now of the patient–analyst pair, the patient's internal phantasy[1] life, and the external reality of past and present. She did not use educational methods, instructions, or reassurances. Rather than rely on suggestion or authority, she stayed with the transference theme within the clinical situation.

Klein believed, as do her followers, that both the positive and negative transference must be analyzed. Rather than seeing the need for a therapeutic alliance from which patient and analyst both worked on the negative, she felt that the entire personality, the full spectrum of emotions and thoughts, were important to understand. Instead of thinking that some patients are too fragile to analyze and therefore must be supported and the defenses strengthened, she thought that proper analysis of the patient's anxieties and troubling phantasies promoted growth and strengthened the ego.

Klein felt that the infant is faced with two developmental levels of experience. She called these "positions" and felt we all are constantly

1 The use of this spelling, in place of "fantasy," indicates the unconscious nature of the process.

moving back and forth between them. The paranoid–schizoid position is the earliest state of more primitive anxiety and idealization. The infantile ego is faced with libidinal desires for knowledge, satisfaction, and gratification. At the same time, aggressive drives aim to do away with these needs in oneself and others. These conflicts between the life and death instincts are difficult for the mind to deal with, so certain defense mechanisms are used. Splitting, projective identification, denial, and idealization are common ways of coping. Love and hate, good and bad, are artificially separated. The ego and the object are split into good and evil. All mental activity begins to revolve around this internal situation.

Later, with positive internal and external experiences, the ego starts to integrate. This new depressive position ushers in a time where ambivalence is possible. Finally, the self and the object are felt to be not all good or all bad, but a mixture of the two. Separation, difference, and imperfection can be tolerated. Mourning is the new developmental task as the ego feels capable of hurting its objects. With whole-object functioning, reparation, guilt, and forgiveness are possible. If one loves and hates the same person, ambivalence is achieved and complex internal and interpersonal negotiations are necessary, instead of a black-and-white world. The paranoid–schizoid position is mainly a pre-Oedipal two-person experience while the depressive position is home to the three-person, Oedipal conflicts.

Melanie Klein extended Freud's principles of theory and technique but kept in line with his basic tenets. She put clinical life into his ideas about unconscious conflict. To her, these were not biological urges in mechanistic conflict over sexual gratification. Klein felt the mind was full of dramatic phantasies, with different aspects of the personality in union or in battle with different aspects of important persons. She called these unconscious representations of loved and hated persons "objects," to make it clear they were internal images, not actual people. Klein showed, through her analysis of children and adults, that there is a internal theater full of ghosts of ourselves and others that are in constant relationship to each other. These unconscious relationships are played out in the transference and throughout daily life. Therefore, how the patient relates to his boss, his wife, his children, his co-workers, and his analyst all give clues to the conflicts, anxieties, and defenses in the unconscious. Just as Freud had pointed out, Klein felt these phantasies were a shifting, dynamic record of actual external events, heavily distorted by the wishes, fears, and conflicts of the ego.

Melanie Klein was strongly influenced by Freud and tried to keep her theories close to Freud's core methodology (Klein, 1926; Schafer, 1994; Bion, *et al.*, 1961). Indeed, Modern Kleinians are, as was Klein herself, extending Freudian thought rather than offering a paradigm shift (Stein, 1990; Segal, 1974).

Regarding the practice of Kleinian analysis, Schafer (1997) states:

> It is assumed, first, that whatever the analysand says or does rests on a substructure of unconscious fantasies, and analysis proceeds by interpreting these fantasies at propitious moments and appropriate levels . . . It is also assumed that the analysand's saying or doing anything in the analytic situation implies something about her or his experience of the relationship with the analyst . . . Thirdly, it is assumed that rather than highlighting what is conventionally realistic, adaptive, and role-appropriate, the analyst's interventions should more or less subordinate these details to interpretation of the unconscious transference fantasies by showing how these "realistic" factors are being used seductively, offensively, or defensively as vehicles or props.
>
> (p. 6)

Most contemporary psychotherapy approaches, practiced by either analysts or psychodynamically oriented therapists seeing patients once or twice a week, are based on the three schools of psychoanalysis maintained in the British Psychoanalytical Society. These are the Freudian, Kleinian, and Middle schools (see below). Kleinian analysis is currently the most prominent mode of psychoanalytic practice in the world, followed by Freudian. Space does not permit an exploration of some significant figures in the history of American psychoanalysis. However, many of these US leaders were influenced by these three schools.

When Melanie Klein arrived in England and began teaching at the British Psychoanalytic Society, Anna Freud was the recognized leader. As analysts began to appreciate Klein's views, there was a tension within the institute. After a series of conferences in which the two camps made their differences clear, the Society decided to divide the teaching tracks into two paths: the Freudian and the Kleinian.

Eventually, a third track was added. These analysts called themselves the Independents or the British Middle school. The Middle school tends to center the psychological treatment around the environmental and relational aspects of a patient's history. Interpretation is not used as much and the general idea is that the patient must regress to their internal point of trauma. With a supportive, therapeutic environment, the ego can then "get back on track." Again, space does not permit a more thorough review.

The Freudian school is based on Sigmund Freud's and, later, Anna Freud's view of the mind. This is a focus on intrapsychic and biological drive gratification and the analysis of defense. Analysis is centered around the understanding of impulse, drive, defense, and compromise. Chapter 1 outlined the major clinical and theoretical themes within the Freudian camp.

The Kleinian school aims to analyze unconscious phantasies, and the dynamic internal world made up of self and object representations that operate within a matrix of drives, defenses, and internal bargains between self and object or parts of self and parts of object. The Kleinian view is that the biological drives (the life and death forces) exist and are channeled into mental representations called phantasies. These phantasies color the ego and make for countless dramas between internal views of self and object. The word "object" is the Kleinian (based on Freud's usage) method of drawing a distinction between a conscious awareness of an external person and the internal, unconscious image of the self or another important figure. Interpretation of the patient's phantasies and the transference, as well as defenses and compromise formations, is the goal of analysis.

From her work with children, Melanie Klein had discovered that anxiety was important to focus on from the very beginning of a treatment. Therefore, her interpretations were aimed at the patient's anxiety, usually about the analytic relationship. Klein found that these types of interpretations reduced anxiety. She also thought the negative transference had to be addressed from the start for an analysis to be effective. Once this occurred, there was more room for the patient's love for the analyst to become known (Hinshelwood, 1991).

Klein in 1943 wrote:

> From my work with children I came to certain conclusions that have to some extent influenced my technique with adults. Take transference first. I found that with children the transference (positive or negative) is active from the beginning of analysis, since for instance even an attitude of indifference cloaks anxiety and hostility. With adults too I found that the transference situation is present from the start in one way or another, and I have come, therefore, to make use of transference interpretations early in analysis.
>
> (unreferenced quote found on website)

Klein made interpretations to the patient based on her belief in the totality of transference in the analytic situation. She stated in 1952:

> we are accustomed to speak of the transference situation. But do we always keep in mind the fundamental importance of this concept? It is my experience that in unraveling the details of the transference it is essential to think in terms of total situations transferred from the past into the present, as well as of emotions, defenses, and object relations.
>
> (Klein, 1952a, p. 55)

In making her interpretations, Hinshelwood (1991) says:

> She [Klein] noticed that the reactions of the patient were more significant than his conscious responses. The unconscious meanings of the

association that comes immediately after an interpretation is more important than any conscious agreement or argument.

(p. 19)

Segal (1974) states:

> [Klein's] interpretive technique [with children] was based, as with the adult, predominantly on the transference, and by transference I do not mean here-and-now interpretations, but suitable links being made between the here-and-now, the child's inner world of phantasies, and its links with external reality, present and past. Klein used no educational methods, gave no instructions, nor reassurances.
>
> (page unknown)

In 1926, Klein pointed out that:

> [child and adult analyses are] essentially the same. Consistent interpretations, gradual solving of resistance and persistent tracing of the transference to earlier situations – these constitute in children as in adults the correct analytic situation.
>
> (p. 137)

Here it seems her technique is not so different than Freud's. Indeed, she strove to remain close to Freud's main theoretical and clinical ideas.

Later, in 1946, Klein offered more specific information on her methods of interpretation:

> I have repeatedly found that advances in synthesis are brought about by interpretations of the specific causes for splitting. Such interpretations must deal in detail with the transference-situation at that moment, including of course the connection with the past, and must contain a reference to the details of the anxiety-situations which drive the ego to regress to schizoid mechanisms. The synthesis resulting from interpretations on these lines goes along with depression and anxieties of various kinds. Gradually such waves of depression – followed by greater integration – lead to a lessening of schizoid phenomena and also to fundamental changes in object relations.
>
> (p. 21)

In 1957, Klein wrote about the technical difficulties, the goals, and the components of making an interpretation:

> Our attempts to help the patient to integrate only carry conviction if we can show him, in the material both present and past, how and why he is

> again and again splitting off parts of his self . . . The anxiety that prevents integration has to be fully understood and interpreted in the transference situation. I have earlier pointed out the threat, both to the self and to the analyst, arising in the patient's mind if split-off parts of the self are regained in the analysis. In dealing with this anxiety one should not underrate the loving impulses when they can be detected in the material. For it is these which in the end enable the patient to mitigate his hate and envy.
>
> (p. 226)

The persistence of the analyst in attending to the particular nature of both the patient's anxiety and the patient's love, hidden among the more blatant hostility, is just one of the clinical treasures in Melanie Klein's interpretive stance.

Etchegoyen (1991) writes:

> Klein interprets in a special way – a way that is different from that of others, although it is not easy to indicate what its peculiarity consists in. Klein interprets more frequently than other analysts, and her tactic consists in interpreting (at least in the child) as soon as possible. If the patient contributes material, she considers that this attitude is born of his positive transference. To delay interpretation will only lead to situations of anxiety and resistance. If anxiety and resistance appear spontaneously, then there is greater reason to interpret in order to allay the former and reduce the latter . . . Klein followed her method, undaunted. It consisted in the end in interpreting the fantasy that was operating (as she saw it) and the anxiety that interpretation could awake . . . risks are real and in some measure inevitable in Kleinian interpretation, which should be weighed against the undeniable virtues of this way of operating. It consists of interpreting with no other commitment or goal than that of making conscious the unconscious, without allowing oneself ever to be led by complacency and weakness, without fearing the consequences of saying what the analyst considers is happening in the mind of the analysand, and which he ought to express.
>
> (pp. 415–416)

Clearly, Klein followed Freud's basic ideas in formulating interpretations. However, she made particular emphases and certain new extensions. She felt that interpretations should focus on the transference nearly exclusively. This was to be done in the here-and-now as well as in genetic reconstruction. Phantasy is a primary shaper of the transference. Therefore, interpretation of phantasy material was vital. To Klein, interpretations were to aim at the principal anxiety the patient was experiencing. Therefore, in place of strict defense analysis, Klein emphasized analysis of both defense and anxiety. While this at times meant deeper and faster interpretations, usually it meant more complete and complex interpretations. The patient's total internal experience was sought after and then explained to him. The patient's affect, phantasies, and total relationship to the analyst were considered the pathways to making the most useful interpretation at the most useful moment.

Chapter 3

The Modern Kleinians

Rather than describing a particular group of people or a certain school of any given country, I use the term "Modern Kleinian" to denote those therapists and analysts who use a particular approach to the clinical situation. This approach is grounded in Melanie Klein's original theory and technique, yet has grown to be different in some ways and expanded in others. Spillius (1988) writes:

> Most of the basic features of Kleinian technique, as Segal notes, are closely derived from Freud: rigorous maintenance of the psychoanalytic setting so as to keep the transference as pure and uncontaminated as possible; an expectation of sessions five times a week; emphasis on the transference as the central focus of analyst–patient interaction; a belief that the transference situation is active from the very beginning of the analysis; an attitude of active receptivity rather than passivity and silence; interpretation of anxiety and defense together rather than either on its own; emphasis on interpretation, especially the transference interpretation, as the agent of therapeutic change. There is particular emphasis on the totality of the transference . . . the term is used to mean the expression in the analytic situation of the forces and relationships of the internal world.
>
> (pp. 5–6)

I think these basic tenets of Kleinian work apply to weekly and twice weekly sessions as well. One premise of psychoanalytic therapy I believe in, as a result of clinical experience, is that a reduced frequency does not necessarily preclude the establishment of these other factors. Transference is present in all relationships regardless of how often the two people meet. In the analytic situation, the analyst tries to highlight transference, explore it, and analyze it. While easier when meeting someone frequently, this can often be done effectively with patients who attend only once or twice a week.

Certain themes have emerged in Modern Kleinian thinking. Spillius (1988) continues:

> destructiveness began to be interpreted in a more balanced way. Second, the immediate use of part-object language diminished. Third, the concept of projective identification began to be used more directly and explicitly in analyzing the transference; similarly ideas on counter-transference began to be used more systematically . . . fourth, there began to be increasing emphasis on acting-in, meaning living out experiences in the transference rather than thinking and talking about them, and more emphasis also on the patient unconsciously putting pressure on the analyst to join in . . . Most Kleinian analysts . . . think that explicit linking with the historical past is a crucial part of the psychoanalytic process which greatly enriches the meaningfulness of the psychoanalytic experience and gives the patient a sense of the continuity of his experience.
>
> (pp. 7–15)

Roy Schafer (1994) has written a comprehensive article outlining the British modifications of Klein's approach. While I find his summary outstanding, I wish to widen his scope to include the present day climate of Kleinian thinking. It is no doubt true that one may find a particular track of Kleinian thinking being represented in, say, South America, London, or Italy, which is different from Kleinian thought in another country. However, I think it is fair to say that Schafer's summary can include most of today's Modern Kleinians regardless of geographical location.

There is no consistent information as to a significant geographical difference among Kleinian schools. The two-volume set edited by Kutter (1992) examines the international climate of psychoanalysis. It shows that while the historical development of Kleinian thought in some countries is somewhat dissimilar than in others, the difference appears to be more quantitative than qualitative. Klein's influence is currently notable in Belgium, Italy, England, France, the United States, Switzerland, Argentina, Brazil, Colombia, and Venezuela.

Freudian thought may differ in emphasis throughout the globe, but it remains an agreed upon approach to the mind. Similarly, Kleinian practice today can be thought of as still generally representing the main tenets of Kleinian thought even while modified in various ways by geographic locations.

In short, what is remarkable about Schafer's paper is not its geographical focus, but its helpful review of current Kleinian technique and theory. While he does propose, "to distinguish this group from the Kleinians of South America and other parts of the world whose technical work and thinking is, on my understanding, different enough to warrant a different presentation" (p. 411), I think the differences are of emphasis rather than belief. Etchegoyen (Benveniste, 1998) was asked in an interview what differences exist between Latin American Kleinians and London Kleinians. He responded:

> it is a good question, but a difficult one to answer. All psychoanalysts that accept the theory of the schizo-paranoid and depressive positions, unconscious phantasy, internal objects, projective identification, primary (or endogenous) envy and, of course, that both the ego and the object are present from birth, are Kleinians. Furthermore, from the point of view of technique, Kleinian analysts do not wait to interpret, and they interpret impartially both the positive and the negative transference. In this sense there is no difference between the London and Latin American Kleinians really. But there are differences in some details. To start with, the first generation of the London analysts were direct disciples of Klein and they were our teachers. There are now Kleinian analysts in many Latin American countries. Naturally they are not all the same. Coming back to the question about London and Buenos Aires, I would say that the London Kleinians are more rigorous and militant. Buenos Aires Kleinians are perhaps more permeable to the thinking of other authors and they have, in my view, a more consistent theory of countertransference.

Therefore, I use the term "Modern Kleinian" to denote analysts from any part of the globe who treat patients according to the theoretical and technical principles set out by Melanie Klein and then extended and elaborated on by her followers. I believe these principles also apply to the practice of psychoanalytic psychotherapy and therefore represent a particular group of psychoanalytic psychotherapists as well.

Schafer (1994) states, "Just as ego-psychological technique is radically different from, but still continuous with, Freud's first technical efforts, so this modern Kleinian work is radically different from Melanie Klein's first work though still continuous with it" (p. 410). He goes on:

> The external world is treated in the consulting room rather like the manifest content of a dream: as an arena in which the problems of the internal world are represented and played out . . . These Kleinians usually view their analysands either as lodged somewhere between . . . or fluctuating desperately between [the paranoid–schizoid and depressive positions] . . . confronted in his or her internal world by two painful possibilities, the first being the persecutory anxiety that is outstanding in the paranoid–schizoid position, and the second, the guilt and feelings of devastation in the depressive position. In the paranoid–schizoid position the focus is very much on aggression or self and other-directed destructiveness, much of it in the form of envy and fear of envy, and on grandiosity, while in the depressive position the focus is on love, understanding, concern, reparation, desire, and various other forms of regard for the object as well as on destructiveness and guilt . . . Mature functioning rests on one's having attained an advanced phase of

> the depressive position in which object love and sublimatory activity are relatively stable; however, regressive pulls are never absent.
>
> (pp. 411–412)

Modern Kleinians use countertransference as a tool to understand the patient's use of projective identification, which is often a primary method of intra-psychic communication. The patient unconsciously positions negative or positive aspects of his self or his internal objects in the analyst for a variety of reasons. These motivations include control, reparation, caring, protection, disposal, and aggression.

Regarding current trends in Kleinian interpretation style, Schafer (1994) writes:

> [The Modern Kleinians] no longer engage in rapid-fire, symbol-laden interpretations of whatever manifest content comes their way, being rather measured in the speed and quantity of their interpretations, as well as oriented toward gathering immediate evidence on which to base each aspect of their interventions. They favor "showing" over "telling" what's what.
>
> (pp. 412–413)

Hinshelwood (1991) summarizes some ideas about the more Modern Kleinian approaches:

> Kleinian technique today emphasizes (i) the immediate here-and-now situation, (ii) the total of all aspects of the setting, (iii) the importance of understanding the content of the anxiety, (iv) the consequence of interpreting the anxiety rather than the defenses only (so-called deep interpretation) . . . in the last two decades, based on the understanding of projective identification and of acting in the transference, [technique] has focused instead on the way these processes in the analytic setting defend against the patient's experience of dependency and envy in the here-and-now.
>
> (p. 23)

Part II

The patients

Helping people within an analytic perspective

Chapter 4

The difficult patient and the psychoanalytic approach

Most current thinking in the mental health field is a product of descriptive psychiatry. As a result, symptoms are highlighted and the value of psychodynamic theory and psychoanalytically based treatment is virtually ignored. When examining patients' personality problems and symptom profile from a Kleinian/Freudian perspective, case-specific and dynamically useful approaches to patients become clear. While severely neurotic, character disordered, and psychotic patients all exhibit certain symptom clusters and personality patterns, how they arrived at that psychological place and how their phantasies and defenses shape their current internal–external life is special to each case.

Theory allows one to conceptualize a problem, formulate the intervention, and understand the outcome of the intervention. The general premise of psychoanalytic theory is that behavior, moods, and interpersonal interactions are a product of the unconscious. The better one understands the unconscious processes by which a patient organizes himself or herself, the better chance one has of assisting that patient. Using Sigmund Freud and Melanie Klein's concepts of the unconscious, the analyst can more easily and effectively work with all types of patients. Indeed, this holds true whether one is conducting home visits, play therapy, supportive counseling, parenting classes, or support groups, or running a homeless shelter. The analytic stance is helpful whether one is working with neurotic, borderline, narcissistic, psychotic, or even brain damaged, drug addicted, or criminal patients. In short, once the problem is truly understood in both its internal and external manifestations, the analyst can offer the best possible treatment for that particular patient.

Who are the more difficult patients? First of all, we must all acknowledge that there are specific types of people we don't work well with. This is not a disgrace but merely a fact. There are also people with whom most of us would have a hard time working. Freud's clinical emphasis was on patients who suffered from three types of neurosis: the hysterical neurosis, the anxiety neurosis, and the obsessional neurosis. In the contemporary clinical setting, psychoanalytic theory now provides us with a great deal of information about character disorders and psychotic dysfunctions. Kleinian theory examines the way the person's anxieties will push the ego to adopt certain defenses and character postures. While there is no cookbook style of treating patients, psychoanalytic methods of understanding the mind provide the clinician with specific tools that help when working with difficult cases.

In applying a psychoanalytic diagnosis to a patient, I think of the primary way that patient is relating or reacting to me, which in turn is a result of how they are relating to their internal world. The Kleinian method emphasizes these internal, intra-psychic relations, which produce repetitious patterns of interpersonal interaction.

In the Freudian view, the difficult patient has an inordinately strong drive, wish, or phantasy. This creates conflict with external reality and the aspect of the ego that sides with reality. As a consequence, the ego constructs an elaborate system of defenses. When these solidify into a rigid, chronic pattern that is used in almost every situation, we say that person has a character disorder. A neurotic patient may be able to erect defenses to contain threatening wishes and conflicted phantasies. The containing is accomplished by the creation of an unconscious compromise formation that tries to satisfy the mind's competing demands. The compromise can produce observable symptoms. However, these defenses are somewhat flexible and don't dominate all of the person's relationships.

In terms of Melanie Klein's model of the mind, the healthy individual has introjected sufficient good objects to build a firm ego with ample reality testing, sublimation, and symbol formation. Splitting and projective identification are used, but in moderation, and the containing and detoxifying function of the mother has been internalized. Therefore, internal conflicts and paranoid or depressive anxieties are handled, managed, and worked through by the ego.

Most of the more difficult patients we see are lacking in all these areas. The ego is fragmented and lacking in ample good objects. Therefore, the ego feels overwhelmed by bad objects and relies on excessive splitting and projective identification, as well as idealization and manic reparation. This creates a vicious cycle that leaves the ego clinging to very static and infantile patterns of coping with internal anxieties and external problems.

One neurotic patient came to see me with a bridge phobia. She gradually came to understand that her change in career from bank vice-president to being a partner with her husband in a small business left her feeling dethroned. When her husband asked her to deliver a set of papers to a client, she drove off and came to a bridge and immediately had a panic attack. She was conviced she would fall off or jump off the bridge. She had to be walked off the bridge to safety. In treatment, we discovered how she was furious at her husband for treating her like an "errand boy." She felt her rage at him was unacceptable, as he represented her hated yet longed-for mother. This internal conflict with her husband stirred up this strong, archaic anxiety which was displaced, externally, onto the bridge. She also could feel cared for by the person who walked her off the bridge.

This material illustrates the unconscious translation of certain unacceptable drives, affect states, and internal object relations into something that the mind finds more tolerable: a compromise formation. Her symptom allowed for emotional gratification of her desires for love and her feelings of hatred. With a bridge phobia, her husband had to deliver the papers himself and in this manner she defied his authority and came back into power. The husband had to be the "errand boy" instead. However, she felt quite guilty as she saw her husband as a whole person, not just all bad or all good. Thus, her fear of jumping off the bridge was an act of reparation, a making up, for her angry feelings.

Difficult patients, who tend to be more troubled and fragmented than this patient was, are individuals who are unable to contain or process primitive conflicts and phantasies. They lack the ego's symbolic function. To their way of thinking, there are only all-bad or all-good objects. "An eye for an eye" is the basic approach to relating. Persecution is the primary anxiety.

This is illustrated by a patient who after five years of treatment continues to tell me how "mean" I am to her for using "special techniques of the mind", hidden cameras, and "psychological punishments" to achieve my "special purposes." We gradually understood her life-long bulimia, her delusional fears of me, and her chronic patterns of alienating everyone in her life as a repetition of certain phantasies. She craved to be close to me, but was scared of being abused and rejected. Therefore, she maintained a sadistic control over me, intra-psychically and interpersonally, but was fearful of losing that control and being abandoned and attacked. As a result, she engaged me in ongoing battles of power in which one of us was always being blamed.

The difference between these two patients is that the first one is able to use reality and the external environment to develop compromises to her conflicts even if they are pathological. Her symptoms were circumscribed and the rest of her life functioned quite well. The second patient was lost in her internal world of persecutory and controlling objects and unable to connect with reality or with her analyst in a way that might begin to reverse the frightening repetitious cycle. All of her relationships were marred by this paranoid perspective.

The difficult patient struggles with making use of the observing functions of the ego. In its place there tends to be a regression to early object-relations and a loss of symbolic function due to excessive aggression, projective identification, and splitting. These dynamics make for a lack of good objects to fortify the ego. Normally, the observing and symbolizing ego provides the ability to understand that one is overreacting and to be curious about that.

The analyst often has to become the observing ego for the difficult patient in the beginning stages of treatment by interpreting the primitive object relationships that disable the object's ego. This sets a foundation for hopeful internalization by the patient of the therapist's analyzing and observing functions.

Freud (1917) felt that normal human activity revolved around the arousal of an unconscious wish or phantasy, the unconscious conflicts regarding those impulses, and a compromise formation created by the ego's defenses. In healthy individuals, the compromise works out in an adaptive manner most of the time. In neurosis, the compromise is often the symptom. This was the case with the first woman and her bridge phobia. The second patient had psychotic symptoms that were harder to understand. This is because the difficult patient is usually a person who has adopted a pathological system of internal bargains and contradictory struggles that are brittle, scattered, and chaotic. In addition, the difficult patient is functioning in more disorganized and dedifferentiated regions of mental life. Klein has shown how these psychic states are linked to more primitive phantasies and fixed internalized object relations.

There are particular clinical situations that, when the transference is left unanalyzed, tend to foster pathological entrenchments. Without ongoing sensitivity to the patient's phantasies and defenses, the treatment can easily become stuck. Acting out that goes unattended leads to difficult impasses. Acting out is the use of action or behavior as a method to avoid the expression of emotional states through language, affective experience, and rational introspection. It is the avoidance of actually experiencing the emotion or thought. Freud (1914) spoke of this as the difference between remembering and repeating.

Transference is the living out, interpersonally and intra-psychically, of an internal, historical, relational matrix. Klein demonstrated ways in which the ego will erase, destroy, or disguise links between cognitive functions and object-relations. Therefore, the concept of deficit is better understood as active self-destruction for the purpose of defense. Disorders such as psychosis, attention deficit disorder, obsessive compulsive disorder, and substance abuse, which are normally treated with medications or manipulated with behavioral therapies, are sometimes better approached with this perspective. In Freud's day, hysterics were treated with electricity, hypnosis, and narcotics until Freud invented the talking cure.

Many difficult cases are clinical situations in which the links between the internal past, the external present, the desired future, and the therapeutic relationship have not been identified and worked through. Enactments are common with more difficult patients and often create difficult cases. The problem continues in the present through action, without any change or modification. In other words, there is an enactment or re-enactment of an intra-psychic phenomenon without an understanding of it in the context of the therapeutic relationship. Examples include an analyst who becomes distant and withdrawing, re-enacting the patient's internal relationship with an unavailable parent. Equally problematic is the analyst who rushes in to soothe or rescue the patient, thus acting out the patient's wishes and demands rather than analyzing them.

Interpretation of both the positive and the negative transference helps clear the path to working through of core phantasies. Avoidance of either positive or negative aspects of the transference by the analyst can foster a therapeutic impasse.

As mentioned in Chapter 1, interpretation is the primary tool in psychoanalytic therapy. Interpretation, not only of genetic material but also of the current transference relationship, brings unconscious material into consciousness through the vehicle of language. More importantly, and in line with Freud's structural model, it makes clear the patient's core anxieties and the methods they use to defend against those ego and object fears.

Interpretation is a linking of the past, the present, and the hoped for future within the therapeutic relationship. The analyst explains to the patient the meaning of a previously misunderstood, unknown, or warded off psychic situation, bringing attention (through language) to the patient's wishes, fears, defenses, and compromises. The analyst provides interpretations about the distorted nature of intra-psychic object-relations that are grossly manifested in the medium of the transference and extra-transference. In other words, the observing ego is supported as a result of exploring and analyzing the deeper unconscious phantasies and anxieties.

The difficult patient is often given supportive counseling as the treatment of choice under the logic that they need to have their ego defenses shored up, that they need help in containing things, and that they need help in learning to manage their life skills. I believe this is usually a combination of the acting out of the analyst's own anxiety and misplaced reliance on Freud's early topographic model. If the theory is that id impulses are not being repressed adequately, then the ego would need to be strengthened. In addition, so-called supportive therapy is usually a focus on external events and symptom reduction by suggestive and coercive means.

In contrast, psychoanalytic therapy focuses on internal conflict as well as the unconscious meanings that are assigned to interpersonal relationships. Supportive counseling is often the promotion of a positive transference without interpretation of it, based on the ill-informed idea that one shoud help the patient "put a lid" on their troubled mind. Again, this is a misreading of Freud's early work on abreaction, in which he thought the patient just needed to unleash or discharge their pent-up emotions. According to this model, patients should either be pushed to "let it all out" or "keep it all in." I believe supportive measures, parameters, and non-analytic interventions are only useful to the patient if they help pave the road toward exploring transference phantasies and increase the patient's ability to participate in the exploration of internal object-relations dynamics.

In trying to define psychoanalytic therapy, the following points arise. The analyst is neither caretaker nor detached scientist, but a new, consistent, and interested object. The hope is that a therapeutic alliance will form that will foster a new object-relations situation. This new relationship is in constant danger of contamination by archaic transferences which must be interpreted as they occur. Gradually, the new and modified relationship is internalized. This is not an artificial "re-parenting." Rather, the patient achieves increased awareness of both internal difficulties and external reality as another person, with all the fallibility of any human, helps point out their deepest fears, hostilities, and desires.

The primary goals and methods of treatment are always the analysis of the transference and of the resistances, especially with the more difficult patient. This is best done within the context of interpersonal patterns and intra-psychic phantasies, both regarding the therapeutic relationship. Any resistance to the exploration and understanding of the transference must be analyzed. The transference is where the action is with all patients, but is vital to address with the more disturbed patient.

It is important to note that making the patient feel better is not the goal of psychoanalytic treatment. Psychoanalytic treatment can provide the patient with a method of self-understanding that creates a more competent adaptation to life, but comfort would only be a potential by-product of that understanding. To truly know oneself, including unconscious motivating factors that shape most interpersonal and external situations, is the potential gift of psychoanalytic treatment.

In today's private practice setting, most of our patients are character disordered, borderline, or even psychotic. Rarely do we see neurotic patients who are mildly hysterical or obsessive and have no other complications. Research (Friedman *et al.*, 1998) shows that the typical patient in a private practice setting suffers from at least one major affective disorder as well as at least one personality disorder.

Character disorders are ego-syntonic. Therefore, such patients don't want help with their personality, they usually just feel the world isn't taking care of them properly. They want us to side with them against the bad objects in their minds. This is the result of splitting their object into all-good parts and all-bad parts.

Suggestion and manipulation (including "homework exercises," hospitalization, enlisting family help, and so forth) are sometimes unavoidable. However, it is still vital, when possible, to find out how and why the patient needed to force the treatment into being one of suggestion and manipulation.

The treatment goal is exploration and reorganization of psychic structure, yet these types of patient push for us to use ineffective interventions based on old ideas of abreaction and suggestion. They are used to the quick fix. They find a psychological patch for their problems with a sexual, drugs, alcohol, food, or emotional rush.

Kleinian theory and Kleinian clinical practice emphasize the understanding of each patient as an individual. Rather than have rigid groupings of symptoms that define each patient, the Kleinian therapist looks for a personal profile in each individual. Certainly, there are specific groups of symptoms and character traits that tend to go together. However, those same groupings can have different internal meanings for each patient. The nature of unconscious phantasy and the various methods of defense make each patient unique.

Melanie Klein and her followers explored character pathology in the context of the paranoid–schizoid and depressive positions. In the paranoid–schizoid position, we encounter psychotic, borderline, and narcissistic characters and we understand them differently than ego-psychology does. In the depressive position, we see patients who have Oedipal, neurotic problems and are hysterical and obsessive. Most of the time, there is a overlap of the two combined with fluctuations back and forth.

Therefore, the patient's personality must be analyzed as a special and unique set of phantasies, anxieties, and defenses that occur as in a constellation that emerges within the transference/countertransference relationship of analyst and patient.

One patient always seemed to have bad news to relate. She said she knew she was prone to being "negative," but there was something more to it. Over the years, she engaged me in a way where I was the ear to her endless tales of sorrow and crisis. I felt a prisoner to her stories. Given how she acted so involved when telling them, she seemed to enjoy these stories of pain and disappointment. I began making comments about how she seemed to enjoy being the bearer of bad news. This led to her telling me of a memory. As a child, she witnessed her neighbor's dog being run over. She remembered a feeling of delight and excitement over telling the neighbor the bad news. My patient went on to tell me how she enjoyed renting sad movies about the Nazi death camps. The movies made her cry but also gave her a "special" feeling.

I interpreted that this pain and sorrow was her connection to me as well as a weapon she used to protect herself. Without it she would feel helpless and alone. She would lose me and feel vulnerable. My patient agreed and went on to tell me how as a child she spent hours every day listening to her mother talking about various tragedies. Consequently, she and her mother developed an intense bond over relating the latest crisis or tragedy from their lives or from the news or from the neighborhood gossip. It was as if they tried to outdo one another on who could tell the worst story. This was a highly emotional tie between mother and daughter. Many of the mother's stories were about how unhappy she was in her marriage. When I interpreted the romantic, intimate nature of this bond of suffering, my patient told me, "I love that. I loved it growing up. I relish others' pain. Mother and me would get so excited over it. Feeling sad seems exciting." I said she might use this way of being to take her own helplessness and pain and turn it into something she feels in charge of. My patient said, "Yes. I make it work for me!"

This woman would be hard to catagorize in strictly psychiatric terms. She initially came to treatment feeling depressed, sleeping most of the time and feeling suicidal. In the transference and in most of her relationships, she got people to tell her what to do and treat her like a helpless kid. Diagnostically, she was masochistic, sadistic, depressive, dependent, and histrionic. However, these descriptive terms merely give a hint of very particular sets of phantasies, anxieties, and defenses that made up her internal world. Therefore, the immediate here-and-now transference was the best diagnostic tool on how to proceed moment-to-moment, while keeping in mind an overall picture of the general diagnosis.

Kleinian analysts think that particular phantasies and pathological ego defenses come together to make character constellations. These are pathological mental organizations that operate in rigid, destructive manners. This is an internal struggle that spills into interpersonal patterns. Therefore, character makeup and character pathology is understood as organized phantasies and defenses that the ego uses in most situations to negotiate intrapsychic object relationships. The moment-to-moment analysis of each patient's unique transference method of relating and organizing the therapeutic relationship gives the best clues to how to help them work through the anxieties and conflicts that constrict their life.

Chapter 5

Keeping the analytic focus

Many of our cases come into treatment with important external issues that are very overwhelming. These environmental conditions can be severe and cause despair, fear, and anger. After working with such patients for a period of time on these outside situations, the analyst may notice other more characterological problems. Indeed, it is often the case that the presenting issues were simply the tip of the iceberg. Deeper personality conflicts and internal object-relational standoffs are frequently found.

It is this dual track of external stress or trauma combined with internal chaos that makes our most difficult cases so challenging. In a perfect world, an optimal and successful course of psychoanalysis would help resolve both areas. The analytic method provides the best way to focus on how these two arenas coincide and how best to work through and integrate the problematic aspects of each dimension. The Kleinian view, based on Melanie Klein's expansion of Freud's work, is that the patient forms a transference to the analyst from the moment they think of or imagine entering treatment. This is part of the concept of the total transference. It means that everything, at all times, is shaped by the patient's unconscious conflicts and phantasies. But the difficult patient's intra-psychic struggles can make it impossible to access either the external or the internal in a way that leads to healing and understanding.

With some patients, there is a combination of resistance to inner exploration and an early termination that shapes the treatment into a more symptom-focused, external centered relationship. This may help the patient in many ways, but also leaves them untouched on deeper psychological levels. This can be frustrating to the analyst and self-defeating to the patient. However, the patient's particular object-relations dynamic can lock the analytic relationship into this limited, one-dimensional view. The analyst can only do their best to provide the analytic environment, explore the nature of these specific transference standoffs, and work to accept the limitations while seeking to stretch their boundaries. Part of the counter-transference work for the analyst is to realize the positive benefits these types of patients do receive, while remaining loyal to always offering the patient more if he or she is able or willing to take it in. This is a balance between needing to reach an idealized vision of cure and always striving for optimal growth within the broad potential for psychological advancement found in all our patients.

In our private practices, we often encounter a patient who draws us into intense and confusing transference–countertransference situations, only to leave treatment abruptly in the same troubling way. These stormy clinical climates are the outgrowth of certain strong conflicts and phantasies the patient is overwhelmed by and enlists us into. Can these brief connections or disconnections really be called analytic? Rather than trying to classify our time with such patients as either psychoanalytic or not, leading to unhelpful political debates, there is a more flexible approach in which the analyst can strive to maintain an analytical focus even in the most difficult clinical settings. This provides the patient with the optimal clinical experience. Whether they are able or willing to take in these new perspectives, different object relationships, and fresh insights is not something the psychoanalyst can control, but certainly every practitioner can strive to offer such perspectives and insights.

The idea of maintaining a psychoanalytic focus is more difficult if we meet with a patient for only five or ten sessions. Yet some patients who engage us for several years can still test the very foundation of our therapeutic goals. Certain external criteria such as frequency, use of couch, method of termination, and other elements usually considered essential for psychoanalytic practice are found, in actual practice, not always necessary to maintain an analytic process. Clearly, many patients present with such troubled external circumstances and complicated internal views that no real progress could ever be made. Yet this is not a determination that can be made ahead of time. We can only assess the patient's psychological profile as we go and within the context of the transference–countertransference experience. Even in a very constricted situation with less than optimal conditions, the analytic approach can help patients make significant changes in their lives. How a patient interacts or reacts to the usual conditions of treatment, including suggested frequency, use of couch, and so on is part of how the analyst can begin to understand the nature of that patient's current object-relations.

The following case material will be presented in order. The first case will represent the briefest encounter, which never solidified into an ongoing analytic enterprise. It would be understandable to say it was not analytic in any sense. However, it is the type of clinical situation that all analysts in private practice have to deal with. The next few cases represent analytic situations of varying frequency and duration and they showcase the types of difficult clinical experiences that analysts have in day-to-day practice. Nevertheless, the Kleinian psychoanalytic method is employed and shown possibly to help the patient. The next to last case is of a patient who remained in treatment significantly longer: even though she struggled with very difficult transference conflicts and unconscious phantasy states, she was able to make positive use of the analytic approach. The last case shows a continued analytic focus on the remaining paranoid–schizoid and depressive issues even in the last session of a long and successful psychoanalysis.

Case 1

Sometimes the analyst takes part in a brief, chaotic slice of a person's life without much chance of establishing even a short-term therapeutic experience. Fortunately, this type of "here today, gone tomorrow" patient is not the norm. But all analysts in private practice have the troubling and frustrating encounters from time to time.

Alice came to see me for help with what she called her "intense stress" and a feeling that "everyone has it out for me and I am always last in line in life." During the first interview, she rattled off a flurry of problems, failed relationships, unfortunate career decisions, and general despair. Alice had been in various forms of psychotherapy many times before and was currently on two medications for mood stabilization.

She told me she had been sexually abused by her stepfather as a child and felt neglected by her mother. Also, she had just been laid off at her job. On top of all that, her husband had just announced he wanted a divorce. Alice cried and raged, pleading with me to tell her what to do. I was supportive and let her know I thought she must be very upset and was obviously overwhelmed by all these events. Also, I responded by addressing the transference. In all her stories, she was the victim. It sounded like this might have become the character plot she was most used to as a way to navigating the world. I told her this and interpreted that she now was asking me to run her life, again making herself powerless and passive. I told her I thought there might be other ways to cope that would feel more empowering and solid and we would need to explore that together. She seemed to understand this and gave it some thought.

On her second visit, Alice told me she felt much better and was starting to look for a new job. She already had a few leads and was somewhat hopeful. However, she told me she "still felt lost and depressed" and she yelled out in fury that she wanted to kill her husband. After talking a bit more, she added, "I know you will lock me up if I really try and kill him. I don't mean that I will actually do it, but I want him to suffer. I hate his guts!" Most of this session was taken up with Alice telling me what a terrible person her husband was.

Hours before her third session, Alice called and left a message. She cancelled the appointment and said she felt "way better" and now felt "in control of her life." I left a message indicating she might want to explore her situation a bit more before ending. She never returned my call.

If I had to speculate on this abortive treatment and tried to examine my contribution to its outcome, I would make one guess. This woman was very disturbed and seemed to fluctuate in a very manic and persecutory way of experiencing her objects. Alice saw the world as a place in which she was the victim and passive follower of others. So, when I made my initial interpretation about there being other ways to be in which she might feel more empowered, I wonder if Alice took me to say, "you should start to act and feel more empowered." If so, she may have put that costume on and begun to perform for me, thinking she should immediately be cured to please me. Obviously this is speculation without much data to go on, but this is the type of strange questioning and confusion the analyst is usually left within such brief and chaotic encounters.

Case 2

The typical analyst in private practice sees many cases in which the patient has such an intense investment in maintaining their psychic vision of their objects that it is virtually impossible to change their psychological perspective. The skilled analyst can observe what the transference dynamic is and can start to understand how the patient enlists him or her as a player in their phantasies. But, with these difficult cases, it proves useless to engage the patient in reflection or thought over action and reaction.

Unfortunately, there are frequent situations where the analyst may feel like a squad of dive-bombers appears out of the blue, flies by, drops its cargo of explosives, and flies off never to be seen again. On occasion, the analyst may be able to move quickly and have a modest impact on this type of patient, but often the result is less than satisfying.

I began meeting with a couple for marital work after the husband utilized the eight free sessions offered by his employer. In short order, the wife told me she "didn't have much hope for the marriage" and didn't think the husband was capable of change. It seemed that for the last two years of their three-year marriage, she felt very pessimistic about the relationship and its future. When we explored what exactly brought them into my office, it was clear they did have problems, but the mutual difficulties seemed typical of many couples: lack of clear communication, indirect expression of emotions, and petty fights over housework and bills. As we started to look at these very manageable problems, the wife's pessimism took over, overshadowing these more normal marital bumps in the road and revealing a more insidious issue.

She told me she thought the marriage was "hopelessly flawed," that her husband "might be trying to improve but it's obvious he can't ever see past himself," and "there wasn't much point in trying to fix it." When I tried to explore the details of this depressing and aggressive view, I was blocked by the sheer conviction of her stance. She told me that she was sure her husband would never be able to change enough to make her happy. When I asked if perhaps change was needed on both sides, she told me there was nothing wrong with her, but her husband was a person who had "serious character flaws" and that was something that could never be fixed. I pointed out two things. First, I observed how she seemed very removed from her feelings, talking to me in a mechanical, logical manner and disconnected from any emotional bond with her husband. I added that even when he began sobbing as she declared how hopeless the marriage was, she seemed almost unaware of him on an emotional level. Secondly, I noted how convinced she was that it was impossible to change and how hopeless it all was. I interpreted that she was so convinced and declarative about it that she left no room for the possibility of change. I suggested this might be an important avenue to investigate.

Immediately, the husband said he knew exactly what I meant. He said, "She has always said it is too late, it is hopeless and what is the point. I try, but it is never enough for her." The wife responded, "Well, you are right. It isn't enough. I don't see any change from your side. The problems we have, that you said you were willing to work on, are all still there!" He replied, "First of all, I don't think that is true. We are making some progress. Even deciding to come here was a good step. And, you are saying it is all my fault. But, there are two of us here. Secondly, we just started realizing there are problems a while back, can't you be patient?" The wife responded in a cold and detached way: "There has been plenty of time and it is evident to me that if there was going to be a change, it would have happened by now. I don't think you are capable of change."

Very soon, the wife's conviction of her object's inability to serve her and soothe her properly took over the transference. By the fourth session, she was unhappy with the "lack of change" that I provided. She said she "saw no point in continuing," since it did nothing to help. At the fifth session, she calmly stated she thought divorce would be the best step to take, since the marriage was "clearly no better than before." She and her husband attended two more times before stopping altogether.

From about the second to the seventh and last session, I interpreted to the wife that she was convinced that I, like her husband, was failing her. I interpreted that I, in her experience, was not providing her with what she wanted fast enough and that I seemed unable to be trusted or to be depended on. I pointed out the parallel to her disappointment in her husband for seeming to do nothing to change the situation. I also made the observation that she gave me and her an impossible task that we would certainly fall short of: to make a dramatic change in two or three short visits. She responded, "Why is that impossible? It is all there in front of you, now you just have to act. If you can't help in that period of time it is simply indicative that you can't help at all."

I continued to interpret her devaluation of me and noted that she didn't really give me a chance so that I was not included in the picture from the beginning. I tried to emphasize the way she saw failure in her objects ahead of time and how she would not budge on that. She would not let the hope of change enter the equation. I interpreted that she used distance and logic to neutralize me and create a ghost of my analytic abilities. So, she castrated me ahead of time and then felt disappointed and dismissive that I could not be strong enough to serve her properly. While I believe most of my interpretations were accurate and made with compassion and timing, she would have none of it.

This intense, no-give transference was the major problem in the marriage. From what I could observe, I think the reason the marriage hadn't broken up years earlier is that the wife was successful in getting the husband to do her bidding. And, up to now, the husband had never confronted the wife on her narcissistic way of relating. Now, the husband, usually a quiet and subservient man, had brought up his feelings of unhappiness with her. This probably disturbed the narcissistic balance this woman maintained in her inner life and now she demanded he double his efforts to serve her and prove his love. She seemed to feel that her objects were destined to fail her, no matter what, and they could only temporarily convince her otherwise. This dread and anxiety were projected and she quickly induced her objects to be anxious and scurry about desperately trying to save the day. This was certainly the countertransference I felt and then utilized to make some of my interpretations. When the husband called to tell me they were not coming back because his wife felt it was a "waste of time," I felt he was apologizing for his pit-bull puppy accidently taking a nip at me and also telling me "welcome to the sinking ship." So, as a psychoanalyst, I was able to detect, organize, and speak to the transference, some of the defenses, and some of the anxieties present in this couple. However the nature of the wife's phantasies, her need to control her objects, and the way they provided each other an airtight sadomasochistic match made a true exploration, let alone a working through process, out of the question.

Case 3

Psychoanalysts frequently engage in brief therapy, but not by choice. Certainly, some psychoanalysts have developed theories and clinical frameworks for psychoanalytic oriented brief therapies. What I am exploring is the interactions with patients who take control of the analytic situation and make it into a brief and often unproductive encounter by a combination of particular transference perspectives, certain interpersonal maneuvers, and by their premature termination of the treatment process.

Joy was a thirty-year-old single mother who came into treatment because she was concerned about her seven-year-old son. Joy told me, in a distant and almost irritated manner, that her son had mentioned thoughts of suicide on and off for several months. When I gathered more information and started to get to know Joy, I noticed that she described things and related to me in a highly rigid, logic-bound, and controlled way. The words and terms she used made it seem like we were in a stuffy business meeting, even though we were talking about her troubled son and her own life stress. I made this observation to Joy, pointing to it with curiosity. She was surprised to hear my assessment and quickly told me she didn't see anything wrong with "efficiency and precision."

By the end of the first session, I thought her son's thoughts of suicide might be triggered by Joy paying more attention to her new boyfriend than to her son. When I told Joy this, she said it could definitely be true, but surely he "ought to be able to deal with it." Now, on one hand, there was this cold and selfish attitude. At the same time, she appeared to offer her son the opportunity to talk with her and express his feelings. However, it sounded like the son was left in the same dilemma I was: Joy invited a sense of warmth, openness, and willingness to change, but she ultimately blocked any true emotionality or exploration within the relationship. I promptly referred her son to a child analyst and continued seeing Joy in the hope of helping her with parenting issues and exploring other areas of her life that might be problematic, such as her standoffish and intellectualized way of viewing life.

When I asked about her background and upbringing, Joy told me in a matter-of-fact way that she had a "normal childhood." When I asked what she felt was normal, she told me her parents loved her, they were never violent or abusive, and they taught her and her four siblings "good manners and how to get along in the world." It seemed hard to get details of this ideal sounding experience. Also, Joy presented it like a laundry list, efficient and dry. So, I told her it seemed she didn't have much feeling about something so nice, so I wondered if there might have been something difficult to bear in her history. Joy said, "Oh, sometimes I was a little lonely, but no. Nothing really. Everything was fine." I asked about the loneliness. It turned out that Joy's parents told her they were overwhelmed by the stress of parenthood and needed some respite. They said they needed their relatives to help out. Strangely, to solve their problem, they had Joy spend three weeks a month at her aunt's, which was in a fairly distant city. This was from age five to age sixteen.

Over the next four sessions, I spoke with Joy about how she must have dealt with this troubling childhood experience. We explored her thoughts and feelings about why she was chosen as the one to send away, why her parents seemed overwhelmed in the first place, and how she felt being with her aunt during most of her youth. Certainly, Joy used her mechanical, sterile approach to ward off most of her awareness of this traumatic time and shared her feelings with me in a spirit of denial, intellectualization, and projection. However, she did seem to start to open up to her internal experiences and tell me about her need to be in control and to focus on "taking care of business" so as to not "dwell on those undesirable areas," as she put it.

Joy was fairly amenable to my suggestions that her detached and avoiding emotional state might be affecting her parenting abilities. She was grateful to learn that she could prevent her child from having the same type of loneliness she endured, simply by being more aware and curious of her own emotional state and thereby becoming a more present, helpful, and compassionate parent.

During the half-dozen meetings I had with Joy, I became aware of the cold and detached manner with which she treated her objects and herself, much like she had probably felt treated by her parents. She looked at human interaction, relationships, and indeed love as simply something to do well and efficiently and then check off the list, so as to move on to the next assignment. So, I wasn't surprised when, at the eighth session, she told me, "I want to tell you how grateful I am for our work together. These meetings have really put me on the right path. I feel I am better equipped as a mother and ready to live life in a better way." Based on my countertransference and the way she was saying this to me, I said that while I appreciated her feelings and agreed that we were making important progress, she had checked me off her to-do list and was ready to move on to something else.

Joy was able to take in my interpretation without defending against it. She replied, "Yes. I know what you mean. It is true. But, in my world, things have to be really bad to warrant help. My son certainly needed help and now he has it. But I don't see why I need to keep coming." I interpreted that her tough skin approach might be the result of having to deal with feeling rejected and unwanted in childhood and that she now might feel she was being a burden on me if she admitted to wanting or needing anything more. Joy thought about it for a bit and said that I might be right, but she still couldn't justify seeing me, that "things just weren't life or death enough."

So, Joy did break off the treatment. At the end of the eighth session, she thanked me again and told me she could really see some differences. "I am less uptight with my friends and I don't take work so damn seriously anymore. And, like I said, I think my son and I are getting along better. You are a smart guy. What you say about the importance of feelings and working with them seems right. If we ever need more help, we will call you."

Joy was someone who had a brush with the analytic method. She and her son gained some benefits from it, but it is hard to say if they will be temporary or lasting. Certainly, I wanted to continue providing Joy with an avenue to explore and work with her internal world. She made the decision to end, probably because I introduced a new way of relating to herself and her internal objects that was both gratifying and anxiety-producing. Unfortunately, the anxiety and the time-tested approach to life she was used to won out.

Case 4

Martin was forty years old when he came to me for help with his anger. He was up for possible promotion at his university job. He felt he had worked hard and done everything his supervisor had suggested in order for him to be the best candidate for the new position. Given the way he described this, I interpreted that he seemed to be bitter and resentful that he had done what he could to please his supervisor and then felt unrewarded. Martin responded in a manner that was to remain constant throughout the year we spent together.

On one hand, Martin could reflect on himself, looking introspectively at how he was relating to his objects. On the other hand, he had a persecutory and masochistic vision of the world that he was sure was real. There was nothing to reflect on. He was simply being bullied. This made for a difficult transference in which he frequently felt I was not siding with him and therefore dismissing and even ridiculing him. Then he would be angry with me, just as he was with his supervisor. So, in the countertransference, I felt bullied either to side with him as a friend or to disagree with him as a foe. There was not too much in the middle.

Over time, Martin told me how his alcoholic father demanded that Martin always do things his way. This seemed to unfold in two ways. First, Martin felt his father always criticized him for having his own ideas, often yelling at him and calling him names. As a result, instead of pursuing his own ideas, Martin would try to follow whatever his father said he should do, basically being a carbon copy of his father. But when Martin tried to abort his own identity to imitate his father, instead of getting praise he would be told he didn't do it right or that he didn't complete the task. So either he sacrificed his own mind for the sake of pleasing his father and was criticized, or he stuck with his own mind and feelings and was punished.

Bit by bit, this background information came alive in the transference. Whenever I would make comments, observations, or interpretations, Martin took it very poorly. Regardless of how careful I was in wording things, he would feel I was putting him down and suggesting that he do it my way. My own tension in being careful about how to speak to him showed me, via the countertransference, how he felt under his father's thumb. In other words, projective identification dynamics led to him flipping the table on me and becoming the bully rather than the victim. So, his reaction to me as a bad object, another version of a rejecting father, was the core of the transference and therefore its analysis was the goal of the treatment. This work, the gradual exploration and analysis of his transference phantasies, was very tricky. We would make progress and work as a team, noticing his vision of me, or his supervisor, as another angry, bossy father and the alternative version in which he treated me or others in an exacting and negative way that put him in the role of father. But then, as an abrupt reaction and defense, he would begin taking my curiosity and observation as a realistic attack and trauma. He told me I controlled him and was forcing him to see everything my way. My alleged restriction and domination of him was a central aspect of the transference, making our analytic work one step forward and two backwards.

After one year of my meeting with Martin at a once a week frequency, this near-psychotic transference state pushed him to abort treatment. Martin's state of anxiety was overwhelming and the paranoia he felt from seeing me as a controlling father led him to see termination as the only logical choice. Even when he left, he could still access a piece of reality when he said, "I know what you mean about how I am seeing you with the glasses I was wearing when I grew up. I know you are not really like that, but my feelings are so strong I can't help it. I really do feel like you want to control me and I am sick of it. Why can't I have a say? Why don't you respect my opinions? I am tired of feeling under your thumb." This affect switch was quite common over the course of his analytic relationship. As he relayed his reflection on these intense feelings, they took over, so by the end of his statement he was no longer reflecting on his distortion; he was convinced I had him "under my thumb." This shows the fragile and fragmented sense he had of himself and of his objects.

After a year of meetings, I certainly felt this was an abrupt ending, leaving us dangling with much unfinished business. With no way of telling, I do think that if we could have met more frequently and for several more years, we could have healed this wide gap between persecutory transference conviction and a working through and integration of conflicting object-relations. A pessimistic way of seeing this treatment would be to say that I became one more critical and dominating authority figure in this man's inner perspective and that he wasn't a candidate for analytic treatment to begin with, due to his severe sadomasochistic outlook. While this is true in some respects, some therapeutic shifts did take place. As discussed, there was an ongoing exploration and reflection on his way of seeing and relating to himself and others, even though this process was erratic and unstable in consistency or depth. Externally, there was a degree of change as well. Martin now reacted less severely to his supervisor and other authority figures at work. He took things less personally. He felt more confident about his own ideas and desires and less obligation to give them up and please others. Also, when dating, he started to be less controlling and less critical. All these external shifts point to some level of internal restructuring, which is always part of the analytic goal.

Case 5

Ruth was thirty-six years old when she started seeing me for anxiety problems, including panic attacks. Five years later, she was still in analytic treatment and doing much better. The symptoms of panic, social discomfort, and performance anxiety at work were now very much in the background, substantially reduced. Now, she is married with one child and another on the way. Ruth's brother is dying of cancer and the brutal grieving process has been part of our current work. Also, we are exploring her life-long sense of alienation from her parents, primarily her mother. Ruth feels she always has needed to adapt to what mother wants her to be. Over time, we have identified a phantasy of being lost, banished, or harshly rejected for not adhering to what mother wants. This phantasy fuels a fear and sense of confusion over what she really wants in life and what her own identity really is or could be. Diagnostically, Ruth is a slave to her internal objects and is convinced she would be attacked and abandoned if she tried to be separate or different.

Over the course of her analytic work, we have identified a specific way in which she deals with this fear, an internal strategy she has developed. By relating in a distant, somewhat aloof and intimidating manner, she manages to get people to let her be herself. Since this is a fragile defense, Ruth becomes alarmed and angry if anyone questions her ideas or views.

Over the course of her life, these psychological factors affected all her relationships. Therefore, they currently taint her analytic relationship. This transference situation was a powerful factor, probably the most influential, in shaping the nature of her analytic treatment.

The first element colored by Ruth's internal world was the frequency at which we met. When she told me, at the very first meeting, that she only wanted to come in "every once in a while," I tried to explore it analytically. In other words, I tried to find out what psychological, unconscious dynamics might be at play. Initially, Ruth responded with external, concrete reasons such as driving distance, conflicting appointments, rigid work schedule, finances, and so forth. I told her I respected all these difficulties she had but I also thought we needed to meet as often as we could to give us the best opportunity to learn about and change her problems. So, I suggested we meet once or twice a week for a period of time and then reassess our schedules. I thought she would benefit from coming in more often, but I was trying to negotiate with her transference conflict about making a commitment and feeling obligated. Whether directly interpreted or not, Ruth's internal view of the analytic situation already steered it in a certain direction, in this case the frequency of visits.

Over the next five years, our meetings varied from once a week to twice a week and back, and sometimes only every other week. Along the way, we did learn a great deal about what frequency meant to her. She told me she was afraid of using the couch and coming in "too often" as it meant she was crazy. Also, "anything could happen with that Freudian stuff." This was part of a vague fear and paranoid vision of our relationship as dangerous or at least untrustworthy. There was a fragile bargain in Ruth's mind, which I interpreted as Ruth thinking of herself as OK when coming in once a week or less often, but suddenly sick, disturbed, and very vulnerable if coming in two, three, or four times a week. This same phantasy applied to using the couch versus sitting on the sofa.

There was also the idea that if we met more often, I would have more of a chance to ridicule her. I interpreted this to mean she was embarrassed and confused about her thoughts and feelings, that seeing me more often would expose her to these troubling parts of her mind and personality.

Finally, the issue of control was very important to Ruth. In her mind, increasing the frequency was the same as losing control. She felt she should have complete control in our relationship and coming more often was equal to letting me take over and possibly manipulate her. Only when she felt that the need for coming in more was her own decision would she think it was a safe or plausible idea. She was very concrete about it and saw the analytic treatment as an "apply when necessary" sort of relationship. So, her fear, paranoia, and need to be in charge of her objects influenced and sometimes paralyzed my ability as a psychoanalyst and it prematurely defined, even distorted, our relationship.

If I tried to explore these matters or make transference interpretations about them, Ruth often became verbally combative, defensive, and even physically intimidating. Even when I tried to bring up how I felt my interpretive hands were tied this way, she felt I was wasting her time with my agenda and ignoring her needs. So, in the countertransference, I felt the need to be careful, hold back, and measure my words. Here, my patient's internal phantasy world impacted the transference in a way that affected my behavior as an analyst, immobilizing parts of my interpretive approach.

This aspect of the interface between my patient's object-relations and the analyst's ability to proceed analytically was gradually worked through by exploring her paranoid vision of me. Many of the interpretations I made were taken as an attack, a judgment, or evidence of my uncaring stance. However, during the fifth year of her analytic treatment, some changes took place. I became more brave and daring in terms of deciding to try again. In other words, I had felt like retreating or giving up the transference investigation, due to her constant intimidation and rigid control. However, I gathered myself and began to slowly risk making more transference-based interpretations, and the response was encouraging. Ruth reacted just as abruptly and aggressively as before, but now I stuck with it more than before. Instead of diving into the safety of my own withdrawal, I dodged the transference-related bullets and kept going. I asked Ruth to please tell me exactly how she felt I was being so nasty. I asked her to tell me what each word of my interpretation had meant to her. So, I used an approach similar to dream analysis, an inch-by-inch exploration of each piece of the puzzle and the associated symbolism or projection process. What I gradually found out was that Ruth took every opportunity to fill in any ambiguity or vagueness in my comments with her persecutory fears.

One example of this was when Ruth told me, "I don't think we have much of a connection. As a matter of fact, I don't feel connected to anyone. I think there is no way for anyone to really understand what I feel, since there is a big wall there. No one can get through the wall to get to me." I replied, "I can tell you want someone to find you, to connect with you, so there must be an important reason you put a wall up to keep me and others away."

Ruth became loud and hostile. She said, "Why the hell are you judging me like that? What kind of therapist are you?" Taken aback, I waited until the smoke cleared and then asked, "What did I say to make you so angry?" Ruth answered, "That is very obvious. You said I put up a wall, like it is my fault! You always say things like that. You take what I say and use it to blame me." In this tense atmosphere, I listened closely and then replied, "Help me understand. When you said no one can get to you because of the big wall, it sounded like they can't get to you because of something you have put up to keep them out and maybe to keep you safe. I could be wrong, but that is what it looked like to me. I guess the wall could just have been put there by someone else and you feel stuck behind it. But, that isn't the way I heard it. So, I am not sure why you are so upset." Ruth replied, "Well, you didn't explain it like that. Now it makes more sense and we can talk about it. But, you don't explain things a lot. You leave out parts when you say things, you don't explain it so it doesn't make sense." I interpreted that she became worried or scared when it wasn't all spelled out and then she filled in the holes with ideas and feelings that scared her even more. Ruth replied, "Well, that is your fault. Why can't you just be more clear?" I said, "I will try and be more clear from now on. At the same time, I think it will be valuable to understand how you fill in the unknown with feelings that scare you." Here, I tried to acknowledge my possible contribution to the confusion and to Ruth's feeling of persecution. At the same time, I remained steady with my interpretive investigation, which I felt was very important and more accessible in the moment than many other times in the past.

Ruth responded, "OK. That sounds like a deal." There was a period of silence that felt comfortable and relaxed. I interpreted, "This seems like a moment of connection, a moment without the wall." She nodded yes. After another moment of silence, Ruth began to talk about how alone and hopeless she had been feeling as her brother died of cancer. She began sobbing. This was only the second time since I met Ruth that she shed a tear. I felt it was a remarkable moment of connection and integration with her internal objects and with her analyst, clearly the result of our in-the-moment analytic work. The exploration of her vision of me as attacking and judgmental led to an increase in trust, which allowed her to open up about her dying brother.

Since this period, I have been able to do more interpretive work with Ruth and she has been more able to internalize and integrate my comments.

Now, if Ruth had been attending treatment four or five times a week on the couch, would these types of breakthroughs and growth spurts have come sooner or been bigger? I think they might have. However, as with many patients, the underlying object-relations and defensive patterns shaped or forced the treatment process into a certain pattern. Part of working analytically is to identify this unique imprint and how it shapes the transference and countertransference dynamic. Then it can become easier to interpret, or at least more clear how best to interpret, those internal characteristics that the patient imposes on the potential of the analytic relationship.

This case illustrated how productive psychoanalytic work can occur even when constrained or confined by a patient's object-related phantasies and internal relational world. While the patient's transference and unconscious vision of the world restricted the frequency and use of couch, these external elements did not prevent a genuine psychoanalytic experience from taking place.

Case 6

Joe was a fifty-year-old man with whom I had conducted a seven-year psychoanalysis. The bulk of the transference and his core phantasies involved seeing me as a stern, judgmental father who disapproved of any autonomous thinking or independent, grown-up behaviors. This was a replica of his relationship with his father, who was very rigid and intimidating when Joe was growing up. Throughout the treatment, we made difficult, slow, but positive strides in understanding this recycling, repeating object-relationship. We succeeded in changing much of its place in Joe's internal world. We had mutually decided to end our meetings, feeling that while more of the same type of work could be done, Joe had made significant strides, felt much better about himself, and interacted with his external and internal world in a much more balanced manner.

Part of this progress was that he could accept me as a more supportive, encouraging father figure in his life. By this I mean that his phantasies of me, in the transference, became flexible and positive rather than stringent and harsh. While I had not in reality become more or less supportive of him over the seven years, his image of me had mellowed considerably. Joe still worried about my reactions to his being adventuresome, "wild," or vibrant in his life. His masculinity was something he now could be more openly proud of, but it still could break down into more of a paranoid, or at least superstitious, view of our relationship. Bit by bit, Joe's view had changed and he saw me as a more accepting, interested, and even encouraging supporter of his maleness and his whole identity.

In our very last session, Joe lay silent on the analytic couch. Then, he shared several different but linked thoughts. First, he brought up a sado-masochistic scene from a television show he enjoyed the night before. It involved a cozy scene of Norman Rockwell-type family harmony that suddenly turned ugly and violent. Joe thought it was hysterical and brilliant. I interpreted that he still hoped for us to be a close, cozy family, but wondered if it could turn ugly. Yet, he could now see it from a safer distance, own his aggression, and share his enjoyment of it. Basically, he was telling me how he enjoyed his own strength and even liked the role of angry father for his own. Joe replied, "You are right, absolutely right! It is just still hard to admit it."

Next, Joe talked about his enjoyment of a TV series much like *The Godfather*. The series revolved around a violent Mafia family headed by a man struggling to shake off the emotional scars of growing up with a violent and critical father. Joe discussed the details of a few shows. I interpreted how Joe was now able to express the more aggressive, worldly side of himself to me without the fear of me "putting out a contract" on him. I added that he was also exposing the loyalty and playfulness he felt with me, the same loyalty he described in the show's character. Joe said he felt there was that element of closeness and some kind of bond that he would miss. "We have been through a lot together!" he said.

After a pause, Joe associated to the image of a wild animal in a cage. He said it was a cage I had built to trap him and he was in there, struggling to get free. I interpreted that his fear of being a whole person, his fear of his aggressive side, his fear of his maleness, and his fear of his love toward me had created that cage. The cage provided a comfortable, censored, safe place from all that, but it severely restricted him too. Now he was ready to try life outside the cage, despite his conflicted feelings and fears.

Toward the end of the session, Joe said, "I am thinking about how I would really like to shake your hand as we part and tell you 'thank you.' But I am afraid you would see it as a gross boundary violation, just wrong and inappropriate. You would be offended and even irritated or angry. I can realize, logically, that you are not as rigid or uptight as that. I do see you now as much more of a flexible guy, but emotionally I am convinced it would be wrong, a mistake."

The history of the transference and the working through process with Joe had included both depressive and paranoid–schizoid anxieties. We had reached a significant level of psychological integration and a healthier balance of object-relations dynamics by the end of the treatment. When Joe spoke of causing trouble by shaking my hand, I felt there were remnants of both internal states still operating. I interpreted that he imagined the paw of the wild, caged animal reaching out to touch me for love and connection, but he worried that he would leave me wounded or hurt as a result of his need and desire. This was the depressive aspect of his concerns. Also, I said that he worried his gratitude would be misunderstood, judged, and punished, that I would retaliate for his violation. This was more an aspect of his paranoid–schizoid functioning.

Joe told me I "knew him all too well" and that while these fears were indeed present, he "felt better equipped to move through them and take care of business." So, a long and fruitful journey came to a close. Joe got up from the analytic couch, we shook hands, he thanked me, and we parted.

Discussion

In all these cases the analytic approach was used, but keeping the analytic focus was difficult because of the nature of the patient's pathology and specific phantasies. These types of cases are common and, if studied, may help the analyst understand how to maintain the psychoanalytic focus even in stormy or less than optimal conditions. Certainly the first couple of cases could not be called a psychoanalysis. However, the material shows how the analytic approach may offer help and sometimes facilitate change in quite disturbed patients who have a hard time settling into the regular setting of analysis. Even in clinical situations where there is virtually nothing to make the treatment be termed a psychoanalysis, keeping an analytic focus may help the patient in some small ways and may help the analyst to avoid countertransference acting out.

Even though most psychoanalysts in private practice are familiar with the types of difficult cases presented, it is interesting to notice the lack of investigation in the analytic literature. This may be a collective dismissal of vexing clinical work that is ignored under the umbrella of "non-analytic" work. A survey of the past fifty years of more than ten psychoanalytic journals reveals virtually no articles with titles including such terms as "crisis," "stalled," "emergency," "infrequent," "modifications," "failed," "failure," and so forth. The only references to the word "brief" are when the therapist or analyst decides ahead of time to offer only five or ten sessions to the patient, calling it "brief therapy." So, it seems important to take a look at what is a part of most clinicians' work day, even if it doesn't fit neatly into an ideal or standardized method of viewing psychoanalytic treatment.

The analytic focus is the simplest method of exploring this. By "focus," I mean the degrees of interest and exploration and interpersonal/intra-psychic stance we take in relation to the transference, the defenses, the patient's unconscious phantasies and the themes within them, the counter-transference phenomenon, and the method of psychological repetition that plays out in the patient's object-relational world. These many factors can push the analyst off course, away from an analytic focus.

Karon (2003) discusses the importance of basic listening and communication in order for the analyst to aid the patient properly. The idea of dynamic listening seems so simple, but is really a critical element of maintaining a true psychoanalytic focus on the patient and their treatment needs, especially with the more difficult patient.

Each and every patient we see requires us to focus on the basic principles of transference, defense, phantasy, and unconscious process. However, certain very troubled patients struggle with such intense psychological issues that they make it a continuous task for the analyst to stay on course within the analytic field of understanding. The idea of maintaining an analytic focus is especially helpful when one is pushed off course by the vexing, chaotic, and unpredictable dynamics some patients bring into the therapeutic relationship. These types of patients fall into a broad range of disorders, including addictions (Smaldino, 1991), those patients lacking the subjectivity and objectivity of triangular space (Britton, 2004), patients with a "nonresonance response" to relational connection (Joseph, 1993), those with severe Oedipal disorders (Boswell, 2002), countless variations of paranoid–schizoid malfunction (Klein, 1946), primitive states of loss (Waska, 2003), and mental constructs that are rigidly controlled by pathological projective identification mechanisms (Waska, 2004).

Many of the patients seen by analysts in outpatient, private practice settings are suffering from chronic and severe conditions. More than 10 per cent of patients fit the more chaotic and unsparing psychiatric criteria of borderline personality disorder (Widiger and Francis, 1989) and many of the rest have other sorts of personality disorders and mood dysfunctions. These types of troubled individuals favor more primitive defenses and regressive methods of relating. Keeping the analyst focus is very important when dealing with these types of problems. The analysis of the transference is particularly hard with these patients and without ongoing analytic focus can deteriorate into mutual patient/analyst acting out. In particular, these patients can resist the acknowledgment of the transference (Gill, 1979), erasing any as-if aspect to the treatment and simply reacting to the pull of primitive phantasies in highly defensive, combative, and fragmented ways.

It is critical to come to terms with how to address these difficult patients and stormy clinical encounters. By applying a flexible or elastic analytic model to these frequent and common situations, the analyst can better work analytically with whatever internal climate the patient brings into the office, rather than trying to force a predetermined model of the mind or model of treatment procedures onto the patient and therefore limiting that particular patient and analyst potential. In this sense, a treatment may be considered psychoanalytic at one point in time, supportive counseling at another moment, and psychoanalytic psychotherapy at yet another juncture. Instead of this being a theoretical confinement or judgment, it can simply be the naturally fluid movement of a patient in analytic treatment. The fluctuation of the patient's inner world and how that shapes the transference and countertransference can simply be a helpful determinant of what the most present and current unconscious forces are to be understood and worked with.

Today, psychoanalysis faces a climate of crisis as a profession. Hopefully, this period of turmoil will push the profession to reflect on itself and remember that psychoanalysis is a method of healing for those in distress. Rather than focusing on rigid criteria that are helpful in training situations, such as frequency and use of couch, the aim of day-to-day treatment should be the analytic method: analysis of transference, the interpretation of unconscious conflict, exploration of defenses and phantasies, and the working through of patterns of relational repetition. The public, our prospective patients, and our profession all could profit from remembering that psychoanalysis is a discipline built on common sense, communication, honesty, compassion, and exploration.

Robert Pyles (2003), the past president of the American Psychoanalytic Association, states: "Psychoanalysis today is under siege. We are fighting for survival, the survival of our profession and of our ability to deliver quality care to our patients" (p. 23). Pyles is addressing many of the external factors facing the profession, which are indeed critical. However, the more inward components of our work and how we are in the consulting room with our patients are part of how to work with this dilemma. We must prove to ourselves and the general public that psychoanalysis is a method that makes sense and provides healing.

The case material presented in this chapter was ordered in degree of difficulty with regard to maintaining the analytic focus. This difficulty was usually the result of multiple factors, including abrupt termination, frequency issues, acting out, countertransference conflicts, diagnosis, and external factors such as insurance benefits and employment. However, each case demonstrates the importance and benefits of maintaining the analytic focus. By doing so, both patient and analyst can frequently find some reward, even in the most modest of circumstances. Also, these cases show the utility of the analytic approach across the spectrum of different clinical situations.

Chapter 6

Difficult but worth the effort

Theoretical concerns

A person's innate libidinal and aggressive object-related phantasies create states of attachment that are often in conflict. These internal experiences are continually frustrated and gratified by constitution, environment, and evolving internal object-relationships. This leads to a further complexity of phantasies and affect states that then fuel or constrict the mental matrix once again. People relate to one another through these highly idiosyncratic core phantasy patterns. The particular and unique unfolding of this intra-psychic and interpersonal connecting makes for a special fingerprint in the analytic setting. Each patient is unique; each transference is new and specialized. The transference phenomenon is a constant in the human experience (Bird, 1972) and the psychoanalytic method is dedicated to the exploration and understanding of this phenomenon by the use of interpretation.

Optimum and ideal treatment usually consists of maximum frequency, use of couch, and successful termination, but use of the couch, frequency, diagnosis, or method of ending do not necessarily define a treatment. These are variables that are clinically fluid and have different meanings for each patient. Novick (1988), Earle (1979), and Glover (1955) are among various authors whose research points out that the majority of analytic treatments are discontinued rather than successfully terminated. This often involves acting out on the part of either patient or analyst and should be understood and worked through, but more often than not it goes unexplored. In addition, even when addressed analytically, acting out and discontinuation can be unavoidable. Some patients' resistance to the exploration of their transference reactions makes the treatment difficult. It is as if the patient is declaring the bulk of their psychic life off limits. This resistance is often in the form of an acting out of transference phantasies within and outside the analytic situation.

These troubled and troubling patients create turbulent and often incomplete treatments that go unexamined in the analytic literature. However, these difficult cases and their vexing transference relationships embody a set of dynamics worthy of study. This study can provide better answers as to how best to aid these individuals who need our help so much, but seem to challenge and fight our efforts so strongly.

The contributions of Melanie Klein

Noting that certain patients rely on splitting mechanisms to project their transference feelings into the past or current external world, Melanie Klein (1952a) stated:

> Reports of patients about their daily life, relations, and activities not only give an insight into the functioning of the ego, but also reveal – if we explore the unconscious content – the defenses against the anxieties stirred up in the transference situation . . . he tries to split the relations to him [the analyst], keeping him either as a good or as a bad figure: he deflects some of the feelings and attitudes experienced toward the analyst on to other people in his current life, and this is part of "acting out."
>
> (pp. 55–56)

Hinshelwood (1991) states:

> The practice of Kleinian psychoanalysis has become an understanding of the transference as an expression of unconscious phantasy, active right here and now in the moment of analysis. The transference is, however, moulded upon the infantile mechanisms with which the patient managed his experiences long ago.
>
> (p. 465)

The concept of acting out the transference can be useful in defining the nature of a treatment and understanding how a patient either works with or reacts against the analyst and the analytic situation. In some cases, this acting out can limit the analytic relationship and/or cause a premature termination.

In this chapter, I am highlighting those patients who are so paranoid, narcissistic, and often aggressive that a treatment process cannot be sustained. While most break off the analytic relationship long before it could be termed a true course of psychoanalytic therapy, I do notice valuable work taking place some of the time. Even in the most chaotic and briefest of meetings, we often learn something. Sometimes the patient feels helped in some capacity. Therefore, even momentary psychoanalytic encounters and aborted treatments should be written about and studied.

Rather than viewing patients as untreatable because of diagnosis, we must be more understanding of what may be preventing that particular analyst and that particular patient from being able to work together in an analytic manner. Klein's idea of transference acting out seems to help explain many of these clinical roadblocks.

How the patient's phantasies shape the analytic encounter

The analyst engages the patient with the tools of psychoanalysis: curiosity, exploration, and interpretation of unconscious processes. The patient expresses himself in some idiosyncratic manner in relation to the analyst and the analytic situation. It is the nature of the patient's unconscious phantasies and their unique patterns (character structure) that determines how that patient unconsciously configures the analytic procedure, not external factors such as frequency.

If the analyst provides the steady encouragement of free association and consistently examines the transference, anxieties, and defenses, the patient will invariably manifest particular responses. In other words, given the same stimulus, patients react differently.

One group of patients attach their inner focus onto the analyst, developing a strong analyst-centered transference. These patients' transference acting out is usually at a minimum and the analyst's interpretations are able to contain and assist the patient in working reflectively. The mutual working through of the core transference phantasies and feelings constitutes what we can call a rather integrated, successful treatment process. Using us in this way, these patients develop intra-psychic change, personal insight, and an increased awareness of reality.

Another group of patients will express a more generalized transference to their environment, which becomes highlighted within the analytic situation. Normal transference experiences are brought to the surface in a broad perspective, including an analysis of external matters other than the patient–analyst relationship. Acting out would be present and at times formidable, but it doesn't overwhelm the analyst or patients' ability to think in a reflective and exploratory manner. Working through involves a combination of intra-psychic and interpersonal issues, so many of these treatments involve much work on general, pervasive, internal phantasies and not as much work on the here-and-now transference phenomenon within the patient–analyst dyad. The potential result of such a treatment is interpersonal growth, behavioral change, and increased insight into aspects of one's personality.

A third group of patients show an active tuning out or fighting against any awareness of internal experiences. These patients relate in a highly concrete way to the analyst. This is where acting out dominates the relationship. Here, the ego uses denial, splitting, manic defenses, and destructive levels of projective identification to ward off the experience of the object and the realization of separateness, attachment, or need for the object. These patients adopt a passive yet demanding role and often demand to be given love, pills, or advice. The potential benefit of such a treatment, if kept at such a pathological level, is some degree of behavioral change and temporary shifts in cognitive thought processes. Unless constantly reinforced by an external force or authority, these gains often fade. Introjection of the analyst as an authority figure may sustain the behavioral change, yet without independent thinking.

How a patient reacts to the analytic method has much to do with the nature of their internal anxieties. Kleinians understand these anxieties as part of two developmental positions. Whether a patient is functioning chiefly within the paranoid–schizoid or depressive position will determine how they make use of the analyst.

The use of interpretation to explore and work through the transference, together with the analysis of the resistance to that exploration, is the goal of treatment. Frequent visits and the use of the couch usually help facilitate that goal, but are not the essence of it. This is similar to Gill's (1984) point regarding the "extrinsic" factors in psychoanalysis. By and large, the extrinsic factors help propel whatever momentum is already there. Therefore, I ask patients to come often and use the couch and I immediately position myself to the understanding of their internal phantasies and their transference manifestations from the very first session. I use interpretation as the method of communicating with the patient from the start and assume they are or can be capable of working within this psychoanalytic environment.

Again, we must be elastic in both our clinical work and our theory building. Difficult patients are individuals who will probably engage a number of therapists over the years and may eventually create a long-term relationship that leads to a successful termination. In between, however, the journey will be erratic and the analyst must be flexible in order to provide that patient with an analytic experience.

As Oremland (1991) has outlined, the technique in psychoanalytic psychotherapy and psychoanalysis should remain identical. It is not the analyst that determines the difference in relatedness, but the nature of the patient's phantasies and their acting out of them through projective identification mechanisms. The nature of a patient's phantasy world, their internal self-and-object theater, acts in conjunction with their current level of ego strength to foster a certain degree of attachment or non-attachment to the transference figure of the analyst. The patient will move toward or away from the analyst as their primary internal object. Of course, this is a relationship full of contradictory and ambivalent feelings. However, there is a threshold at which the patient will be able or unable to tolerate the presence of the analyst in their mind. We hope that with therapeutic understanding and the tool of interpretation, traumatic and intolerable phantasies will gradually be modified. In this way, we can enable tediously positioned patients to better tolerate the analytic procedure.

Nevertheless, some patients are in the grips of such severe paranoid–schizoid anxieties that they just cannot maintain an ongoing internal or external relationship to the analyst. These patients usually act out as a way to maintain some degree of inner safety and control. They use extensive projection, denial, and splitting to dilute and destroy any evidence of a connection to the analyst. They are unaware of any feelings or thoughts about their relationship to the analyst. Again, interpretation is the key to slowly establishing trust in some of these cases. Some of these patients are so overcome, or flooded, by their transference feelings that they have a psychotic reaction. Here, the acting out is carried out by destroying internal bridges between reality (the analyst) and the ego.

Case material

The patients who enter treatment and quickly establish a stormy or very tenuous transference based on internal chaos and conflict are living with great anxiety. Their lives are shaped by phantasies that feel overwhelming. After engaging with the analyst, they often leave after a few months. These treatments are unsuccessful in shifting the patient's personality structure. However, some interpersonal changes may occur. Clinically, the analyst attempts to engage the patient in an exploration of his mind and its conflicts, while simultaneously trying to analyze his acting out and his unconscious attempts to destroy the link between ego and object.

Some of these patients will attend for a year or more, but they manage and control the level of attachment in the transference by refusing to come frequently. This type of acting out is not usually amenable to interpretation as it is based on tremendous narcissistic and paranoid resistance.

Oscar

Oscar told me, "the world is a place where people just eat each other, sucking each other's blood. The only work that is left goes to illegal aliens who will take low pay. It is just a matter of time before it all collapses. There are too many people all fighting to get what they want. People continue to make fun of me because I am a little carpenter and they think I am unable to make it, and maybe they are right. I am getting taken advantage of right now because I didn't get these people to sign a contract. But, if I had tried they would have just laughed in my face and hired someone else. Everywhere I look someone puts up a barrier to prevent me from getting anywhere. It's all about money. Everyone just wants the buck!"

Usually Oscar talks like this for twenty or thirty minutes and ignores or deflects any comment I may make. Then he starts to feel bad and apologizes. He tells me how he has made a "5 per cent to 25 per cent rate of progress" and cites examples of his recent successes. At this point he will then digress back into trying to convince me of the world's evils. Here, I believe he temporarily shifted from aggressive and paranoid phantasies to primitive depressive anxieties. He felt he had hurt me and tried to make up by citing his progress. Then, he went back to his more core feelings of persecution and anger.

I suggested there must be an important reason why he wants to show me the doom and gloom in his life. I thought he might be trying to warn me what to look out for and show me how much he needed my help. Oscar said he must look out because in the future all these bad things will overcome him: "it's just a matter of time." I suggested he come in more often, but he refused to come in more often than once every two weeks. He said he must use what he learns out in the world or it won't be worth it and that he needs the time to think about what he learns and then use it. He says "two weeks is just about right, by then I really need to be here." So, he had everything carefully divided or split into thinking vs doing, outside vs inside, treatment vs real world, etc. He seemed to worry about mental contamination happening through the mixing of these two camps.

Oscar's persecutory anxieties were too overwhelming. He tried to manage them by keeping his distance from me with words and with attending infrequently. I suggested this to him but again he deflected my comment. I saw him for almost a year and I used an analytic approach. He was unable to tolerate any direct closeness for fear of attack. Yet he so wanted comfort, help, and understanding in his nightmare world that he drove over three hours of a round trip to see me. However, he reached a psychic crossroads where he would have had to engage more with me to receive what he desperately needed or he would have felt empty and alone. At this point, the anxiety won, and he left.

In terms of progress, I think Oscar achieved some internal feeling of safety and attachment from his time with me. I don't know if that would have lasted or not, as it was never processed or explored. I feel he probably achieved a temporary intra-psychic quieting of his paranoid–schizoid anxieties. Externally, he was able to be more interpersonally appropriate with his customers and friends. This may have had a more lasting quality, as a behavioral change.

Steve

Steve was a middle-aged man I saw for five years. He maintained a sense of control over me by coming in only once a week and by discussing only topics that he had already decided on and thought through on his own. When I suggested he come more often or that we discuss any topic that might occur to him, he quickly reacted as if we were in a power struggle. My countertransference was of being strong-armed.

Steve's father was a stern and distant man. He felt that Steve was not manly enough. Steve's mother alternated between smothering him in a highly sexualized way and shunning him with cold indifference. Initially, Steve spoke mostly about his chaotic marriage. Two years later, he was discussing the breakup of that marriage and his attempts at dating. Any effort to expand his career options, increase his dating, or otherwise move toward the world and out of his schizoid shell brought on intense anxiety.

Gradually, toward the fifth year of treatment, he was able to speak more about his lifelong anxieties and his inability to be close to women. He was unsure of how to relate to others and was afraid of being rejected or criticized. Nevertheless, he tried to date but it was in a counterphobic sort of way where he would act overly masculine and macho. He was quite split off from his feelings and rarely spoke of our relationship.

On one hand, he began to explore some of his internal fears and phantasies. On the other hand, he mostly remained fixed on daily situations and refused to acknowledge his inner experiences of himself or of the analytic relationship.

Eventually, he revealed that he secretly took drugs and dressed up as a woman. Steve would take out his vast collection of women's undergarments, put some on, and watch himself masturbate in the mirror. He said he felt "merged" with "the woman" in the mirror. He felt in perfect unity with his sexualized ideal. This would clearly take on psychotic proportions. He saw the woman in the mirror kissing him and fondling his penis.

I felt an eerie lack of relatedness working with Steve. He acted warmly toward me as long as I did things his way. My countertransference was a nervousness and a feeling of "why are we meeting?" It was difficult to speak with him about abstract concepts, especially about his feelings. I was usually anxious and tense when I met with him. During our time together I was quite cautious about exploring our relationship because of his obvious agitation. During the last year of treatment, I tried to engage him in more of an investigation of how we were relating and how he experienced our time together. But he became more and more angry and paranoid. He stopped the treatment in the fifth year, citing money problems and a feeling of gradual independence. He said he was "ready to try it on his own." Looking back on his case, my sense is that I did not fully understand the degree of psychotic fusion he maintained with his internal mother. This was a way to avoid her abandonment and attack. He acted out the perverted union with her to avoid feeling attacked and suffocated by her. Also, he experienced my curiosity as both a sexual invasion and a pulling apart of him and his mother.

Steve made most of his progress in the interpersonal realm. He related to people more freely, had far fewer panic attacks, and started to see women as potential friends. While he began to understand his character makeup and the nature of some of his unconscious phantasies and fears, his shifts were primarily interpersonal and behavioral (an adaptation versus a working through). His sexualized fetish remained in place as an intrapsychic compromise with his seductive, attacking internal mother.

Zack

Zack was a thirty-year-old gardener referred by his lawyer after being arrested for making hundreds of obscene phone calls. He had a history of petty theft and drug use.

He appeared very nervous and talked without stopping during the first few months. While he seemed quite intelligent and able to make links in the material, he also seemed infantile and simplistic. Also, he often negated any insight that seemed to accidently leak out of him. With only a high-school education and a great reliance on television for information about "what the right way" is, he reminded me of a character in the movie *Being There*.

Zack said he made obscene phone calls because he was afraid of being rejected. Therefore, he "got over the hard part" by not letting the woman see him. He would call and pretend to be someone the woman knew. He then aroused her with sexual talk until there was mutual masturbation. It was only later that he let them know who he was and gave them his name and phone number. This led to several invitations from the women for face-to-face meetings. He claimed his intent was not to harm anyone and if the woman was angry or offended he apologized and hung up.

Zack felt shunned and judged most of his life, mostly by his father but by others as well. He felt close to his mother but punished for that intimacy by his father. His father and mother were chronic alcoholics. By Zack's account, his mother would become loving and friendly when drunk and his father would get enraged at seeing them together. When I asked if he thought his father was jealous, he said "no, just sickened!"

Zack was emotionally immature and unmotivated. At the same time, he could be articulate and occasionally seemed interested in exploring his thoughts and feelings. He developed a transference of me being the all-wise doctor who could tell him about the mysteries of his mind. This shifted to a view of me as an untrustworthy authority-figure and jailer. He was irritated to find out that he would need to be an active participant in the therapeutic process.

He wanted to control and own his internal objects, yet felt he was a little boy who was humiliated and ignored by his father. This was projected into the transference when he got me to set rigid rules about fees and schedules due to his disregard for my needs. He went for months not paying me, citing countless excuses and assuring me the check was in the mail. I felt used and disrespected by him and found myself becoming more and more of a policeman in the treatment. Through projective identification, I received a taste of what he felt like and I was pushed into becoming more like a controlling and dominating father.

Just as he managed to gather information about women when he called them and then used the information in a way that frightened them and left them feeling controlled, he found ways of gathering information about me. It was actually more guesswork, based on narcissistic phantasies about sexualized control. Zack asked me how my family was doing. When I asked what he meant, he told me he noticed I drove a four-door Buick, therefore I must have children. At the end of a session, which was the last in my evening schedule, he said, "we are the only ones in this whole building!" I was uncomfortable and worried about my safety. I told Zack he was controlling me as he had the women on the phone. He was unable to discuss this and neutralized it as "nothing important." I felt this acting out was a combination of him trying to be close and affectionate with me and a way to control, manipulate, and intimidate me. In this sense, he was simultaneously projecting different aspects of his ego and his internal object into me and our relationship.

Zack had to find a way to control and intimidate the object, which defended against how dependent and desperate he felt. He was scared his object would control and abuse him. This was somewhat traceable to a narcissistic father who always picked on him and an alcoholic mother whom he had taken care of and possibly become overly intimate with when quite young.

Throughout the treatment, Zack continued to abuse drugs and manipulate women via obscene phone calls. As soon as he wasn't mandated to see me, he stopped coming.

This was a treatment that had definite periods of psychoanalytic work, yet was best seen as a counseling situation. While Zack was able to explore his unconscious life, he acted out to such an extent that any true insight or analytic collaboration became impossible. His aggression and perversion won out.

Betty

Betty was a thirty-year-old African woman I met with once a week. She worked as a secretary and told me that her boss was verbally abusive. Although Betty felt he had helped her out when she "really needed it," she thought he took advantage of her. Her husband, an alcoholic, treated her in a demeaning manner, finding fault with everything she did.

Betty came to see me as a result of the trail she had blazed through medical practitioners and therapists who saw her for assorted somatic complaints and chronic anxiety. She had been given many tests, which always showed sound health. Betty said she had a case of chronic "nerves." Statements such as "I feel like I will fly apart, I am afraid of being out of control. I am so alone in this world and the fear has never gone away," were her associations to nonspecific terror. She spend many sessions telling me about her health. She was fearful of ailments that are usually thought of as incurable and catastrophic (i.e. cancer, AIDS, brain tumors, and so on). These seemed to be pre-genital anxiety states of unregulated and unmanaged affect triggered by infantile experiences of sensory overload. Correspondingly, my initial countertransference reaction was of being both overwhelmed and held at a distance. Her anxiety produced a defensive shell which made our relationship sketchy and brittle.

It became clear that this woman had been the witness of many traumatic events over the years. Whether these were phantasies or recollections of real events was not the point. She felt like a passive witness, powerless and at the mercy of the environment.

Betty's childhood was cruel, oppressive, and scary. Her father was uninvolved and passive, yet he may have also been molesting the children. He was frequently a silent witness to his wife's violent attacks on the children. Betty's mother would beat the children for no apparent reason with sticks, brooms, pipes, and fists. It was not uncommon for the children to have large welts on their backs and legs. During Betty's latency and teenage years, the abuse took on a different mode. Betty began to notice the violence in her extended family and in her community. Her actual beatings reduced in frequency, but she began to notice more violence around her. There was an escalation of civil war in her part of the country. There was regular gun-fighting and nightly curfews for several years and she witnessed many of the confusing and bitter realities of wartime life.

When Betty told me of the violence she witnessed, I felt numb. No doubt I was finding ways of disassociating, much as she did. It was a struggle to stay present with her at these times. It also seemed she was beating me numb with her tales of horror. Stories of wife-beating and rape were common. Details about blood pouring out of a cousin's ears, screaming wounded people outside the house at night, and a brother-in-law hanging himself in the garage took up many sessions.

Betty played the role of victim and martyr. She would say that if she was a better mother, a better lover, a better cook, and a prettier woman, she would not be abused by her husband. However, this sounded and felt like a "throwaway line."

Betty spoke of her body in a gloomy way. "I feel so tired, my bones ache. My muscles feel slow and I feel really heavy." When I asked her if she placed importance on self-care through exercise or diet, she replied, "I must take care of my boss, my husband, my family, and everyone else. I never have time to do anything like that. Anyway, I am just a lazy person to begin with. I have always been that way." Her self-depreciating style was used to negate the treatment. Even her thoughts of suicide were laced with traces of this. She told me, "I would probably mess that up too, I am such an idiot."

Betty's sadomasochistic personality quickly became the theme in the transference. The helpless, needy, and confused little girl part of her was symbiotically bound to an angry, selfish, cruel, and critical mother part. She also remained stubbornly loyal to the detached and distant father object. She limited us to external events and refused to acknowledge the phantasies she had about her objects, including us.

This was a case in which the patient's internal acting out of her phantasies and transference feelings kept the treatment externally focused. She recounted her trauma and grievances in a way that excluded me. This was no doubt out of fear of being re-traumatized, as well as a narcissistic way of controlling her objects and making me feel as helpless as she did. Betty kept the treatment in a supportive counseling mode, where she quietly demanded answers and soothing reassurance. She left after a year, citing lack of funds due to having to pay other people's bills. Therefore, she ended the way she began: passive and victimized, unable to connect with a hopeful ego-ideal or to a phantasy of a durable and useful object. Overall, she felt less at the mercy of others and was less concerned with her physical condition. However, she remained in the cross-hairs of her internal objects.

Bill

Bill was a middle-aged lawyer who came for help in understanding his inability to commit to the woman he was engaged to. He had been dating another woman and each woman knew of the other. When he came to see me, both women had threatened to leave him for good and he was unable to decide between the two. Early on, we identified one relationship as the sexy, exciting, but hollow one and the other as the logical, secure, but boring one.

I met with Bill for nine months, once a week. Issues of conflict around dependency and a marked sense of never being appreciated quickly became our focus. These feelings were equally spread out over the transference as well as our discussions about his work life, current family situation, childhood, and his indecision with the two women. In other words, we consistently explored and worked with his phantasies about himself and his internal objects as well as how he projected these anxieties and conflicts. He developed enough intrapsychic momentum to investigate his inner thoughts and feelings about dependency and rejection as they played out in our relationship and other areas of his life. Using these criteria, we were conducting a psychoanalytic psychotherapy.

For financial and emotional reasons, he decided to not continue the work but wanted to feel able to return at some later time. After nine months, we ended the treatment under the mutual agreement that he had resolved his presenting problems but still had more work that could be done. I pointed out that he wished to move ahead in life and gain a better sense of autonomy, yet still be dependent on me. He also feared I would control him if he was dependent, so he in turn tried to be self-sufficient. This phantasy left him feeling insecure and angry. His early termination was an unconscious bargain that he struck with himself to try to deal with these factors. I felt he both succeeded in changing some of his more acute fears and conflicts and managed to con both of us into feeling "all was well and good." He left treatment a week before his wedding date to marry the woman he had been engaged to. Bill thanked me for my help and told me his plans to have children and settle down. Years later, a patient who knew Bill told me that Bill was enjoying his marriage, had several children, and seemed very content.

John

John was a psychotic man who was arrested for running down the highway naked while masturbating. I saw him sitting up, two times a week, for five years. He would not lie down on the couch for fear I would either rape him or kill him. Early on, he was convinced that I was an agent of Satan, or perhaps Satan himself. He so desperately wanted to be close to me and to learn how to have a girlfriend that he was able to struggle with his intense anxiety about being with "the enemy." Even though he tried to control me in many different ways and approached our relationship as a cat-and-mouse game where someone was going to get eaten, he still wanted to learn how to be close. This was the extremely conflicted repetition of desire and fear that he experienced with a psychotic mother and an abusive father.

Gradually, we came to see how he felt I might be like his mother, who without warning would beat him, or like his father, who without warning would caress his genitals. When dating women, John feared he might attack and rape them.

Our time together was focused on understanding the nature of his phantasies, as they manifested in the transference and in his attempts at dating. By the time he terminated, he no longer felt I was Satan and he was able to date without fear of hurting women. He also had gained a good deal of understanding about himself and how his mind operated. This led to other positive changes in his life.

Chapter 7

A mixed bag

The realities of private practice[1]

Last week, I conducted the last session of a successful analysis with a middle-aged man who came to see me six years ago for feelings of panic, anxiety, and failure. Diagnostically, he was an obsessive neurotic with narcissistic features. We met multiple times each week and he used the analytic couch. He paid his bill on time and rarely missed a session. Through an ongoing analysis of the transference, dreams, extra-transference material, and genetic reconstruction,[2] he achieved a major shift in his psychological structure. When he left, after a thought out and agreed upon termination period, he had made significant changes. Issues of loss, power, competition, and envy had radically improved. As a result, his external life was blooming. He had found a very suitable mate, gotten married, had his first child, and made important advances in his career. When the analysis ended, we both felt very satisfied and proud at the tremendous shift in his life.

While being a part of this success was very gratifying, this type of patient and this type of treatment outcome are not the norm in my private practice. Most private practice patients (Friedman *et al.*, 1998) are more disturbed than the patient I just described and therefore produce a more taxing and less tidy outcome. By facing this reality and trying to better understand what really goes on in psychoanalytic practice, we can better serve our patients and be less overcome with countertransference troubles.

Caper (1992) has explored the idea of what is really curative about psychoanalysis. He thinks the analyst's job is to help the patient identify

1 This material was first published in 2003 as "A mixed bag: the realities of psychoanalytic practice", *American Journal of Psychoanalysis*, 63(1): 49–67.

2 "Genetic reconstruction" is a psychoanalytic term that refers to the way the analyst attempts to reconstruct, through the patient's associations, dreams, and transference material, the family dynamics and major themes that shaped the patient's upbringing. The way the patient remembers those family dynamics and the way they convey them to the analyst are best understood as comprising actual historical facts blended with and distorted by unconscious phantasies and feelings.

and integrate split-off, projected, and denied aspects of their ego. To achieve this limited treatment goal, the analyst must avoid the omnipotent zeal of assuming the power of curing the patient. This cure is often an unconscious manipulation in which the patient is molded into the likeness of the analyst. I think Caper has done an excellent job at simplifying and clarifying the essence of psychoanalytic practice. We strive to help the patient put the pieces together, to integrate what was not only broken by circumstance, but torn apart by the ego itself. Caper emphasizes that this is the goal, but we must remember we will never reach it in any idealist, fully complete way. The best results in any treatment will be a better integration, never a full one.

Rothstein (1994) has written about the importance of maintaining a psychoanalytic view of all patients' problems and advocates psychoanalysis as the preferred method for all his patients. He believes that even if a treatment starts off without the usual elements of a psychoanalysis such as frequency, use of the couch, and so forth, the analyst must steadfastly work toward those elements.

While I would enjoy reaching all the goals Rothstein sets, I believe it is more realistic to say that using a psychoanalytic approach in a once a week treatment with an acting out patient who ends therapy abruptly with only some presenting problems resolved is still a psychoanalytic process and possibly a successful one at that.

Even when addressed analytically, acting out and discontinuation can be unavoidable. Many of these cases involve individuals who routinely make internal bargains with themselves whereby they are able to make some progress in exchange for some amount of commitment to a repetition compulsion. At some point, this unconscious bargain breaks down and the ego resorts to action (either physical or psychic) as an emergency measure to ward off overwhelming persecutory or depressive anxieties.

Unfortunately, some of our training, some of our literature, and our own phantasies contribute to an elusive quest for an idealistic patient and an ideal form of treatment. This sets us up to feel impotent and frustrated with our patients. Rather than feeling like we are failing and rather than seeing our patients as failing, I think psychoanalysis should be seen as a method of helping that will always produce mixed results, and rarely produce a total cure.

In a perfect world, we hope for a patient who can afford to pay our full fee, come every day and on time, not act out, work through their problems in an insightful way, and terminate in a way that leaves both parties fulfilled and satisfied. The cracks in this wonderful, wishful picture are countless.

The obstacles to helping a patient are often overwhelming and are frequently a taxing mix of internal and external blockades to healing and integration. Scheduling is usually difficult. Most of the patients I see work a nine-hour day, commute for an hour home and have family responsibilities or night school. Their cars often break down.

Many are single mothers or young adults who have small incomes and large debts. Bankruptcy, unpaid taxes, overused credit cards, and looming student loans make paying for therapy difficult. Quite a few patients would never be able to see me at all were it not for their employee assistance insurance benefits. Of course, this means they have between three and twenty visits a year and then they are cut off. These are all external factors.

Depression, acting out, panic attacks, masochism, obsessive or narcissistic control issues, and psychotic delusions are all internal states that conspire to make it hard for patients to attend and complete long-term psychoanalytic treatment.

Rather than feeling frustrated at not being able to practice an idealistic psychoanalysis with non-problematic patients who always pay our full fee and pay on time, show up for all their appointments, work through all their problems, and terminate when all parties feel it appropriate, practitioners can take a different road. I think the psychoanalytic approach is well suited for the realities of day-to-day private practice work (Waska, 2000). This clinical reality includes a less than perfect analyst who does his or her best to help an often quite disturbed and emotionally turbulent patient who may improve enough to go on leading a more satisfying life. However, this will often be a life still haunted and hindered by the ghosts that brought them to treatment in the first place.

So, one of my goals is to offer hope to the frustrated therapist and make a stand for the benefits of psychoanalytic work as it really happens, however limited it can be at times. To this goal, I think it is helpful to explore case material where the treatment obviously lurched and sputtered along, sometimes managing to cross the finish line and sometimes not.

Case material

Melanie

Melanie, a nervous looking woman in her late fifties, came into treatment for "panic attacks." She was a paranoid schizophrenic with loose associations, persecutory projections, delusions, and auditory hallucinations. These symptoms dramatically improved over the time we met.

As she was growing up, her older brother routinely beat her and criticized her. Melanie's father was an alcoholic who was not often home. Her mother seems to have been distant, hostile, and critical of both children, but especially Melanie.

After barely completing high-school, she married an abusive man who was rarely home.

When in her mid-twenties, Melanie began to feel disoriented and intensely anxious. Escalating ideas of being followed by the police led to her first hospitalization.

In her early forties, her husband died in a car accident. One or two years later, she went on disability because of escalating feelings of fragmentation and thoughts of suicide.

When I met Melanie, she had been on disability ten years and had tried many types of psychiatric treatment over the previous three decades. She has been hospitalized several times over the years. Melanie had tried biofeedback, rapid-eye-movement therapy, hypnosis, pharmacological therapy, cognitive-behavioral therapy, twelve-step programs, and various 'new age' therapies. Her experience with at least six previous psychotherapists had been a general over-involvement on the part of these therapists which promoted Melanie's excessive dependency, hostility, and devaluation of the treatment. She would appear in crisis, and the therapist would become anxious and overly suggestive and friendly. Then Melanie would feel great hope, followed by feeling disappointed and betrayed.

One observation I made was that Melanie felt that having her own thoughts and feelings was equivalent to being alone, in danger of attack, and "crazy." She feared she could never receive help or assistance and would "fall into the black hole forever," which was her way of describing a terrifying experience of fragmentation and disintegration. These anxieties led to loneliness, desperation, and hopelessness. Fear of loss of the object was analogous with loss of self. Her primary defenses were projective identification, splitting, devaluation, and denial, which made her thinking concrete and non-symbolic.

When I first started working with her, Melanie frequently perceived her bodily sensations as indicators of catastrophic mental phenomena. When she ate some spoiled food and had a stomachache, she was sure she was "being pulled into a bottomless pit and falling into hell."

Intense states of anxiety occasionally brought on diarrhea and the bowel urgency was experienced as a fundamental fragmentation of her mind. She would call me in panic and disorientation. Upon describing her fears, we could see that she needed to go to the bathroom. Initially, she could not identify her bodily sensations and instead experienced feelings of annihilation. Over time, our understanding led to a gradual internalization in which she was able to think, "I think I may be feeling sick to my stomach, maybe I need to take some medicine." Later, she could start to wonder why she had started to feel so anxious in the first place. She began to deal with her somatic symptoms from a psychological perspective.

When I interpreted her fear, anxiety, and desire for a connection with me, her confusion over bodily states, and her terror about uncovering topics that she felt were "off limits," she usually was able to reintegrate herself and return to functioning. When her anxiety was not excessive, she gradually was able to provide her own observations and interpretations. Recently, Melanie has been exploring her fear of making progress and her fear of either killing the object or being killed by the object as a punishment for having an identity.

After five years of analytic treatment, Melanie has made much progress. A gradual working through of some of these overwhelming anxieties has allowed her to make some friends and to have actually completed several courses at a local college. She is thinking of interviewing for a job and no longer engaging disability. Her internal struggle of persecution, loss, and fragmentation has decreased. She is more aware of her own contributions to these intra-psychic conflicts.

Todd

Todd was in his thirties and had been married for ten years. He had three children. After his wife threw him out of the house for his drinking binges, he came to me for help. I saw him for several years, twice a week. Diagnostically, Todd's drinking diverted attention from his perversions, which in turn were a coping mechanism for his paranoid psychosis.

Todd was raised in a religious family. Commenting on his Catholic upbringing, he said, "the entire family was under heavy duty repression." I said, "I guess your parents thought God doesn't like feelings."

Todd was one of seven brothers. They were raised in one bedroom, with separate bunk beds. Without my asking, Todd volunteered that there was never any sex play or masturbation in the cramped bedroom. I followed up his comment by asking him about his sexual history as a teenager and young adult. Todd blurted out, "I was really naive, I didn't even know what a homosexual was until I got to high-school." This thinly veiled fear of his own homosexual feelings seeped out in other conversations over the years.

During high-school, Todd began experimenting with drugs and alcohol and isolated himself from his peers. He had a girlfriend for one year in his late teens. He seemed puzzled as he told me that the only part of the relationship he remembered was having sex. I said, "Maybe your feelings about the relationship had to be erased, or repressed like in your family."

For most of his adult life, Todd had worked in the construction field. He drank heavily for years, but the last several years were marked by more and more binges.

He told me he had what he called a normal sex life in the marriage. Todd said, "You know, it is like most marriages. The wife gets it when she is in the mood and the husband has to wait till she is in the mood." Todd felt his wife was fat and not too attractive, but he said she was "OK" and "worth keeping."

Todd told me his wife was fed up with his drinking and his masturbation habits. I asked for details. He told me that when he "discovered" masturbation, he felt a new world had opened up. "I think it is great. Once you realize how great it is, you can't stop doing it! I usually do it every morning when the family is asleep. Also, I do it in the shower, in the living room, in the kitchen, or wherever feels right. I try and only do it every other day, except when I go on a roll and do it several times a day. It is the perfect mate. They don't talk back and they are ready to go whenever you are." His use of "they" referred to the women he fantasized about while masturbating.

His son walked in on Todd masturbating in the living room, and Todd told his son it was a normal activity. His wife told the son that his father was a pervert. As Todd told me more about his masturbating, it became clear that he often spent hours each day under his house, in a crawl space, drinking and masturbating.

During one session, I questioned Todd about taking his young children to see the "R" rated movie *Cape Fear*. This is a violent film about a male predator stalking a young girl, trying to rape and kill her. Todd became defensive at first, saying the movie was a realistic example of life and his children ought to see how life really is. I suggested the movie might be a representation of his own emotional experiences growing up. Todd didn't pursue that line of thought. However, he has since asked me what I think about other movies and has taken my advice that there are ratings on movies for a reason. Clearly, I combined a suggestion with an interpretation. This is a parameter that went unanalyzed.

Over the years of treatment, Todd told me about being watched by the CIA and constantly having to battle the agents of the FBI, who would sneak looks at him through his bedroom window to catch him having sex. He felt the FBI kept a file on him because his oldest son was so intelligent. Todd explained how they keep records on smart people to see if they are headed into any sort of deviant activity.

I helped him deal with these delusions by giving him advice as well as interpretations. These interpretations were of the transference and the extra-transference. Because of his potential for emotionally harming his children, there were times I resorted to more interactive, non-analytic counseling.

After three years, Todd stopped coming. He said he felt better and he could no longer afford it.

By taking a mostly psychoanalytic stance, I think I was able to help Todd in many ways. He felt less paranoid, less anxious, and more in touch with reality. He drank less and resorted to masturbation in the crawl space only under significant periods of stress. His marriage seemed more balanced and Todd was a more available parent with more realistic ideas about his children's needs. Overall, Todd's anxious, psychotic state improved quite a bit. At the same time, his fundamental psychological problems remained and his basic paranoid state was unchanged. However, psychoanalytic treatment brought a significant degree of relief to his life.

Compared to the case of Melanie, Todd did not do as well in achieving structural change. Both patients were quite disturbed, although Melanie's symptoms were more somatic and Todd's took the form of acting out and perversion. I used the same degree of flexible technique and analytic focus with both individuals. Melanie came to understand herself more and therefore felt more independent and in charge of her life. Todd achieved some important symptom relief and behavioral management skills without as much insight.

Stacy

Stacy was a woman in her late twenties who came for help with her depressive feelings. She had never been in treatment before and I saw her several times a week on the couch, for four years. She was seen for ten dollars per session since she was either jobless or working at very low-paying jobs. Stacy had a history of prostitution, drug use, erratic employment, and short-lived relationships. Upon my request, she stopped using all recreational drugs, with the exception of marijuana. The family history she gave me was among the worst I had ever heard. All the children were repeatedly molested by her father and frequently beaten by her mother. During her adolescence, her father raped her several times at gunpoint. The family was extremely poor and constantly moved from city to city.

Diagnostically, Stacy was a borderline patient. She was impulsive and suffered paranoid delusions and fears. In the first year, we dealt with her psychotic, persecutory phantasies. These faded in the second year. In the transference, she had to convince me of the evils of the world and the evils within herself in the hope that I might pay attention and come to her aid. Also, she was at times convinced I disliked her and at best put up with her. During the second year, she started to have more mixed feelings toward me in which she imagined how we both cared for each other, but felt angry and deprived as well.

Excerpts from the second year of treatment

P: I do not want to talk about anything! (*Long silence*) I do not want to spend much time on this, but I guess I want to talk about this guy that I met recently. He has come into the place I work a few times and we have started talking. I kind of like him but whenever he starts to talk to me I get really nervous and start talking a mile a minute about anything and everything, but never about anything important.

A: Like you do in here when you feel nervous and afraid that I will reject you?

P: Yes. I am sure he thinks I must be some sort of freak for doing that. I never ask him questions about himself. I just talk about myself and other stupid subjects. I am sure he will get tired of that and decide to not be around me anymore. I think that is a way I end up having people not want to be around me. But I can't help it. It just happens. I get nervous.

A: You are scared that I or other people who are important in your life find you uninteresting or selfish.

P: Well yeah! Why wouldn't you be disappointed in me? You probably think all sorts of things, like "why the fuck can't she just talk about what is important instead of all this stupid shit!"

A: So, you worry I think many negative things about you.

P: Yeah!

A: Like what else?

P: You probably think I am lazy, fat, out of shape, not intellectual, not motivated, negative, not going anywhere in life, always picking shitty people to be with, that I am boring, and not a hard worker. Do you want me to go on?

A: Is that how you see yourself?

P: Probably. (*Starts to cry*) I just think you will see what I tell you as stupid and unimportant, insignificant, and crazy. Like I am making a big deal over nothing. It doesn't really matter anyway. No matter what I talk about, it doesn't really matter.

A: If you think I will belittle what is valuable to you, it would be very hard to risk sharing yourself with me. You want me to care, but worry I won't.

P: Yes. I do want that, but I can't see how you could respect a shit like me.

A month later

P: I think you can be cold and indifferent. You never show me what you really think or who you really are. I feel like you don't care and that maybe we are not a good match. Then again, I don't seem to be able to find a good match anywhere. People are just shit. It always turns out that way.

A: You see me as uncaring and not interested in you?

P: It isn't what I think, I know it! It is obvious you don't care.

A: Yet we continue to meet and seem to get somewhere.

P: Yeah, but you are not warm. I need someone who is warm and shows they care.

A: Perhaps you want these things from me but are also scared of getting them.

P: That is absolutely true. If you were really warm and showed your feelings I would probably run out the door.

A: Lots of mixed feelings you're having. You want my love but fear it too. You are scared of being cared for so you are quick to reject it.

P: No shit, Sherlock. Well, whatever. See you next time.

Stacy ended her treatment when she was accepted into a distant college. As a result of our work, she had become emotionally stable and decided to pursue higher learning in college.

I received several letters updating me about her new life. She was able to settle into the routines and frustrations of student life, found a loving boyfriend, and eventually re-entered treatment. When I said goodbye to her, she had achieved a better understanding of her self, was better able to manage her impulses, and had stopped replaying her traumatic background within much of her current life. Our exploration and working through of portions of her phantasy world resulted in significant structural change.

Chapter 8

Gone but not forgotten

A new look at difficult cases[1]

Although it is taxing, confusing, and frustrating, I am invested in working with patients who are so paranoid, narcissistic, or borderline that their treatment cannot always be sustained. Most break off the meetings long before it could be termed a true course of psychoanalytic therapy, but I notice valuable work taking place some of the time. Even in the most chaotic and briefest of meetings, I often learn something. Sometimes, the patient feels helped in some capacity. Therefore, I believe that even momentary psychoanalytic encounters and aborted treatments should be written about and studied. These fragmentary treatments occur in everyone's practice. We can ignore them, but they will continue to occur for all of us. It is better to reexamine them and understand what processes might be taking place.

Rather than viewing patients as untreatable, I believe we must be more understanding of what may be preventing the analyst and patient from being able to work together in an analytic manner.

Many of these patients never make it past the first phone call. We struggle with them on the phone for one or more calls. Then, they either make an appointment but never show up or decide they don't need to come in after all. Some will begin treatment, establish a very precarious and rocky relationship to the analyst, and abruptly stop coming. These are often individuals who are more narcissistic or manic. They come to therapy to regain their narcissistic footing and leave when they have their illusion of power restored. Finally, some of these patients engage the analyst for a period only to stop treatment abruptly, even after many months or years of progress. These tend to be people struggling with more paranoid and masochistic problems. Rather than being overtly sadistic, they are covertly controlling and manipulative.

As a group, difficult patients show commonalities. All have suffered some degree of external trauma early in their life and are gripped by pervasive

1 Originally published in 2001 as "Gone but not forgotten: a new look at difficult cases", *Psychodynamic Counselling*, 7(2): 159–176. www.tandf.co.uk/journals/titles/14753634.html

feelings of envy, aggression, and alienation. Externally and internally, loss is a central theme and projective identification and splitting are the primary tools used to counter these threats. Attachment to the object is their fulcrum of conflict. Loss of the ideal object and attack by the bad objects are a constant unconscious worry. Loss is an intra-psychic principle in these patients' lives. In addition, they usually have histories of abusive or neglectful relationships with their primary caretakers early in life. Many report a sadistic and rejecting mother. They also feel that their fathers were either absent or neglectful. In these ways, the impact of the internal on the external and vice-versa shapes these patients' intra-psychic experiences in a particular manner.

Hanna Segal (1974) spoke to this:

> it is essential for the infant's favorable development in the paranoid–schizoid position that good experiences should predominate over bad ones. What the infant's actual experience is depends on both external and internal factors. External deprivation, physical or mental, prevents gratification; but even when the environment is conducive to gratifying experiences, they may still be modified or even prevented by internal factors.
>
> (p. 39)

Again, one factor that seems prominent is a primitive phantasy of loss and persecution. The issue of unconscious loss of and attack by the primary object becomes a cornerstone in the transference relationship. I believe that Melanie Klein's ideas about ego development and internal object-relations help us deal with these patients' dynamics.

Klein described how the ego constantly projects its introjected good objects, which in turn color how the ego perceives the world. The ego then takes them back in, which colors the internal world. Loss of the good and helpful internal mother leaves the ego overcome by its own tension, envy, and aggression and therefore vulnerable to the threat of bad objects. Klein (1936) has shown that fear of the loss of the good maternal object, internal and external, is mixed with feelings of having destroyed her. The loss is therefore a punishment from the object. My view is that this is true for the depressive position but that other anxieties regarding loss dominate the paranoid–schizoid position.

While projective identification and introjection normally serve to build the ego up and fill it with enduring experiences of trust and safety, projective identification can also serve as the primary cause of this core ego collapse.

Klein's theory of the mind is particularly useful with difficult patients as they so often rely on primitive methods of relating, organized around splitting, manic defenses, and projective identification. They are organizing their internal experience within the paranoid–schizoid position.

In this more primitive experience, the ego feels supported by good part objects that suddenly shift into multiple persecutory part objects. This is the result of excessive hostility in the ego that the ego transports via projective identification and introjection into an experience of angry, attacking objects ready to devour a helpless ego. At the moment these processes occur, the ego loses contact with the good part objects and is left alone to fend off attacking maternal part objects. This is the point of loss in the paranoid–schizoid position.

In the depressive position, the ego feels it has hurt or damaged the object and feels guilty. In the paranoid–schizoid position, the ego feels it has killed off the one thing it must have for survival. In the depressive position, the ego feels the object will punish the ego in some way for its crime. The paranoid–schizoid ego envisions a vendetta in which the object returns to hunt down and kill off the ego. Life, death, and survival are the focus compared with guilt and reparation in the depressive position. Projective identification and splitting are used as weapons and tools of survival in the paranoid–schizoid battle with the bad object and as a desperate attempt to prevent the loss of the ideal object.

Many of these difficult cases never make it to the first consultation meeting. A woman called up saying she was suicidal and wanting to cut herself "again." She had been depressed for months and stopped going to work because she "doesn't like the people there." She said she left her car "where it died" and now has to get around by bus. She was sighing and sounded agitated. When I suggested we meet, she said it would be "a hassle" to take the bus all the way to my office. She added that she wants to visit some friends for a week or two and may call me when she gets back. I suggested she had mixed feelings about coming in and feels angry that things aren't going well. Momentarily, she seemed less anxious and less agitated. Then, she asked if we could conduct therapy over the phone and wanted to know how many phone calls it would take before she "would be better." I told her she must have a hard time taking herself seriously. She said she felt unsure of what to do, whether to see me or have a fun vacation with her friends. She told me she would think about everything and call me if she decided to not visit her friends. She never called back.

I think this woman was telling me about a part of herself, an internal object, that she had killed off and left "where it died." She had lost a part of herself; an internal object had died. She wasn't terribly interested in retrieving this split-off aspect of herself, but probably this was a cover for how scared she was to find it and own it. I felt that her contact with me amounted to a massive projective identification process of evacuation. She put all of her anxiety and badness onto me and walked away. This was probably the best she could do at that moment. She devalued me and triumphed with a manic projective identification.

Loss within the paranoid–schizoid position and the accompanying fears of attack and persecution seem to be a principal element in many of these cases. Certainly, patients bring us a mix of paranoid and depressive anxieties (Klein, 1950). However, these patients are consistently struggling with phantasies about what is happening to them and what they are losing, rather than concerns about their objects and how they are affecting those around them. If analyst and patient can manage to stay together and weather these painful and angry feelings, a slow healing and mourning take place. Klein (1950) writes:

> I have found that in adults the success of the work of mourning depends not only on establishing within the ego the person who is mourned (as we learned from Freud and Abraham), but also on re-establishing the first loved objects, which in early infancy were felt to be endangered or destroyed by destructive impulses.
>
> (p. 79)

With the more difficult patients I am exploring, the awareness of these feelings can be so humiliating, threatening, or incriminating that they feel they are fighting for their survival. The analyst becomes anything but an ally. Nevertheless, some of the mourning work Klein discusses is possible. I find that before many of these difficult cases abort, much exploration and some working through takes place. The analysis of primitive paranoid–schizoid phantasies of loss and persecution may not be complete but can be started.

Typically, difficult patients have encountered trouble from an early age and it has usually been a combination of external and internal difficulties. Envy, aggression, and insatiable yearning have mixed with ongoing external deprivation or abuse. These feelings and phantasies bombard the idealized good object and destroy it. Without sufficient strong internalized good objects, the ego's envy and rage take over. Also, due to splitting, the idealized object is a fragile, polarized, and hollow entity. It is literally too good to be true.

During optimal development, an infant and mother are involved in continuous projection and introjection of curiosity, love, need, and desire. This builds up a supply of good objects in the infantile ego and creates a beneficial cycle of taking in and giving love and concern. These good internal objects help detoxify the accumulation of hate, greed, envy, and pain. Attachment to reaffirming and supportive objects fills and fortifies the ego, which in turn shapes psychic structure.

My view is that in the paranoid–schizoid position, the ego's hostility, frustration, and hunger bombard the good part objects. If these part objects are not plentiful, cohesive, and able to withstand the ego's aggression, then they simultaneously perish and then return as bad objects seeking revenge. This is the intrapsychic moment of loss in the paranoid–schizoid position. Projective identification brings out the ego's negative forces and in less than optimal situations, the ego perceives the object to be overwhelmed and seeking retribution. Hope shifts to dread and security turns into danger and loss.

The case of Freddy

This was a case in which the patient made it into my office, but came for only five visits. As with all the cases I am presenting, the case of Freddy could be discounted as a failed treatment with an unanalyzable patient. However, I am proposing that the analyst always engage a patient with the analytic instrument. The procedure may not "take" and flourish, but something may still come out of it. If nothing else, the analyst may learn something that will help in treating the next patient.

Initially Freddy's brother called me twice; later his mother called several times. His brother said that Freddy needed help getting motivated with his college classes. He felt Freddy's problems were chronic and confided that "Perhaps Freddy and his mother are too close." Once the brother felt I could help, he wondered if I could merely talk to Freddy over the phone instead of meeting with him. After I explained the requirements of therapy, he felt more comfortable about Freddy making an appointment. However, this is when the mother took over.

I felt that Freddy's mother was trying to control me and was treating Freddy like an infant. She wanted to know who I was, how I worked, how much I charged, and how long it would take to make her son better. This was all asked in a demanding and somewhat demeaning tone. After what seemed like a long debate, she said she wanted me to see Freddy. At first, she wanted the treatment by phone. When I insisted he come in person and that he call me to make the appointment, she said she wanted me to meet with him that very day. When I told her I could see him in three days, but he would need to call me, she told me she would find someone else. I felt devalued and thrown out because I didn't work to her specifications. In the countertransference, I experienced a sense of loss of connection with this woman and then I felt judged and punished. This was a taste of what I believe her son went through much of the time, on a more intense level.

The brother called about two weeks later and asked if he could make an appointment for Freddy. I suggested Freddy call himself. He did, and his mother got on the line and asked for directions. The first appointment was set but on the day of our meeting she called and canceled, saying Freddy was "too tired." Finally, we rescheduled and did begin meeting.

On one hand, the mother appeared to be quite caring. She did not work so that she could care for Freddy. She drove him to school and to therapy. On the other hand, she denied the severity of his illness. When I arranged for a medication evaluation, she told me she had to cancel because of a tea-party. When she spoke of his hallucinations, she was concerned but felt it was "just his nerves acting up." There was a controlling and aggressive way in which she denied aspects of him and cultivated other aspects. The brother seemed to be the one who realized the severity of the illness and was genuinely trying to help.

Until the patient was in middle school, the family was poor. Then the father managed to change a small business venture into a highly profitable firm. This enabled the family to send my patient to a special private high-school. He felt odd coming from the poor section of town to go to this nice school. Freddy said he felt confident and intelligent until high-school. During high-school, his parents divorced and his grandparents died. After four very difficult years and increasing isolation and odd behavior, his parents sent him overseas to college. He attended classes but quickly became delusional and unable to function. He hallucinated ghosts who wailed, "Take me away!" Clearly, Freddy felt scared, homesick, and angry. These feelings became externalized specters through projective identification, creating a psychotic process.

His mother urged him to move back with her but he elected to live with his father. During the year of being there, he became much more psychotic. At his mother's urging, he moved back with her and she quit her job to care for him. When I met Freddy, he had been with his mother for three months and had just started attending a local college. He no longer had outright hallucinations, but suffered periods of psychotic delusions and verbal disorganization. His mother was scared of him at these times and told me that he became violent. I saw Freddy twice a week, sitting up. When I tried to see him more often, the mother told me there wasn't anything wrong with him, only that he was "lazy." I felt, through my countertransference, that this was a sort of power struggle mother and I were in. She made me feel it was a tug of war over who would own Freddy and his identity.

The treatment

When I asked Freddy to come in, I greeted a man who looked like a mildly retarded fifteen-year-old. I shook his hand and noted a limp, lifeless response. He began by saying he did not know why he had to see a psychologist. "It is not like I ever raped or killed anyone. I masturbated once and I have watched a few bad movies. So why am I here?" I replied, "Maybe you feel as though you have done bad things." He agreed.

Freddy told me I looked like a smug, rich psychologist who was out to take people's money. To him, I only thought of how to get money out of people and I seemed arrogant and superior. He repeated this throughout the hour. Freddy told me of a movie he had seen starring Bruce Willis. A troubled young woman goes to see a psychologist. He makes her attend group therapy. He is mean and ignores her feelings. She hates him but feels trapped. One day, she meets Bruce Willis and he starts to take care of her. He is understanding and helps her feel better. At some point, she finds a knife and kills the mean psychologist.

Hearing this, I felt a bit threatened and hoped he didn't have a knife with him. I said, "You are worried I won't be understanding and that I could trap you and be mean to you. That would force you to be mean back. What you really want is for me to be like Bruce Willis, kind and understanding and able to take care of you." Freddy replied, "That would be wonderful. I feel really good being here. I love it, but it is a perversion. I should be studying hard and doing homework instead of being here." I said, "You feel so good being here but you're worried that you're taking in too much of a good thing and that might cause trouble." He agreed, and said it was too good to be true and was unrealistic. He said he must get back to the real world and study hard all day long. I commented that there might be another side to him, and he interrupted to say, "Why do you think I might be gay?" I said he could be worried that I will see who he really is, unless he works hard to be perfect. Freddy asked, "Can you show me how to succeed in school?" I told him I might be able to help him in many different ways. Later, he explained his goal in school of being a doctor, so he could be successful and make lots of money like I did. "That's what it's all about, isn't it?" When we ended and I told him I would see him next time, he was shocked. He thought that hour was the only time we would ever meet and didn't understand why we would need to meet again.

It was only months later that I had a chance to watch this Bruce Willis movie. I was struck by the fact that the therapist (Bruce Willis) was seeing a patient who was so depressed she killed herself by jumping out his window in the middle of her session. The therapist, now in despair, sought the help of a therapist friend, as he felt to blame. I think Freddy felt he had destroyed his father, causing him to leave the family. His mother was now destroying him. He was worried he would destroy me as well.

In the next session, Freddy seemed to feel more organized and able to track reality better. He told me how he felt omnipotent and godlike in high-school. Feeling superior to others, he didn't study for tests. Later, when he didn't receive the highest marks in the school, he felt ashamed and angry with himself. He told me how he was close to his grandfather, who died when he was in high-school. Freddy said the whole family became cold and distant afterwards, but the death was positive because others gave him sympathy. Freddy let out a diabolical laugh and said this sympathy made him feel secretly superior.

When I brought up his contempt of me in the prior hour, he apologized. I told him I hoped he would try and tell me everything that he felt, positive or negative. He said "OK" with a sense of relief. He went on to tell me how he failed at math classes so he turned his focus to chemistry. Responding to the way he described it, I commented that he was desperately trying to find something to cling to and something that he might be able to feel competent at. He agreed and said he hoped it would work. We discussed his hallucinations and delusions he had experienced over the years. He said he didn't hear things anymore but that when he felt bad there was a special part of his brain that hurt. He pointed to the top of his head. Freddy went on, "There is another unconscious part of my brain that feels great, like almost perfect, when I have a perfect outcome in math." His lack of symbol formation left him with psychotic somatic experiences.

My countertransference was split, much like Freddy's feelings. During both hours, I felt somewhat unsure whether he was really smart and just ignoring and distorting his abilities or whether internal anxiety had so clouded him that he was unable to take in learning. I even wondered if he might be retarded. I also felt he needed and wanted a father figure to care for him but that he might become a hopelessly dependent little child who would never get better. I wondered if he felt his neediness had driven his father away and made his mother angry. In other words, I felt he had projected his abandoned and lonely feelings into his father and felt he had driven him away with his anger and neediness. He was scared to have so much hunger and anger inside of him, which could hurt his objects, so he projected those feelings into mother. Now he felt at her mercy and worried that he had made her angry. Unfortunately, neither father nor mother seemed able to provide Freddy with an adequate mental container to detoxify and translate some of these overwhelming phantasies.

In the third session, Freddy discussed high-school memories of a girl who helped him with math and whom he helped with chemistry. They had a friendship that felt nice. When I asked if he had wanted her as a girlfriend, he assured me that it was merely platonic and that he respected women and thought of family and family values. He went on to discuss his history of feeling odd and out of place. This seems to have started when his father became successful.

Freddy felt inferior to the other students in high-school and felt like a fraud. He began to judge others in his mind and put everyone down. He started to feel superior. I commented that Freddy had felt it necessary to put me down as a money-hungry psychologist who sat smugly in my chair. I emphasized my statement by sitting as he pictured me. He immediately said my comment made him feel totally normal, a "rare moment of normality." I interpreted that he was relieved to see I had survived his attack and that I seemed to understand him and his need to put me down. I said this understanding was important to him. He agreed and said, "That is right. It feels wonderful to me. Nobody has ever been able to understand me or take the time to listen to me. It feels so good. It makes me feel normal." I felt it important to stay in the here-and-now transference material rather than link it to his possible phantasy of having attacked and destroyed his mother/father.

Freddy went on to tell me about his parents' divorce. Then he told me an amusing example of how his mother and her mother seemed identically self-absorbed and obnoxious. He went on to tell of being sent off to college. There he began to stab his arms with a knife and burn his arm with a cigarette. "I had to become strong," he said. I interpreted his wish to become stronger than the pain he felt about the divorce and about being away from his father.

After the divorce, Freddy's father would buy lavish gifts for his new girlfriend. Then Freddy would spend thousands of dollars on a credit card. I said he was trying to be like his father as well as get revenge on his father for leaving the family. He agreed. He then told me of how he would watch X-rated cartoons every weekend and one time he "felt something down here" and masturbated.

Later, he told me of his plans of being a doctor. I said he knew he was fooling himself, but needed something to cling to for hope and the illusion of greatness. I said this was to try to avoid the pain of feeling weak and inferior and all alone. I felt this was more to the point than to interpret his identification with me as a great doctor.

During the fourth session, Freddy told me how he always had trouble in school from elementary school on and always felt inferior and abnormal. He discussed his current struggles with college courses, talking in a tangential and rambling way. I commented that he was hoping to prove his normality through getting good grades. He said his aunt had been different than most of his family and told him after he graduated high-school that he would make a fine doctor or biologist. Freddy looked sad and said she accepted him. He said that memory helped him survive a recent chemistry test. "She told me that even though I was gay at the time, or almost gay." I asked for more information. He went on to say he worried that people saw him as gay and he hated TV programs about gay people. He asked if I was gay and I asked him how he came upon that idea. He rambled on about how he wasn't gay, but he wasn't sure.

Freddy said his mother forbade him to take any human sexuality classes at college. I said he wanted to know about sex and hoped to have sex but didn't know if that was OK with me or his mother. I added that he hoped I would see him as normal and accept him "as is." He brightened and said, "All the other talk is bullshit. This is what it's about. I want to feel normal." Freddy said he worried that since he had taken several English courses already, he could easily be confused for being gay. He joked that Shakespeare might be interesting but you're then branded as potentially gay. He said he felt sorry for a friend who not only had taken several English courses but was interested in theater as well. His reputation was doomed.

Freddy also talked, back and forth, about his ambivalence with girls at school. He wants to hang out and meet them but his mother is there to pick him up as soon as class is over. On the other hand, they are all pretty ugly and all the kids are singing angry rap-music on the sidewalk. Here, I felt he was trying to undo his desires so as to still be loved by mother and not hate her. Finally, he told me how he had tried to imitate several friends along the way, regarding how they talk about girls and how they approach studying. I said, "You are not sure of your own identity and try to wear their identity. You're hoping to trade in the angry parts in your mind and find some peace and feel acceptable." He agreed.

Finally, he told me how in high-school he used to enjoy drawing cars. However, then he noticed that the smartest guy in the class, whom he envied, drew wonderful pictures of castles and scenery. He couldn't understand how someone could study all the time, be so smart, and be such a good artist. He immediately felt his cars were crap and that he was not smart. When his father bought a big nice car, he felt vindicated and equal with the smart guy. He said he saw the car magazine in my waiting room and knew that I put it there to remind him of that, since I already knew these events. I felt he hoped I was an ideal, all-knowing object that he could depend on.

In the fifth session, Freddy told me the story of his parents' divorce. Apparently, his father didn't pay much attention to his business and began to gamble and womanize. Freddy's mother had to study and learn about the business and worked hard to maintain it. After the father continued to have affairs and gamble, the mother divorced him. Freddy described his mother as a long-suffering martyr who always demanded attention and recognition. He said that respecting her for that was hard. I commented that he worried I might be a self-serving person who would demand from him. He said yes, but he felt better about that now.

He went on to say he wasn't sure what to do in school and that he had failed another test in chemistry. He said he didn't know whether he should be a political scientist or a doctor or a scientist like me. Freddy went on to say how Alex Baldwin was a political scientist and he seemed like a fine man except that his eyes were screwed in his head in a strange way.

Freddy told me that he saw his father as a hero. Even though there were things about him that were not too good, Freddy could see how he tried hard and was a good man. Freddy looked sad. I said, "You love him, he is your hero." Freddy cried and said he didn't know if he could be a scientist like me. He didn't know if he could make it in school, but he must. I said, "You hope I will be like a father for you and tell you to relax. That I will accept you whether you are a political scientist or a chemist. You're hoping

I can help you relax about that pressure and help you feel loved for just being yourself, as is." Freddy looked enormously relieved and let out a big sigh. He nodded and smiled. "Yes. Yes, that is what I want – but you are not my father!" I said, "No. I am not. It upsets you that he doesn't think that way. You believe you have to work and study and be a scientist for your father and mother to love you." Freddy replied, "Yes, I do. But I don't know if I can do it. I sit in class and have all these thoughts and I can't concentrate. I sit by myself and pretend to look at the book, but I can't think."

He went on to tell me how he didn't respect his father in the past and also felt very badly about himself. Then he began to feel better about his father and himself. I commented that he felt uneasy if he seemed to be outdoing his father, leaving him weak by becoming stronger. Freddy replied, "I think that answer comes later, maybe tomorrow." Looking back on this, I may have made a more Oedipal-based interpretation and Freddy reminded me he wasn't yet operating at that level.

Finally, Freddy told me a story about a book he said he had read. He said it was a famous novel about a character named Eric Fromm. This was an odd man who lived in the side of a mountain. He was a loner and came down to the village and went to the taverns and collected magazines. The town people thought he was odd and weird. He loved to read and study on his own. He was married to his wife, Polo. She was a complaining woman who felt sour in her stomach and always had some kind of misery to tell Eric about. Then one day he met Polo's cousin. She was uneducated and simple, but Eric felt she was beautiful and nice.

Freddy told me he wants to be like Eric Fromm, because he respects Eric. I commented, "You feel like your mother is Polo and you are Eric. You hope I will realize that part of you is like the cousin and part of you is like Eric." I decided not to comment at that moment on Eric Fromm being me and the nasty Polo part of him. He said he definitely hoped that I would see he was trying to be like Eric and that he felt comfortable with that.

Freddy didn't show up for the next session. I called and he answered. He told me his mother had gone on vacation for two weeks. Freddy had tried to figure out where my office was and tried to call me but didn't have anything written down. The mother apparently had not left adequate instructions. I felt sorry for Freddy and felt we all were now victims of mother. On the surface, she had given up her normal life to care for Freddy and she had sought out treatment for him. On an unconscious level, it appeared that she needed to control him and have him remain with her.

I called a few days later and spoke with Freddy. He told me that he didn't need to come to therapy, that he didn't want to, and that his mother couldn't afford it.

Three weeks went by; I called the mother and she said she couldn't afford the therapy anymore and that Freddy didn't want to come. She said, "What am I supposed to do? I can't make him come if he doesn't want to."

Freddy seemed to feel he had lost his internal father and he feared that a persecutory mother had replaced him. I think he loved his father a great deal and idealized him, but felt a great deal of anger and disappointment in him as well. Fearing he could destroy his father and cause terrible trouble, he resorted to intense splitting. He tried to identify with the idealized aspects of his father but kept running into the bad part of his father that he also internalized. He tried to discharge these conflicts into his mother, who did not provide an ample container. In fact, she only amplified these feelings with her own pathology. Therefore, Freddy tried to save his father but felt abandoned by his idealized version of him. This good aspect of father/self corroded and vanished and was replaced by a bad mother/self object.

Clinical experience verifies what Melanie Klein (1950) has pointed out. Patients are always in some fluctuation between depressive and paranoid–schizoid anxieties. Freddy was no doubt functioning primarily within the paranoid–schizoid position and experiencing life from a psychotic vantage. However, he suffered from intense phantasies and feelings of loss and guilt that were persecutory in nature. He felt, "What have I done or not done that has caused my father to abandon me and my mother to control me." He wondered, "Maybe I haven't achieved what you want or demand of me. Perhaps that is why you have left me and now control me?" These phantasies included an idea that he was only loved if he was in mother's mold, otherwise he was lazy and bad. So, Freddy was overwhelmed by a primitive and persecutory paranoid–schizoid guilt in which he felt he had not given mother, and later father, what they demanded. This guilt was not depressive. In other words, Freddy did not worry about how he had hurt his parents. Indeed, he feared that if he didn't deliver the goods, he would be deliberately abandoned (loss) and then judged and attacked.

In the transference, he feared I would leave him and attack him if he didn't become a doctor/scientist and follow my mold.

This experience of primitive, unconscious guilt, loss, and persecution has been outlined by Hinshelwood (1991):

> The earliest version of this conflict, however, is not a moral sense at all. In the paranoid–schizoid position the conflict is more over the survival of the ego, which feels under threat of death . . . Guilt therefore has numerous tones to it, strung out along the spectrum from horrendous and persecuting punishment to pained remorse, mourning and reparation. At the outset, in the paranoid–schizoid position, guilt is a retaliatory persecution of an unmitigated kind . . . At first this guilt is persecutory and punitive.
>
> (p. 314)

Again, paranoid–schizoid loss and guilt entail loss of the good part objects followed by their rebirth as deadly enemies. Klein also discussed this point in 1935 when she wrote:

> The absence of the mother arouses in the child anxiety lest it should be handed over to bad objects, external and internalized, either because of her death or because of her return in the guise of a "bad" mother.
> (pp. 266–267)

Consistent experiences with durable, loving part objects fortify the ego and move it toward the depressive position with its greater integrative ego functions. These positive developments occur from ongoing introjection and projective identification processes by which the good part objects and the loving feelings from the ego are brought together to bind anxiety and strengthen the ego. Freddy didn't have enough of these positive internal and external experiences. Therefore, he felt at the mercy of his own sadistic superego and his controlling and angry objects.

My patient, Freddy, was clearly able to make use of the psychoanalytic method and seemed to be an excellent candidate for continued treatment. Unfortunately, like many such cases, the process was ended prematurely.

Within the lens of the paranoid–schizoid position, the ego is unable and unwilling to bring the forces of the life instincts and the death instincts together. Due to a strong reliance on splitting and projective identification, these feelings and phantasies are kept apart. This provides a degree of safety for the ego and its idealized objects from the bad and corruptive aspects of the self and one's objects. Until the integration of the depressive position and its associated ego strengths that integration brings, the ego is threatened by any less than perfect perspective.

The infantile dependence on projective identification lays the ground for difficulties around loss. If the ego is too full of envy or oral hostility and the external environment is abusive in some way, the ego may become overwhelmed. The natural developmental use of projective identification and splitting will become heightened to compensate for these conflicts. The result is a world of fragile idealized objects and omnipotent ego states divided off from dangerous, persecutory objects and hostile, sadistic ego states. A vicious cycle is established in which extremes are always crashing into one another and more and more exaggerated defenses must be built. Denial and manic escalation begin to shape the ego's character. The hostility and envy of the ego combine with the fragility of omnipotent objects to produce the sudden and frightening collapse of ideal objects followed (via projective identification) by the appearance of bad, attacking objects. Abandonment and the threat of death become central. Unmanageable anxieties take over and a destructive cycle of projection and introjection take grip over the ego.

Quinodoz (1993) has pointed out that hate needs to be sufficiently linked to love for the object, or the ego imagines itself capable of destroying the object. Without a strong enough fusion of the life and death instincts, the ego feels capable of overwhelming and annihilating its objects.

For most paranoid–schizoid patients, there is no sufficient link between life and death, love and hate, or union and separation. Therefore, the ego cannot feel safe with its core affects and phantasies. To hate the analyst is to destroy the analyst. To love the analyst is to be committed to eternal dependence. The ego feels its essence to be so powerful that it can easily overwhelm the object, losing its precious love and security. Thus, many of these patients are in a constant and unresolvable dilemma. They want to connect to the object but this would entail releasing poisonous desires and phantasies that could destroy the object and cause it to retaliate. The paranoid–schizoid ego imagines not only that it would lose the object through its own toxicity, but that the object would return to exact revenge.

To be more aware of the role of primitive experiences of loss and guilt within the paranoid–schizoid experience may lead to better clinical outcome with these difficult patients who find it so hard to attach themselves to the analytic process.

Many of these aborted treatments do help the patient in some minor way. It may be that the patient was helped to temporarily stave off a total mental breakdown. It may be that they are making their way through a series of therapists and life struggles that will eventually land them into a stable therapeutic relationship. We don't ever really know. All we can do is to try to assist the patient with the tools at hand: the analytic process.

Part III

Kleinians in the real world

Chapter 9

Working from the Kleinian perspective[1]

Melanie Klein believed, as do her followers, that both the positive and negative transference must be analyzed. Rather than seeing the need for a therapeutic alliance from which patient and analyst both worked on the negative, she thought the entire personality – the full spectrum of emotions and thoughts – was important to understand. Instead of thinking that some patients are too fragile to analyze and therefore must be supported and their defenses strengthened, she thought that proper analysis of the patient's anxieties and troubling phantasies promoted growth and strengthened the ego.

We all wish for ideal patients who calmly enter treatment, carefully explain their difficulties, and show honest interest in exploring their problems from a psychological plane. After insightful reflection during consultation, analyst and patients agree on regular visits and the long-term analytic process begins. After several years of successful working-through of core conflicts, patients and analysts mutually agree to a termination date, some three or six months ahead. During that time, they revisit many issues and work through some more. Finally, the last session unfolds and both parties part with some sadness and a great deal of pride in work well done.

This is usually not the case. More often than not, we are grappling with patients who test the limits of our analytic ability and quickly set up battleground conditions within the analytic relationship. If these patients do show up for their first appointment, the mood is one of "What are you going to do for me, doc?" If they continue attending sessions, they can immediately be controlling, challenging, and paranoid in the way they relate to the analyst. Often, rage is the native language and everyone is to blame. When they provide much background, it is often a horrific tale of parents who were alcoholic, psychotic, or physically violent. Sexual abuse is common and divorce goes without saying. Usually, poverty, foster homes,

1 Previously published in 2001 as "Working with difficult patients", *Psychoanalytic Social Work*, 7(4): 75–93.

death of near ones, and total lack of trust and intimacy are all part of the landscape.

The cases presented in the previous chapters show how these types of patient miss many sessions, don't pay their bills, feel dissatisfied with the quality of the analyst in just about any way possible, and abruptly quit by phone message. The analyst is left with an unpaid bill, a charred debris of a treatment, and a pile of uncomfortable countertransference reactions.

These grueling and demanding patients will stop treatment after only two or three sessions. Others may continue for several months or several years. However, the analytic challenge is the same. They all present transferences marked by strong oral desires, cruel superegos, and reliance on splitting, denial, and projective identification. Although these cases are difficult, they often provide the patient with some benefit and give the analyst an opportunity to better understand mental functioning.

Intense struggles with loss, guilt, and paranoia color their internal world. The feelings of loss and guilt are of a primitive nature (Grinberg, 1964) and have to do with persecutory visions of part objects and part aspects of the self. True whole-object relating is not available. The ego is fragmented and left to simplistic all-or-nothing defenses.

These lively and taxing patients can stimulate a wide spectrum of countertransference affects and phantasies including excitement, despair, anger, frustration, the desire to rescue, and the wish to punish. These countertransference reactions parallel the patient's internal turmoil and confusion.

The Kleinian concept of countertransference acknowledges the presence of two minds working within a particular intra-psychic relationship. The patient projects feelings, anxieties, and phantasies into the analyst. This is usually a combination of two elements. The patient has an internal phantasy of controlling, communicating with, or influencing (positively and negatively) an internal object. Also, the patient acts, unconsciously, in subtle interpersonal ways, influencing the external relationship with the analyst.

Analysts, strengthened by their own training, personal analysis, and ongoing self-scrutiny, try to be aware of the various feelings evoked in them. The analyst sees these as important information about the patient's unconscious state of mind. Ideally, the analyst is able to contain these projections, begin to understand them, and gradually offer them back in the form of interpretations. Because of the analyst's own personal struggles and/or the severity of the patient's projective identification mechanisms, the analyst may act out the patient's anxieties and desires rather than contain and metabolize them. Grinberg (1992) has explored this in terms of projective counter-identification. In all cases, countertransference is part of a complex relational system, intra-psychic and interpersonal, that must be analyzed as such.

In normal development, the ego searches out the protection of a consistently present container–mother (Bion, 1962), an object that is accepting and resilient. Difficult patients have egos that feel faced with a Venus fly-trap type of internal container. Rather than containing the ego's affects and raw phantasies for the good of the ego, it is an object that captures, owns, and absorbs the ego. Like the Venus fly-trap, this is an object that reacts to the ego by closing its thorny leaves around its prey, not to offer security, but to grab for itself. Rather than being replenished, the ego faces destruction. These paranoid phantasies of the object are often the result of chronic fears of abandonment, loss, and annihilation. The ego cycles through strong aggressive and fearful phantasies, feeling overwhelmed and alone.

My clinical impression, consistent with Melanie Klein's school of thought, is that difficult patients have constitutional problems of excessive aggression and envy as well as traumatic childhood histories. A combination of external trauma and internal cycles of oral aggression and envy produce a paranoid phantasy based in distrust and despair. In other words, persecutory phantasies of an omnivorous maternal object are the result of actual trauma as well as early infantile ego distortion. Klein explored the multiple ways in which excessive projective identification can discolor the external world and how the external world, in turn, distorts the ego's perception.

My most difficult patients have experienced catastrophic childhoods where not only were they exposed to ongoing trauma, but most importantly there was no one there to help them or to make sense out of it. Instead of the internal and external experience of a loving object that could contain, process, and reformulate their anxieties, these patients were often left to fend for themselves. This leads to combinations of omnipotent manic defenses and severe states of hopelessness and fragmentation.

These patients create short, demanding, and abortive treatments that are easily dismissed as non-analytic cases that don't really count for rigorous study. Nevertheless, I feel these patients actually show us valuable insights into the efficacy of our method and reveal much about the nature of mental functioning. Research, as well as anecdotal data, repeatedly shows that these patients are the bulk of what constitutes outpatient treatment. Up to 90 per cent of all patients in private practice settings (Friedman *et al.*, 1998) have at least one affective disorder and at least one personality disorder. In other words, the "worried well" are not spending their time in our offices now, and it's doubtful if they ever did.

Here today, gone tomorrow

These erratic and desperate patients avoid the pain of loss and the persecutory feelings of envy and superego torment by resorting to rigid manic defenses. They come into treatment for immediate symptom relief. They demand instant cures and assume the analyst will quickly hand over solutions like a bottle of magic pills. Encouraging the patient to explore his or her problems from a psychological and emotional standpoint seems to surprise them and they often feel blamed. Because these patients are so used to using splitting and projective identification to rid themselves of their anxieties, they often react strongly to being asked to take an honest look at themselves. So, when the patient realizes he must participate and investigate his own mind and feelings, he feels cornered or judged. Resistance is immediate and strong. The patient takes every comment or interpretation from the analyst as a challenge or ridicule.

Jerry was a television producer in his late twenties. He came into treatment to see if there was anything in his past that might be affecting his current life. Jerry was into extreme sports such as skydiving and dangerous rock climbing. His motto was, "Drive fast, live for the moment, and get as much out of life as soon as you can." His big goal was to become rich and retire by the time he was 40.

In the first session, he told me he thought he had had a peculiar upbringing and wondered if that might ever slow him down or affect his relationships. I asked him to elaborate. Jerry explained that his mother had been psychotic for most of his early years. She would worry that the neighbors were plotting against her and that agents of the government were spying on her. Because she felt the government was poisoning the food, she would not let the children eat and they became malnourished. Jerry's father left the family when Jerry was ten years old, saying he was overwhelmed with his wife's mental illness. Shortly after, Jerry's mother killed Jerry's younger sister. His mother thought that the government had "gotten to her" and that she was now helping them in their plot. Jerry's mother was taken into custody and the children put into foster care. Jerry's mother killed herself while in custody.

When I asked Jerry how he felt his horrific past might be affecting him now, he said he felt fine and he didn't think it had affected him at all. While understandable that he didn't want to face his overwhelming pain, he could not manage to even acknowledge the possibility of its presence. Indeed, he couldn't even acknowledge his own curiosity of a few minutes ago. He said it was a "non-matter."

Here, I think I was presented with the kind of emotional dilemma with which Jerry grew up. I felt caught in a bizarre bind. If I brought up what he had introduced himself, he acted as if I was doing something bad to him, out of the blue, and he blamed me for it. Via projective identification, I felt the psychotic sorts of twists and turns he had described about his childhood. He brought up intense feelings and ideas, only to then violently project them and refuse to have any further link to them.

For the next two sessions, he was without any affect and had nothing to talk about. When I mentioned that this might be a reaction to telling me about his past, he flatly denied it and assured me of how wonderful his life was. He spent the bulk of the time telling me how independent he was, how perfect his life was, and how he, without question, needed no one. I felt no inroad to work with, so I mostly listened. I felt sad that one person should have to carry such pain and I felt my hands were tied since he had to maintain such tight internal and interpersonal security. Indeed, I was impressed that he actually came to see me in the first place.

If I did make any comment, he told me I was completely off base and went back to tales of how exciting and adventurous his life was. It was no surprise when he announced that he saw no point in seeing me anymore since he now realized how pleased he was with life. "I have got it made. I don't need anybody and I am having the time of my life!" This brittle, whistle-in-the-dark, manic stance was so overinflated that it was impossible to say anything without getting put back in my place immediately. After the third session, Jerry said goodbye and thanked me for helping him see what good mental health he had.

Patients like Jerry seem to have such large segments of their intra-psychic life based around avoiding and defending loss, persecution, and primitive guilt that they are on constant alert. Narcissistic defenses give them a temporary but hollow feeling of safe distance from being exposed to their own devastating inner experiences. The great fear of both loss and attack leads to fantastic levels of manic omnipotence. In the transference, these grandiose ways seem so fake that the analyst feels unsure of how to respond. This is a countertransference response to the patient's projective identification efforts. Projective identification is an internal phantasy that often colors interpersonal dynamics, potentially drawing the analyst into intra-psychic and interpersonal acting out of the patient's unconscious object-relations. The Kleinian literature (Rosenfeld, 1958, 1983; Quinodoz, 1994; De Racker, 1961; Pantone, 1994; De Pado, 1980; O'Shaughnessy, 1983, 1990; Malcolm, 1986, 1995; Malin and Grotstein, 1966; Kernberg, 1987, 1988; Hunter, 1993; Waska, 1998, 1999) has explored and expanded this phenomenon extensively since its introduction by Melanie Klein in 1946. The patient puts confused, helpless, and overpowered feelings into the analyst and maintains a megalomanic, independent stance. This is very difficult for the analyst and pushes him to make desperate attempts to try to change the relationship with suggestion and coercion. Acting out by both analyst and patient is common.

These patients also defend against loss, persecution, and primitive guilt by demanding to be taken care of without reciprocation. Again, when they find out they are being asked to participate and share their feelings or thoughts, they recoil and rebel. They want to be given to; they refuse to give. Indeed, they feel humiliated to share their thoughts and feelings with the object.

The miracle worker

Alice came in for help with feelings of panic. She was a fifty-year-old waitress who had always tried to "stay out of people's way" and shunned any social life. She was content to just be alone at home, watching movies. Alice had some limited success as a painter years ago, but gave it up because it was too "unpredictable." She started to feel uncomfortable when she was promoted to head hostess at the restaurant. This entailed much more direct contact with the public and she was frightened by the pressure and demands that contact seemed to bring. Her insurance provided ten therapy visits.

The first time I met with Alice, I had the impression of someone who felt terribly scared of how demanding and judgmental others could be. She felt people always "dropped" her without a moment's notice, leaving her alone and desperate. I wondered to myself if that would be my fate as well. She said she only worked to pay her bills and had never felt any motivation to compete or climb the career ladder. "I would gladly scrub toilets and never have contact with a soul if I just got paid enough to make my bills."

Alice's background was a combination of minimal achievement and social isolation. As a child, she felt her parents had put up with her and otherwise ignored her. Alice also feared her father. While she didn't come out and say it, I had the sense that her father could go berserk at any time unless Alice was nonintrusive and quiet.

When Alice described her adult life, she mainly talked about a series of low-paying restaurant jobs in which she was at first extremely impressed with some aspect of management or the restaurant's philosophy. After a while, she found out something about the restaurant or its management goals that brought on great disappointment and she eventually left. This was somewhat repeated in the transference.

Alice talked about the various stresses of her job and the ongoing financial problems she was having. She talked in a mechanical manner that left me feeling she was trying to contain and disguise a profound loneliness, fear, and paranoia. Here and there in her stories were little comments about the government, the "system," and the ways that authority is cruel to the "little guy." I proposed that she was talking about her experiences growing up and her internal experiences with herself now as an adult. She quickly denied all of that and said she thought everything was connected to her manager at work. She only felt pressured by the manager to be the new hostess. Alice said she wanted some advice on how to deal with that and how to feel less "stressed out." She said she had thought of suicide for several months and couldn't sleep well. She was ready to quit her job and move out of the city to get away from it all, and if that didn't work she was ready to kill herself. I felt she meant this and would probably carry it out if we didn't manage to reduce her fears.

When I saw Alice the following week, she was quite different. She felt exuberant. She said I had performed miracles. Since our last meeting, she now felt enthusiastic about life, had no anxiety, and was perfectly at peace with the world. In fact, she had taken up painting again. She had already completed one small painting and was busily working on another. Alice said that talking to me and getting "stuff off of her chest" had been very helpful, "just what she needed." She thought that maybe we should stop as she felt so much better. I suggested that sharing her problems might have given her some relief, but maybe there were still reasons she had been feeling so stressed. She agreed and decided to stay in treatment for a while longer.

Alice's manic bliss remained. She attributed her cure to being able to "unload" onto me. In fact, I think she was "unloading" certain feelings and phantasies into me via projective identification. After her ten insurance visits, she stopped. She said she couldn't really afford to continue and felt OK. During those ten sessions, she clearly put me in an omnipotent position. I was the doctor who turned her life around. While she agreed with my ideas about her idealizing me, and the way our relationship paralleled many of her job experiences, Alice still insisted that I had taken the problem away and she was all better now. Here, I think Alice developed a manic defense in which she idealized me as an omnipotent healer–father who understood her in all the ways she wished for. Through splitting, she bonded with this all-good healing object and projected all of her anxiety into the worthless, non-gratifying bad object. Through manic maneuvering, the bad object was then erased by the greatness and power of the good object. This magically took away her chronic fear of being cornered, humiliated, and punished. Her fear of being attacked by her father and by the public at her job was so overwhelming that she had to resort to these drastic measures.

I believe the ten-visit insurance limit affected the treatment and was subsumed into Alice's transference phantasies. I interpreted that she might feel pressured to set unrealistic goals and that she might feel reluctant to depend on me given that she might have to stop coming in so soon after starting. Given her financial situation, I offered to reduce her fee. I explored the potential feeling of shame, indebtedness, and dependence this could bring on. Finally, I wondered if the limits of her finances and insurance plan replicated her lifelong feelings of never quite getting herself or her relationships off the ground to a point of follow-through or success and fulfillment. Alice was able to explore some of these ideas, but mostly relied on denial, rationalization, and negation to avoid her feelings about them. Overall, I think the insurance problem fueled her resistance and her fears, as well as creating a manic flight into health.

Alice seemed to be gripped by deep feelings of loss and a sense that the lost object she longed for could easily return to hurt her. To truly build a link with me and begin exploring these anxieties was too overwhelming. Instead, she kept her distance and remained in control by shaping me into an idol. Once she got her fix from this idol, she could go on independently and feel safe again. However, she retained her lifelong paranoid–schizoid stance.

Paranoid–schizoid patients who are experiencing primitive states of loss, guilt, and persecution resort to these kinds of coping mechanisms. These are dynamic states in the form of internal bargains or strategies to deal with certain self-and-object concerns. Projective identification, splitting, and manic defenses are common. The interpretive stance must be maintained, but how, what, and when to interpret is always a consideration.

I can do it all by myself

One young girl, a ward of the juvenile justice system, was constantly using projective identification, splitting, and omnipotent grandiosity to ward off a combination of feeling forsaken by her objects and terribly controlled by them. After her parents split up, she lived with her alcoholic mother and older brother. She was so defiant that she was thrown out of school and taken away from her mother.

A social worker was able to coordinate funds and a referral for out-patient treatment. When we met, she would belittle me and filled the hours with tales of all the stupid people she had to put up with. She never did any wrong and was simply a victim of others' ignorance and meanness. Sometimes she would not speak at all, refusing to answer any of my comments.

Some two years into her analytic treatment, she brought in two dreams. This was the first time she ever mentioned her dreams. In the first dream, there is a little girl whose mother dies. This girl vows to never talk again. She is taken by force to a psychologist to help her "work on her feelings." The therapist tries to help her but the little girl doesn't want to speak. In the end, she finds a wild mustang horse and develops a deep bond with the horse. Because of that bond, she starts to speak again.

I thought of this dream as a thin cover for the heartbreak my patient felt over losing her father, and most of all, a reliable, containing mother. Fueled by the sorrow and rage at this loss and rejection, she tries to fight back with revenge by vowing never to talk. This was acted out in the transference. She wants help from me (the therapist) to "work out her feelings," but cannot bear to admit her need and desire. Therefore, her neediness is projected into me and she feels taken by force to see me. (The external reality of being referred to me reinforced her internal state of persecution.) In this sense, she retains a masochistic power. Rather than submitting to her own desperation and hunger for a containing, mothering object (the therapist), she shuns me in favor of her own source of power: a wild-spirited, independent mustang. This is a projection of her own narcissistic ideal. Therefore, she finds her voice by bonding with an omnipotent replica of herself.

There were certain technical implications in hearing this type of dream from this type of patient. Since she usually deflected and defaced my direct transference interpretations, I didn't make them. Instead, I spoke to the struggles and dynamics of each character in the dream, without making any reference to her or to us. She responded easily to this tactic, as it didn't cause her to feel challenged or attacked.

She then told me the second dream. She is forced to enroll in a horse-riding school. The mean teachers tell her she must master complex horse-riding trick techniques in order to graduate. She feels sure to fail and is desperate. Then, she finds a wild mustang horse that is not a part of the school. She bonds with it and tames it. She learns the complicated trick-riding on her own and then surprises the school and is allowed to graduate.

I felt this dream was similar to the first one in its manic style. She adopted an independent stance of "I will find my own solution that isn't connected to you." She feels forced to learn how to deal with her mind and to find out how to ride it. So, she rebels and refuses to use any of my horses or my schooling. She schools herself and uses her own horse. These elements of the dream parallel her transference feelings of being under my thumb, forced to look at herself and "retrain" her wild mustang self.

This phase of treatment was a constant battle of one manically independent part of her mind setting out to control, destroy, or deny other more dependent and needy parts of her mind.

Later in the analysis, she was able to explore her fears of "being a baby," needing me, and feeling weak and stupid. She felt this neediness would drive the object away and she would be left alone to suffer. Therefore, it felt safer to act out and at least be in combat with the object rather than risk being rejected, attacked, and alone.

Pain and love always go together

Mary was a young woman who dealt with overwhelming feelings of loss and persecution from a very young age. She had been taken away from a drug-addicted mother and put up for adoption. She was adopted by a family that seemed to use her as an emotional target and wastebasket for all their hostility and anxiety. Her father was particularly violent with her. This chronic emotional abuse was internalized as Mary became embroiled with her body and focused on countless aches and pains. In other words, she turned inwards and used a physical plane to struggle with emotional and mental conflicts. She felt disappointed and attacked by her body. In this physical/mental domain, she became quite sadomasochistic to her internal objects. Ill-health and somatic worries were her close companions. She tried to manage some degree of control, domination, and mastery, by being submissive and victimized by her body and by the people in her life or by having temper tantrums in which she would slam doors and punch walls.

Mary felt no one ever respected her, let alone loved her. She hoped I would put up with her and maybe help her feel less depressed. She believed

I only tolerated her and secretly detested her. After more than a year of mostly acting out her intra-psychic struggles by limiting our relationship to stories of illness and physical pain, she started to talk more about her family, her own feelings, and our relationship. Side by side with this progress, she continued her pattern of missing many sessions, forgetting to pay me, bouncing checks, and cutting herself. She also managed to get herself fired from several jobs, endangering her apartment and our therapy relationship. I interpreted the way she used suffering to keep me distant, to protect herself, to provoke me, and to keep herself attached to the image of a negative-ideal. Mary seemed to feel that with the loss of her positive-ideal parent came a much deeper loss, one in which she lost herself. The treatment was marked by an ongoing lack of commitment, a great deal of ambivalence, and a constant questioning of our worth together. These feelings were sometimes voiced, but usually acted out. After a stormy two-year analysis, Mary abruptly aborted treatment. However, I think we accomplished valuable analytic work along the way.

This session was midweek, in the latter part of our first year together.

P: My father treats me so badly. He always tells me how he hates me and how he wishes he would have never adopted me. (*She just returned from visiting her father. While I feel she is also talking about her relationship with me, I choose to follow her lead.*)

A: You wish he would accept you.

P: Yes. I always felt like the outsider, wanting his love. In public, he treats me nice, but privately he is so mean and abusive. He only adopted me because my mother wanted a child. She couldn't have one and kept begging him to adopt. He says he is regretful he did. He is so vindictive too. If he said, "God help you!," I would know he was really going to beat me and there was no way to avoid it. I still feel worn down by his games. He opens the wounds for his own pleasure. (*I am struck by this graphic image of sadistic torture and make a comment on it.*)

A: You feel like love and pain go together.

P: Yes, I do. They are one in the same. All I can do is to accept it. (*She seems very distraught, but trying to just "tell me the facts" without showing her feelings.*)

A: I think you feel very upset, but you're reluctant to show me. You "accept" it when really you are very emotional about it. You're not sure how I will accept you, if you show me more of yourself.

P: Yes. Also, I worry about if I ever have kids if I could be like him, so abusive.

A: One way you relate to me is with stories of pain and suffering. Maybe that is your way to test me and see if you should reveal deeper feelings. (*I think she is afraid to show me the more father-like sadistic side of herself.*)

P: I think I used to cut myself to escape, to get away from it all. I felt closer to death. Every time you think you're close to being happy, it falls apart. I don't know how to live life with these pieces missing. (*Here, I think my interpretation was helpful because she proceeds to tell me her deep fears of losing contact with her object. She feels she loses touch with life, so she counters by bringing on death.*)

A: It is interesting that with all those feelings of being alone and wishing for something better, you missed several sessions last week.

P: It felt strange. Something is missing. I thought of all I told you, like I revealed way too much.

A: You feel exposed when you're away from me and can't tell if you can trust me. Like you might lose me as a good helper?

P: Yes. But, it is so hard to reach out for help. I am pissed off I have these mood swings. I heard my old boyfriend is getting married soon. That pissed me off too.

A: You told me he dumped you for another woman.

P: Yes. He is so impersonal. He feels nothing. I am nothing but a bad debt.

A: Maybe you are upset with losing the relationship with him and also are upset over us not being together for a while. You have rarely brought it up, but I suspect you are also upset over not being in touch with your birth mother. (*Here, I try to bring together the past, the present, and the transference.*)

P: Yes. Yes. I do feel that way! I just want to feel connected to something or somebody! But don't. I feel I just roam the planet looking for my place, so alone. I don't feel real. I feel like just a visitor on this planet. I want someone to just hold me and tell me it is going to be OK. I just don't know how to open up. (*Crying*)

A: You are opening up right now, to me.

P: Yes, but you don't just tell me it will be OK. (*She wants me to be her ideal good object that makes it all better.*)

A: I can't guarantee it will be OK, but I can guarantee I will be there to help you in the struggle to be OK. (*I am not able to point out her putting me in a dilemma. She can't accept me and my help unless it is to her specifications. In other words, I am either the good object she wants or the frustrating bad object that doesn't gratify her.*)

P: When I see mothers being loving with their kids at the park, I get so jealous! (*Crying*) I wish I had had a parent who could be that way with me! I don't know how to be with people.

A: You feel awkward with me?

P: Sometimes. And I really can't figure out if I want to be with my boyfriend anymore. I just don't know.

A: Maybe you're not sure if you want to risk showing me your feelings and you doubt you can get that kind of good parenting here. Maybe you're angry with me for not being everything you want and so you're thinking of leaving. (I comment on the fear of loss, the paranoia, and the projective identification process.)

P: I have never gotten what I want out of anyone. If anything, people seem to take me and use me and then throw me away.

Next session

P: (*She makes barbed comments about having to pay me, not wanting to, and not having my check. She also says she wanted to go to a show instead of our session.*) I am having such a hard time at work. Nothing is working out. I never have any consistency at work. It's always some kind of chaotic crisis. No one is dependable and when they say you can call them for help they are lying. I am totally on my own there!

A: You are angry with the lack of commitment and connection you have at work. By your angry comments about my bill and not wanting to be here, I guess you feel the same thing with our relationship. You are not happy with the connection we have. Part of you sabotages our time together and part of you is very sad and angry about that.

P: Well, if you don't get something out of a relationship, why bother? Why should I stay if I don't get something out of it? Even if it is me that is screwing it up, it is hopeless and I don't feel like I will ever get better. I feel I am defective merchandise. I have a habit of starting things and then stopping and never finishing. (*She tells me of hobbies she starts and never follows through.*)

A: Maybe this is another hobby you feel like throwing away.

P: No. I like this, it's fun. I like coming here and telling you things. But I think I need positive reinforcement to keep doing things or I just stop. If somebody pushes me and makes me do it, I am fine. If I have to do it on my own, I usually quit really fast.

A: (*Perhaps, since I didn't tell her it's going to be OK, she feels I am leaving her on her own. Also, I am not "pushing her" and dominating her to keep at it. If I won't play the sadomasochistic game, she is angry and ready to stop her new "hobby."*) If I am not coaching you along properly, you might get rid of me.

P: I like to pick on you. (*She acknowledges the sadomasochistic game.*)

A: Are you relating to me like you feel with your father, teasing and getting picked on?

P: No, that wasn't allowed. He could do that if he wanted to but I could never tease back or I would get my ass kicked.

A: So, here you get to show me your love and your anger and how they are mixed up together.

P: I am sorry. I will try and be nice from now on. (*She says this in a way that made me feel she was "just reading the lines," but not really feeling *it. However, I chose to follow the content as it still was a potent statement about our relationship.*)

A: I guess you took what I said as critical and now you're retreating.

P: Yes, I did hear it that way. But, you know, more and more I am starting to just be playful with people. (*Now, I feel she said "her lines" just in case I was like her father, but she also felt we were different. I think, through projective identification, she often blurs the distinction.*)

A: Maybe you're trying to redo the mess you have with your father.

P: We never had much of a relationship. I never felt comfortable around him. I can tease my mother and she is fine with it. We can get along that way.

A: So, you might be testing me to see if I will be like your father or like your mother. Will we be close or will we fight.

P: Yes, I think I am. All my father ever did was make me cry.

Next session

P: (*This is a session after the weekend. She asks me if I "partied" on the weekend.*)

A: You want to find out more about me. Maybe you're feeling more comfortable about our connection.

P: Not fair! I just wonder if you let your hair down. I could never go out growing up. My father wouldn't allow it. The older I got the firmer his rules became. (*So, it seems she wanted to identify with me, as an easy-going person who could "party" and let my hair down without getting in trouble for it.*)

A: Your father didn't like you having your own identity. (*I feel she experiences her objects as abandoning her and attacking her when she maintains her own integrity and confidence.*)

P: Absolutely. Anything I did on my own I would get into big trouble. (*She goes on to tell me how she got into a car wreck recently and how badly damaged her car is.*)

A: (*I think of how her masochistic ways of relating are devices for destroying her independence and her identity.*) I think you are not sure if you can think and feel independently with me. You want to know if I can tolerate your independent thinking or if I will ground you like father.

P: Wow! If I am independent enough will I get a prize? I couldn't even go out of my parents' home if I was wearing shorts. He called me a slut all the time. My shirt had to be buttoned to the top at all times. (*I am thinking about how she is dressed in the session, a low-cut blouse with no bra.*) My father would be so great to everyone in the neighborhood and at his job, but never at home where it counts. Everything was about sex for him. He saw everything as dirty and somehow about sex. In his eyes, I was a slut. If he ever saw me in this shirt, he would beat my ass.

A: So you must be trying to figure out if I approve of you or not. You're not sure if you're showing me too much, with your shirt and with your feelings.

P: Well, those questions do follow me around. I really like to wear sheer underwear and slinky bras. It makes me feel so sexy!

A: You're suddenly getting playful and teasing with me. You want to see if you can trust me and will I be OK with your own choices. Will I be able to handle you.

P: I guess I feel more comfortable with you.

Next session

P: (*She tells me about the movie* Titanic.)

A: The movie is about a couple who really fight for their relationship and how much they love each other. Maybe you're also thinking about how your father doesn't seem to want to fight for you. He doesn't show any commitment to you as his daughter. (*I choose to not mention her ambivalent struggle with a commitment to treatment. These patients use projective identification so much, causing a constant blur of self-and-object, and seem to refuse to take back what they deposit in the analyst's mind. In fact, interpreting the projection too quickly often causes them to become paranoid and defensive. Therefore, it is helpful to assess their level of self–object differentiation and for a while either to make only interpretations that follow the path of the splitting and projection into external objects or to make interpretations based on how the patient's ego now views the object as it remains distorted by those projections. This means a back and forth combination of transference and extra-transference interpretations.*)

P: Yes. I feel that way about my boyfriend too. He doesn't want to fight to save the relationship. I guess I just have to move on. (*She tells me about a friend at work who seems very comfortable in having open dialogues or debates about any subject. This person's ability to allow for diverse opinions amazes my patient.*)

A: You often feel you are breaking my rules with your opinions and feelings and then you apologize. Maybe you wish you could just be yourself and feel safe in doing so. (*I am pointing out her fear of differences between herself and her objects.*)

P: In my family, I always had to follow all the rules or else. I simply couldn't question anything. I was so frustrated and just gave up and went along with whatever it was. It gave me tunnel vision. My father kept me in the dark.

A: Being curious about things when you're scared is hard.

P: Yes. Now, as I start to wonder about things I still wonder if it will be OK.

A: You mean you wonder how I will react?

P: Yes.

A: You're concerned that I could change from someone who listens and accepts you to someone who is critical and rejecting. (*I interpreted the foundation of her anxiety, a paranoid–schizoid fear of loss and persecution.*)

P: You got that one right, Doc!

Discussion

Each case in this chapter shows the dramatic use of manic maneuvers, splitting, and projective identification to manipulate the object and reshape the self. The ego uses these internal dynamics to ward off intense and primitive experiences of loss and persecution.

While these patients are difficult and often unable to stay in treatment, they seem to benefit if the analyst adheres to the psychoanalytic method. With this as a foundation to bounce off, some of these very anxious patients are able to slowly calm down and then begin to explore their internal experiences.

None of these cases can be called complete or successful. However, some benefit was evident, even if it was part of a pathological compromise. Some of these difficult patients managed to use me to repair their leaking, fragile method of coping with a frightening paranoid–schizoid world. In other words, they strengthened their defenses and reaffirmed internal bargains with their intrapsychic objects. Some of these patients are able to open up a bit to a new way of looking at things. Some of them, including the cases I presented, become a bit more self-reflective, make a link between their present state of mind and their family experience, or simply find a better way of containing their anxieties. I was a temporary rest-stop for some of them. For others, I became a new path towards self-discovery, self-healing, and a sense of choice.

In each case, I pointed out to the patient everything I observed and made links to the transference. Even when it seemed better to focus on extra-transference material, I still geared my comments to the dynamic, internal struggle they were in with their own desires, fears, needs, aggression, and conflicting phantasies of self-and-object. This decreased their anxieties and helped them focus on internal fears and conflicts. This led to a certain amount of working-through and adaptation to reality.

Chapter 10

The ideal patient and the realities of clinical work[1]

The difficult patients I am presenting are unable to fit into a standard model of psychoanalytic treatment. They act out and resist, breaking most or all of the rules about what a "proper" patient should be. They are predictably erratic, chronically anxious, and often quite aggressive. As illustrated in previous chapters, this group of nonstandard, non-neurotic patients miss many sessions, are late when they do show up, withhold fees, refuse regular and frequent attendance, and bitterly resist the exploration of any deeper motivations in life.

There are many useful ideas to expain why some patients are self-destructive and strive to destroy the analytic process. Steiner (1987) has investigated the pathological interplay between the paranoid–schizoid position and the depressive position. Joseph (1960, 1982, 1983) has discovered that patients cling to extremely masochistic and sadistic ways of relating and strongly resist the importance of thinking, understanding, and feeling. Rosenfeld (1971a) has written about the death instinct and the chaotic feelings of envy that turn the analysis into a precarious and combative situation. Segal (1983, 1993) has examined the difficulties analysts face when confronted with patients operating within the realm of the death instinct, the paranoid–schizoid position, and pathological projective identification mechanisms. Spillius (1993, 1997) has noted the complexities of cases involving chronic envy of the object as well as self-envy. Bion (1962) warned of the collapse of the container–contained function in analysis, leading to a damaged or aborted treatment. Finally, Rosenfeld (1975) pointed out how certain patients seek to undermine and destroy the analytic process through a cycle of envy and pathological projective identification phantasies.

The patients I am exploring show all the clinical detours, dead-ends, and conflicts that these authors have explored, yet represent the extreme version

1 Previously published in 2000 as "The ideal patient and the realities of clinical work", *Journal of Contemporary Psychotherapy*, 30(4): 381–399.

of that pathology. They quickly and loudly enter and exit treatment, struggling with very intense feelings and phantasies that involve fears of annihilation and an overwhelming conviction that relationships are hurtful and therefore need to be controlled or avoided. Issues of control, combat, and survival color most of their unconscious and conscious lives. Therefore, it is remarkable that they seek help to begin with, let alone remain in the intimacy of an analytic relationship for very long.

It would be easy to discard these difficult cases as people who are unsuitable for the analytic method, perhaps more suited for supportive therapy, behavioral management, or medication. However, I approach these cases with the idea that some important analytic work can be accomplished if both patient and analyst are willing to hang in there and willing to settle for a less-than-perfect outcome.

These cases are almost always borderline, narcissistic, or psychotic. Usually, the patients are still negotiating the perils and anxieties of the paranoid–schizoid position. Symbolism is at a minimum and grossly compromised by the ego's excessive reliance on projective identification and splitting. Projective identification, denial, and splitting blur the distinctions between self and object. This creates high levels of fear and encourages the need for primitive, repetitious defenses, creating a vicious cycle.

During optimal development, repeated contact with good internal and external objects helps to mitigate this cycle. This group of patients lacks this important inner fortification.

A completed psychoanalytic treatment would ideally entail a full structural move from the paranoid–schizoid position to the depressive position. These patients usually end treatment while still struggling with intense persecutory phantasies and a strong dependence on primitive ego defenses.

My experience with these difficult patients is that they are constantly struggling with unconscious phantasies of primitive loss and a self-destructive, persecutory guilt, both of which color the transference. They lose their precarious hold on an ideal part-object and a dangerous and vengeful part-object replaces it. Good turns to bad and trust shifts to betrayal. In trying to cope with the sadistic guilt they feel, they often use masochistic and narcissistic defenses. This primitive guilt includes anxieties about being destroyed as punishment for imagined atrocities rather than depressive concerns about the safety of the object. These are paranoid–schizoid fears about the survival of the ego. Loss of the object is a concern only because without the object the ego cannot survive. True worry for the object and guilt about one's effect on the other crystalize only in the depressive position.

The threat of loss is so great for these patients that their fragile ego is unable to sustain itself. Most flee treatment since they do not feel safe enough to work through these phantasies with the analyst. Therefore, the ongoing, careful analysis of these fears of loss and persecution is critical. By staying true to the analytic task, some of these patients can start feeling safer and more trusting. Eventually, give and take can become possible and negotiation with an equal can seem available, rather than duels with a bully who wants to either take or attack.

An ongoing problem in the treatment of such patients is their constant conviction of the analyst's withdrawal. They react strongly and violently not only to the literal separations of vacation and weekends, but to the perceived moment-to-moment failures of the analyst to understand them fully. The phantasy of an ideal analyst is constantly crumbling through their own aggression and withdrawal, projected into the object. A cruel, attacking, and disappearing analyst replaces the good, understanding, and constantly present analyst. This internal fear requires ongoing, steady interpretation over a long period of time.

Many of these patients are defensively narcissistic and although they suffer these fears of loss and persecution, they insist they have no problems at all, especially no problems of dependence on the analyst. They will constantly resist and deny any evidence that they may need anyone other than themselves. When they begin experiencing some of these terrifying feelings of abandonment, shame, and persecution, they abort treatment. Others become so convinced the analyst is not on their side that they flee to escape the enemy. In other words, the transference becomes real, instead of an as-if experience.

Case material

Ginger

Ginger came for help with her relationship problems and feelings of depression. She had a history of becoming involved with abusive men who cheated on her. I saw her for almost a year. Ginger was paranoid and formed sadomasochistic relationships with the important people in her life.

She was youngest in a very chaotic family. From what she told me, her mother routinely beat all the children and on occasion her father beat them too. The mother often lost control, beating the children for the slightest infractions. Ginger remembered feeling very disturbed about not having her father's love.

While she had no memories of sexual abuse, Ginger was fixated on the idea that her father molested her. She described scenes of "cuddling" with her father in which she suspected sexual violations. I pointed out that she appeared to be in an intense search to find herself the victim of incest. She asked for hypnosis to find evidence of molestation and felt I was not sensitive in trying to help her "breakthrough" to this memory she felt she must have.

Ginger's father was unfaithful in his marriage. In fact, he paraded himself about town with different girlfriends. When he would leave the house to be with other women, the mother would brutally beat the children. Ginger felt she had been the family scapegoat and had countless stories to illustrate this.

My experience of seeing Ginger was of being steamrolled with tales of tragedy. The sheer quantity of stories about how awful her current life was and the constant crisis state she found herself in was amazing. "Why me?" was her motto. I was occasionally successful in interpreting the sadistic endeavors behind this style of relating, but there was always a fresh onslaught. I proposed that this was the only way she felt comfortable because she was frightened of becoming close to me in other ways.

I told her it was safer for her to put the persecution she felt from mother into the father and find him to be the bad one. It was too overwhelming to face her mother as an attacking and betraying anti-caregiver. Therefore, she had to prove to herself and me that it was father's fault.

These types of interpretations were based not only on her associations, but on my countertransference reactions. I felt beaten down and like I rarely had a moment to catch my breath. Only when I took a step back could I see the desperation and panic that accompanied Ginger's aggressive ways. Pick (1985) has described not only the difficulties, but the importance of working through the countertransference. She notes:

> the experience for the analyst is a powerful one. To suggest that we are not affected by the destructiveness of the patient or by the patient's painful efforts to reach us would represent not neutrality but falseness or imperviousness. It is the issue of how the analyst allows himself to have the experience, digest it, formulate it, and communicate it as an interpretation that I address . . . The contention that the analyst is not affected by these experiences is both false and would convey to the patient that his plight, pain, and behavior are emotionally ignored by the analyst. It is suggested that if we keep emotions out, we are in danger of keeping out the love which mitigates the hatred, allowing the so-called pursuit of truth to be governed by hatred. What appears as dispassionate may contain the murder of love and concern.
>
> (pp. 164–165)

By noticing and examining my countertransference, I was able to see how Ginger's constant state of crisis kept us from discussing other matters. In exploring Ginger's negative feelings about her father and her ideas about his abuse and neglect, I pointed out how little she discussed her mother. This was part of her covert and not-so-covert sadomasochistic style.

At times, this sadomasochism would shift into outright paranoid delusions, which was her more core underlying problem.

Summary of two sessions

In the first of these sessions, Ginger told me that she had been reflecting on her relationship with an old boyfriend and how abusive it was. This was about six months into her treatment.

Ginger elaborated on how victimized she felt. She told me she had been talking with one of her friends and felt put down and picked on "as usual."

Ginger told me about a conflict with her landlord and how awful she felt about it because this was to be a place she moved into to "get away" from the horrible living situation she had been in before. She felt she had always been in conflict with her prior landlords and hoped this would be a respite. Yet she felt her new apartment was now just as miserable as the last one.

She asked me why she was always in a bad way and told me how hard she always tried to "just live her life and be happy." She cried.

Then, Ginger said she often feels people don't take her seriously and she finds herself talking "around" a subject. She was able to parallel this to how her mother can't be up-front with anything and speaks about things in a roundabout manner. This was now taking place in the transference–countertransference. We were both not speaking directly to what was occurring in our relationship. It was uncomfortable for us to explore her fears about our relationship, the hostility she felt, and the nurturing she wanted. I felt this was a result of idealization and devaluation: splitting. The balance between good and bad was so fragile and tenuous that she projected that tension into me and I felt the need to proceed in caution.

Once, when I gave her the monthly statement, she noticed an error. She seemed irritated, frightened, and somewhat disoriented by the discussion we needed to straighten it out. She resisted any exploration of her feelings. Next, there was a sudden outpouring of stories in which somebody victimized her. Clearly, she felt I had done her wrong, but couldn't speak to it directly.

Ginger discussed feeling the victim of her boyfriend (me?) and how she felt too afraid of ever saying anything to him, for fear of losing him. Then she discussed the same fears and troubles, but this time about her work situation.

When I asked her to elaborate on the idea that she would be "punished for talking," she told me that her mother would always beat her or yell at her for speaking up about anything and that this made her be "quiet" and "hope for the best."

I interpreted that she was afraid to speak up to me regarding the bill and her feelings about me for fear that she might lose me and be punished. This led to a discussion about how she had an extremely difficult time imagining herself as an equal to others. I commented that she felt she had no rights and therefore was always anticipating victimization. Here, my interpretations were again based on what I felt to be her core phantasy of losing an ideal object and having to face abandonment, loss, and persecution.

In the next session, she discussed her fears about her boyfriend cheating on her. This was a very familiar theme. I made a link to her family history.

I brought up her father's chronic infidelity and how her mother was usually panicked, hopeless, and furious about it. This led to her exploring how she felt responsible for her father's infidelity and how she "could have done something to prevent it." I thought to myself that she may unconsciously wish she could have been sexual with her father, as a way to prevent his unfaithful behavior and his abandonment of the family. This would have prevented her mother from taking out her rage on Ginger.

I decided that to voice this idea would invite her to intellectualize things and to displace her current anxieties into the past. It seemed sufficient to simply comment on the link between her current worries and the historical. However, in retrospect I also think I became part of the cautious avoidance she lived under.

Ginger told me she felt scared about the landlord being in a conspiracy with her neighbor and how both were treating her very unfairly. She relayed an incident about her toilet not working well and how it might have been deliberately broken by the landlord. She told me about a "strange odor" that she felt someone had put into her vent, and several other suspicions she had about her neighbor and her landlord.

Finally, she told me about terrible situations at work in which she felt helpless and victimized. Just when I thought nothing worse could happen, she told me how her car mechanic had cheated her.

We discussed the chronic indirectness, vague uncertainty, and everyday violence that she experienced in her family while growing up. Here, I was making genetic interpretations, rather than here-and-now comments. I believe this was an acting out of her projections into me of fear and avoidance. When I tried to shift my approach to more here-and-now interpretations, Ginger ignored me and quickly got back to telling me stories of how bad her life was. When I pointed this out, she became critical and contemptuous. It was as if she were saying, "Why are you wasting my time with your silly ideas? I want to get back to my important story."

Ginger seemed to use masochism as a thin veil from which to attack me and demand explanations, solutions, and rescue. She was chronically battering me just as she felt battered by her objects. Clearly, she felt all the objects supposed to support her, understand her, help her, and love her failed. We all failed and disappointed her but, much worse, we shifted into scary, persecuting objects. Relating to me in a complaining, demanding, masochistic way was Ginger's best effort at preventing a full descent into losing me altogether and finding a dangerous attacker in my place. Once I started to analyze these feelings and phantasies, she felt I was destabilizing her survival strategy and taking away her power-base. She didn't see us as capable of negotiating or working through these threats, so she fled the treatment.

I believe Ginger and other similar patients are involved in a chronic and intense projective identification process. Ginger tried to rid herself of unbearable trauma by putting it into me. She did not want to understand it or have it returned; it was an evacuation of terrible pain and rage. Rosenfeld (1983) has stated:

> one has to realize that projective identification is not just one single process but includes many different types of projective identification . . . In a previous paper (1971b), I suggested first of all that it was important to differentiate between projective identification used for communication and projective identification used for defensive purposes such as ridding the self of unwanted parts of the self . . . The evacuation–annihilation process has to be differentiated from those projective processes in which the patient tries to push unbearable mental content into the analyst, not for purposes of denial but to compel the analyst to share the unpleasant experiences with the patient. This is often done in the form of an attack on the analyst who is believed to be aloof and not caring at all about the patient but there is also a faint hope that the analyst, through being forced to share this experience of the patient's, may find a better solution to the problems than the patient has done. This behavior of the patient is frequently misunderstood and misinterpreted as being entirely aggressive and as a result the patient feels even more rejected, misunderstood and alone.
>
> (p. 263)

I think I didn't realize that Ginger thinly hoped I would find a better solution. Perhaps I somewhat misunderstood her as entirely aggressive when she was also trying to communicate with me. On the other hand, she seemed unable, due to primitive feelings of greed, envy, and paranoia, to take in whatever I did have to offer in the way of understanding and solution.

In meeting with Ginger, I learned more about how to deal with strong countertransference feelings and how to navigate within a persistent, concrete form of projective identification. I also learned more about the difficulties of working with strong sadomasochistic character structure. I think Ginger was able to feel more confident and less paranoid in her day-to-day living. While her intrapsychic conflicts remained, she seemed to rely less on aggressive projective mechanisms and felt more able to negotiate her interpersonal world. Indeed, when I first met her, she was about to be fired, and she was thinking of quitting school and breaking off her relationship. These situations quieted down and became much more manageable.

This was not an ideal treatment outcome, but a fairly reasonable one given the clinical and diagnostic limitations. I think it is easy for therapists to become discouraged or pessimistic with these types of difficult cases. However, I feel that if one proceeds with the analytic method, focusing on the issues of loss and persecution, one can be cautiously optimistic.

Janet

Janet was a thirty-year-old woman who came to me for help with relationship problems. I saw her for three years. Every six months or so, she would suddenly stop attending. She felt furious with me and feared I was controlling her. Then she would return, suspicious and reluctant.

Janet was raised in a very abusive family. Her father, an alcoholic, was often violent with his wife. My patient witnessed many attacks in which mother was thrown across the room, had her hair pulled out, and was beaten with a pipe. Janet had memories of floating on the ceiling and being a part of the wall during some of these horrific fights. There were many nights when my patient lay in bed listening to her mother's screams as she was beaten.

I had occasion to treat the mother briefly. She was clearly psychotic and spent her time telling me rambling stories about her own hideously abusive childhood and her chaotic marriage. One telling story was how she started hearing children screaming while she was in the back yard. She raced in, looking around for her children. She frantically looked in each room as the screaming got louder. When she passed by the bathroom, she happened to catch a glimpse of herself in the mirror and realized it was herself that was screaming.

Janet's father left the family when she was six years old. He killed himself when she was in her teens. After the father left the home, the mother was unable to manage. The house filled with garbage and child protective services tried to take the children away several times.

Into adulthood, Janet had many relationships with men in which she either tired of them because they were "too normal and boring" or dated "exciting" men who exploited her and with whom she felt trapped. She felt victimized and trapped in her job setting too. In her treatment, she exploited me, felt trapped, and thought I was boring.

Overall, Janet found me irritating, bothersome, and out to criticize her. Also, she saw me as greedy, picky, insensitive, intrusive, unhelpful, and generally not in tune with her. Much of the time she attempted to use me as a narcissistic extension of herself and was upset when she found I had my own opinions. She also felt I was judgmental and ready to betray her and attack her, so she was usually quite defensive. Whenever I remarked on any hint of closeness between us, she was outraged. She tended to be very concrete as her ability to symbolize was degraded by excessive projective identification.

Janet demanded concrete answers on what to do about her life. She saw her actions, reactions, and problems as individual concrete entities. When I attempted to deepen a topic, she became defensive and irritated, feeling I was forcing her to talk about something that she has no interest in and that she had the right to talk about anything she wanted, or not to talk about anything she didn't want to, since she paid the bill. This led to a pattern of her bringing up topics that obviously had an emotional charge for her, but then skipping from topic to topic without much understanding about any of them. When I pointed this out, she felt I was trying to manage her time and direct her hour. At times, this would make her so upset she would walk out of my office.

Summary of several sessions

Janet told me about a party she went to. She said, in passing, that she was worried she made someone angry with an "insensitive comment." I asked her to tell me more about this. She asked why. I observed how she always becomes agitated when I asked her to discuss something in more detail. As a result of this comment, she became agitated. I asked her to tell me more about how she felt and she said I was "stuck" on it. She wondered angrily, "why can't we just move on?" so she could tell the rest of her story. I was not being the ideal audience she demanded and suddenly I was wanting something from her. This was a blow to her narcissistic way of relating and she started to feel attacked.

Next, Janet told me of her interest in a friend and how it felt strange to think of that relationship changing from a friendship to a possible romance. She said thinking of kissing him would change the focus of the closeness, "like it would if *we* kissed." I said nothing, feeling she had handed me a bomb that would go off if I commented on it. Janet told me how this man had given her a vase with two roses in it, one rose being taller than the other. He had told her that the roses represented his hopes for their relationship, that the tall one was him and the other was her. She told me this made her furious. She couldn't stand the idea of him being superior to her by the tallness. Also, she couldn't stand being trapped in the vase with him. Janet felt he had "forced her into this position." As a way to gain back control, she took the roses out of the vase and cut one down to the same size as the other, but this didn't solve the problem. Then, she then put each rose in a separate vase and placed the vases at opposite ends of the room. Now she felt better.

I told her that this man's words had incredible power over her and meant a terrible thing to her. She ignored my comment. At the end of her story, she looked upset and I asked her about that. Janet said she had probably talked too much and made me either bored or irritated. I said that she was seeing parts of herself in me and felt afraid of that. In response, she said it felt like she was being ignored and ripped off when I, or others, talked too much and that she always felt discounted and ignored by her family. She said she wanted to be sure to tell her whole story before the session ran out. The session was indeed almost over. I commented that not only had she told me her whole story but we were able to discuss other factors as well. I suggested that if she were ever not able to finish her story in one session, she could continue it in the next session. I also noted that she was usually five minutes late for her session, and that might be five more minutes for her to discuss things in. I think this was my own defensive reaction to her "I want it all now" approach to the session. I was trying to put boundaries on her greedy and demanding desires, instead of exploring and analyzing them. Janet said she would be furious if she had to wait till the next session to finish a story and that therapy just doesn't seem to work anymore. She also told me that regarding the first five minutes, I was never right there waiting for her the minute she walked in. She said, "If I am late, then you should have your door wide open and be ready to start the second I walk in." She said that therapy was a "rip-off" and a waste of her time.

I felt that once again, I could do nothing right. Here, I had tried to reassure her and be supportive in showing how she could get exactly what she wanted. This, just like my more analytic interpretations, seemed to be the trigger for her to feel immediately disappointed and angry. Behind this, I felt she was scared at how close we were becoming, how much she could lose, and how gravely she could be hurt.

In the next session, she discussed how she used men for her own gratification and how she was "pissed off" that they want something from her in return. (I think this was a comment on her wanting to tell me her whole "story" in the last session.) Janet said this caused her to feel suffocated and pressured and then she would retreat from the relationship, only to be overwhelmed by boredom and loneliness later. At that point she would reinstate the relationship and begin to take what she wanted and needed, and the cycle would continue. She also said that she hated it when the men didn't comply with her demands. I commented on her use of this pattern with me as well. I commented on how she presented it as "no big deal," but might actually be quite upset by it.

She became angry and said it was only a problem when the men didn't comply, and she didn't want to discuss the subject because it was something she didn't want to change. "If the man doesn't like it, he can leave," she said. I said that with the feelings she had discussing this, and with the number of times it had caused friction between us, it seemed like it was indeed a conflict for her. She became very angry and said that if it was a problem, I had caused it. She said, "You taught me to look out for myself, to put myself number one. I like it that way, so if it is a problem you caused it." She then proceeded to ask me what she should do about it if it was a problem, and that once again I had told her she had some problem but didn't tell her what to do about it. She demanded to know what to do about it. Unfortunately, our time was up. She left, acting angry and aloof. Later, she called to tell me I had shorted her two minutes in a previous session and that she wanted some form of payment. This was a way for her to regain the upper hand in a power struggle she felt she had lost ground in.

In the next session, Janet came in looking irritated and tentative. She is usually this way and my countertransference response is to feel anxious and vulnerable. She told me how her whole day had been a series of awful events in which no one did anything right and everyone irritated her in some way. I asked her to investigate her mood a bit by talking more about it. She repeated the idea that everything went wrong during the day. I said that her mood was usually precipitated by her not getting her way. I wondered if something hadn't gone well in our last session. She said, "So what am I supposed to do about it?" She commented that therapy was one of the things that irritated her because she never got any answers. She said, "I resent coming in but I tell myself maybe this time will be different, but it never is. It ends up to be a waste of my time." I said that her feeling of never getting "what she orders" was happening at that very moment, and that she felt left to deal with everything on her own. I asked her to slow down and just talk about her thoughts and feelings as a way to find some insight into these problems.

She began to tell me about her day again, but this time in a very different manner. After exploring various situations she had dealt with during her workday, she realized she had needed to be better organized or needed to communicate more clearly with people. Janet became much more peaceful as she talked. She said that maybe the therapy was at the point where it was getting deeper and therefore slower going. Needless to say, I was quite surprised and pleased at the shift in affect and sudden integration. My previous interpretation seemed to have alleviated her immediate anxiety and persecutory phantasies. I said she had managed to find a new and more peaceful experience of herself and us as she spoke, and that she had created the answer to her own question of "What do I do about it?" We then discussed how she could begin to separate the triggers that threw her into these states of emotional distress from these feelings that she was overcome by. Essentially, I pointed out to her the difference between her internal experience and the external environment that she encountered, and how the two could interact in an overwhelming way. She left the session appearing relatively intact and satisfied.

In the next session, I mentioned that we needed to reschedule one appointment and I offered her several options. Obviously upset, she said she would have to think about it and get back to me. Gripped by her dismissive tone, I acted out her projective identification dynamics of control and power. I asked her if she could possibly make a decision now, as I needed to make other plans as well. I brought to life the power struggle she felt in so often. Janet responded by saying "Forget it, just drop me from that appointment altogether." I realized how I had tasted her internal experience of being controlled and then I retaliated. She looked furious and I asked her to explore this. As usual, she denied any sense of anger.

Next, Janet started discussing how she was aware of "doing her pattern" with current boyfriends. She would see a man as perfect, begin to bond with him, find imperfections, and then angrily leave. At that point she would become lonely and find another "perfect man," or forget the last man's faults and go back to him. We talked about her need for perfection and her attitude of "If I can't have it my way, I will throw it away." While this attitude had been clear in the transference for many years, it was new for her to talk about it.

At this point, I brought attention to how she felt out of control with our appointment time and, since it was not perfect, she had thrown it and me out. At first, she fought this by telling me that she didn't have to do anything she didn't want to. But then she calmed down a bit. She talked about how she felt that she had always been controlled and not given what she really needed so she was "pissed off and vowed to never let that happen again." She said she needed to "find perfection and find it now!" Janet felt I was asking her to compromise on her appointment time and she would not have anything to do with it. I said she felt insulted and was trying to exact a revenge. She agreed. I commented on how her method of interacting with me and others sabotaged herself, noting that in the past she had canceled out of revenge and then wasn't able to come in right away when she wanted to and felt unfairly punished. She agreed, and we negotiated a new time.

In the last five minutes of the session, she regressed to her usual approach of viewing me as an unhelpful, critical, and distant enemy. I think this was because she felt I had exacted revenge on her by getting her to talk so openly. Suddenly, Janet demanded answers on what to do with her life, told me that therapy was constantly ineffective, that she was on the verge of quitting, and that I was no longer helpful to her. All this was done with great anger, bitterness, and control. I said she needed control and seemed to need to turn her achievements into failures. I commented on her shift from a collaborative stance to an offensive one in which she felt victimized and wronged. Now she demanded recompense. These interpretations seemed to contain her a bit, but still she stormed out of the office, glaring as she went.

In the next session, Janet came in and told me how angry and unhappy she had been. I asked her to tell me more about it. She said she was angry because "everyone was messing up and not doing it right." She quickly informed me that she was canceling our next appointment because, "even though she didn't want to," she had to pick up some friends at the airport. Then she told me a long story of how someone had "stolen" her parking spot. I asked her more about her feelings as they were so severe. She told me that everyone was just thoughtless and stupid and that it constantly affected her. I asked Janet if she felt this same way when she made mistakes, and she said no. I asked why and she said that she knew hers were honest mistakes but other people made mistakes because they didn't care about her. With this she sobbed. I commented that she expected and longed for perfection in others, but then was repelled and infuriated by a less than perfect object. (While I didn't directly interpret how she felt *I* had stolen her parking spot/analytic appointment, we seemed to get to that phantasy anyway.)

Then I said that she wanted me to be omnipotent and have all the answers, but when she demanded them from me and found that I didn't have them, she was furious and rejected me. She agreed and said that she would like to understand this more and learn how to deal with it. In the next breath, she began to press me for the solution to these patterns and demanded that I tell her what to do. I suggested she slow down and that what we had been talking about was happening at that very moment. She seemed to calm down a bit and said, "I would like to keep my appointment please, my friends can take care of themselves." Later that day, she called and told me that the dentist called her to remind her that she had an appointment at the time of our meeting, so she canceled our meeting and told me she would see me the next time.

Brief summary of a session one year later

Janet said she wanted to save some money in case things "got rough" and she needed to pay off a medical bill. She therefore wanted to cut back her treatment. When I started to ask questions about her finances and her other concerns, she became very agitated and told me it was none of my business and that nobody had the right to ask about her money. At that point, she said that she decided she would quit altogether since she knew that coming less often was "just a waste of time anyway." (This was a sarcastic statement based on a discussion we had at one point about frequency. I had suggested that coming less made it a bit more difficult to get to important matters.)

At this point, I said she was ready to flee because she felt she had no options. She agreed, but proceeded to tell me more about her irritation about therapy. I said I was curious that if finances were indeed a concern, why hadn't she considered asking about a temporary fee reduction rather than limit herself to having to giving up her treatment? Janet said she refused to put herself through "that type of humiliation." "It would be better to just not come in." We managed to discuss this a bit and I pointed out her fear of rejection and her fragile sense of safety within our relationship. She became calmer and started to ask about the idea of a temporary fee reduction. I mentioned that I would like to have a sense of her overall financial picture to help me understand what her condition was. This threw her into a rage and she told me that "she should have known better than to waste her time talking to me" and that I had confirmed her idea that I would sit in judgment of her and her needs. Janet said if that was the way it was, then she didn't need to be wasting her time in therapy and that she had already been considering seeing someone else who charged less. While it was difficult for me not to get caught up in her drama, I was able to say that she was very afraid I would scrutinize and reject her if she opened up and became vulnerable. In fact, she was already feeling, through projective identification, vulnerable to me not providing the perfect container for her to be any way she pleased. She continued to assail me with her accusations and said she would be quitting "at least for a while." The session was over and she left. We had a brief phone call the next day in which much the same theme occurred and she told me she was "quitting for good."

While she did not return to treatment, I have since found out that she was able to see me as more than just a bad object to reject. Over the years, she has referred several co-workers and friends to me, always telling them, "He is really good and helps you figure things out!"

Janet had clearly profited from her treatment. She stopped her longtime cycle of dating abusive and unavailable men and married a gentle, understanding man. She became a loving mother. She found a better job with supportive co-workers. She no longer felt suicidal, no longer had debilitating bouts of depression, and no longer starved herself to lose weight. She was more tolerant of others and much more self-reflective. At the same time, major paranoid–schizoid conflicts continued and primitive compromise formations remained. She continued to use some limiting and self-destructive defenses and was still ruled at times by primitive feelings of loss and guilt.

Janet used narcissistic defenses against the pain of losing her ideal object. In addition, she feared being held accountable for the destruction of that object. She was so angry and devaluing of her objects that she knew on some level she was responsible for their failure. Still, she felt a primitive persecutory form of guilt that made her scared of what would be done to her in return. She felt such pressure to be a "good little girl" that she had to evacuate that pressure into the object. Therefore, she felt surrounded by demanding, judgmental objects that she ultimately had to flee from.

Difficult cases that never get off the ground, or seem to "crash and burn" after some period of rocky treatment, are opportunities for analytic research. These patients will continue to come to our offices so we need to understand them and find ways of helping them. The best course may be simply to do the best analytic work we can while accepting that they will abort the treatment without much of a shift in their internal or external experience.

Gary

This was a case that failed to solidify or stabilize due to the patient's acting out, the intensity of his persecutory phantasies, and my failure to address the transference fully.

Gary was a forty-year-old man who came for treatment of what he called panic attacks. He had been a drug addict and alcoholic for many years and had been diagnosed with a rare blood ailment. Medications were expected to extend his life by five or ten years.

A family adopted Gary when he was one year old. His new mother, a severe alcoholic, masturbated him, fondled his anus, and beat him regularly. Gary would say, "She just wanted me from the waist down, she felt the rest was a waste of time." His father was a passive man who stayed in the background. His brother began a life of crime at an early age and ended up serving life in prison. When they were growing up, this brother would sodomize Gary at night.

I met with Gary for four years. However, he would often storm out of my office and not return for several months. When he did attend, he might suddenly stop showing up and never call. I would have to call him and "remind" him of his next appointment. His drug addition and paranoid delusions made it difficult to meet consistently and frequently. I hospitalized him twice for psychotic decompensation. He heard voices most of the time, but when he was intoxicated they overwhelmed him. He would cause public scenes, leading to his arrest. He was very concrete and became anxious when I tried to explore his feelings. He used bizarre references and self-help mysticism to fill our time and ward off any relational connection that seemed too dangerous. Except for one-night-stands, he was a recluse. While he had held a job as a clerk for many years, most of the time he was on disability.

Gary had a symbiotic relationship with his mother, who was now demented and lived in a hotel. They talked daily and he wished he could live with her. He felt there was no point in living, other than to try and be close to her and be accepted by her. He would become angry when I suggested he might have trouble sharing his thoughts and feelings with me. He mostly discussed his current problems with his mother, his job, or drug use. He saw the world as against him. When he was not in some sort of crisis, he pursued gratification and escape through one-night-stands, alcohol binges, and drugs. He often put me in the role of a "shoulder to cry on" and others as the "bad guy," all in a very superficial manner, but this shifted to the opposite without much warning. Gary was on a combination of anti-psychotic medication, antidepressants, and anti-anxiety pills.

Summary of one session

Gary was in the midst of a six-month on-and-off-again drug and alcohol binge. At the same time, he managed to achieve a more advanced position at work. The drug and alcohol escapades left him so badly off financially that he filed bankruptcy. Two days before this session he had been using crack cocaine, his drug of choice, and had to sell some of his furniture to procure it. He arrived to the session after drinking a few "cocktails" which he felt put his "anxiety" to rest. He told me that he had called in sick to work again and he didn't understand why he continued to "drag his ass through the garbage" and "put himself through hell." He told me that he was very tired of the voices he heard that told him he was a bad person. Gary felt the only things that stopped the voices were earplugs, long walks, or alcohol. He had previously managed to get the earplugs lodged inside his ears for several days and had to have them surgically removed. He told me that it also helped to gorge himself with huge amounts of food. This made him sleepy enough to drift away from the voices. He said that he was aware that the voices came from "inside his head" and told him that he was a bad person, but that when he was under stress or taking drugs he began to hear people around him having group discussions about how bad he was. He also felt that people in my waiting room were probably talking about him. I asked him if I was adding to his feeling of being put down. He told me he didn't feel I was because he was "able to see my lips and therefore could tell what I meant."

Gary said he was fed up with having to please people and was feeling so low that he just didn't care anymore. He said he felt like a survivor and wished he could be dead instead. I said that perhaps he felt under pressure to please me and perhaps he felt he was failing that obligation. He responded by discussing how much he hated himself. I also made remarks about how the voices were similar to how his mother would relate to him. I proposed that his guilt about not wanting to visit her might recently have led to the feelings of self-punishment he was now under. I said that he put his anger and neediness into me, and that he now felt trapped in a cycle of trying to please his mother and myself but felt like we would never be satisfied. He responded mostly to the last comment and then left the session early, which was common. He said his head was spinning and he needed air.

Gary was overwhelmed by fears and phantasies of an object that sadistically failed him, conning him into believing he could find love. Suddenly, that object seemed to transform into an abusive and cold object. This occurred in the transference, where I turned from special helper to cruel betrayer, someone "not on his side." He saw his co-workers, boss, psychiatrist, and his drug buddies all in the same light. Most importantly, this was the internal and external experience he had with his mother.

Gary did benefit from his treatment. He made fewer suicide attempts, he managed to work much of the time, he maintained some friendships, and he made efforts at reducing his drug and alcohol habit. Also, he gained some understanding of his internal anxieties and phantasies. Overall, treatment helped him to manage himself better. However, his intra-psychic conflicts were fundamentally unchanged and his life was maintained rather than improved. This may be the best we can do for some patients.

Chapter 11

Brief and atypical encounters

By now, the reader can see how the highly motivated neurotic patient who is willing and able to attend four or five sessions a week, on the couch, is a rarity in typical private practice settings. Many studies show that this type of ideal case represents a small and decreasing number. Vaslamatzis and Rabavilas (2001) echo some of my ideas when they note:

> The development of psychoanalysis has traditionally been based on "neurotic" patients (usually hysteric, obsessive-compulsive, or depressive) and the classic analytic setting. However, since 1960 there has been a gradual shift in the population who seek psychoanalytic therapy. Patients with a history of trauma, unstable relationships, and chaotic erotic lives, with narcissistic vulnerabilities and psychosomatic symptoms among the problems, now request psychoanalytic help.
>
> (pp. xi–xii)

Unfortunately, psychoanalytic training institutes have not kept up with this trend, as reflected by little change in the core course work and the supervisory choices of what constitutes an analyzable case. While candidates learn about personality disorders and psychosis, the message is that working with these difficult patients requires an approach that cannot really be called psychoanalysis. Psychotherapy or supportive counseling are often brought up as terms to embrace this uncertainty when dealing with atypical cases. Subtly or not so subtly, the candidate learns that psychoanalysis and the analytic method in general are not helpful for these patients. I think this is a disservice to the strength and breadth of the psychoanalytic method and to the many patients that can and do benefit to some degree from our services.

From my own experience in a training institute that was working toward acceptance into the International Psychoanalytic Association, there was much to-do about separating the training in psychoanalysis from psychoanalytic psychotherapy. This was discussed in such a way that one could only conclude that psychoanalysis could be contaminated by this other species, unless properly separated and protected. Yet the main observable difference between the two modalities as presented in the training tracks was seeing the psychotherapy patient twice a week versus four times a week. From a diagnostic perspective, the sicker patients were funneled into psychotherapy cases. But the theoretical and technical approaches taught in the classes were the same. Indeed, all candidates attended the same seminars except for the case conferences. My point in describing this situation is that the separation into two tracks for training purposes seemed to be motivated by political factors. However, the fact that all candidates were taught the same technique and theory shows that on a unspoken level, this training institute realized that the psychoanalytic method is what works for both groups of patients.

So, political allegiances and rigid rules about external criteria such as frequency, diagnosis, duration, and use of couch get in the way of studying the benefit of the analytic method for the patient most likely to been seen today.

Most analysts in private practice know from experience that while many cases are very difficult and disorganized from start to finish, the analytic method offers a great deal of healing and help to most patients. Some of these patients are able to make more use of it than others, but it seems only fair to offer them the opportunity instead of prejudging them to be unable to utilize the experience due to their lack of adherence to certain rigid criteria, questionably necessary in the first place.

I do think the optimal setting for analytic treatment involves high-frequency visits, use of the couch, and a substantial duration. However, I also know from clinical experience that many patients, including the very disturbed and disturbing, benefit from the analytic method even without those criteria. When I see these patients evolve and benefit in a similar way to more neurotic patients in a more classical setting, I think it is fair to call both treatments psychoanalytic.

Kunst (2002) makes a compelling argument for the benefit of working psychoanalytically even under less than optimal conditions. He states:

> Even without the benefit of the standard psychoanalytic frame, deeper contact with the patient's unconscious can be made. One can facilitate a mind-set, in all sorts of treatment situations, in which every interaction and intervention is directed toward understanding the unconscious, developing curiosity about one's internal world, learning to bear rather than off-load psychic pain, and committing oneself to emotional development rather than immediate relief of anxiety . . . in these and other ways, an analytic culture can be cultivated even when so many prohibitive factors predominate.
>
> (p. 164)

The main point I think it is helpful to note is how Kunst is comfortable calling his method "psychoanalysis." He does not become buried in the esoteric or political debate as to what it means that he sees his patient only once a week, or if that patient is overtly psychotic at times. He, as I am stressing with my own work, advocates the analysis of the transference, the exploration of unconscious phantasies, a working with defenses, and the integration of split-off aspects of the patient's personality. This is the genuine benefit that psychoanalysis can offer in the real world, even in challenging circumstances and settings.

The strict definitions of what constitutes psychoanalysis, usually measured in external terms; the narrow band of diagnostic categories deemed appropriate; and the discarding of clinical data from less than optimal treatments are all part of an attitude that will ultimately lead to the demise of the profession. This stance certainly leaves many patients without the help they need. Freud believed in helping the mentally suffering individual by using a method centered in the exploration of the unconscious mind. Reviewing his cases, one is struck by how flexible and open he was in applying the analytic method.

To be more flexible and openminded about what constitutes psychoanalysis, one must reconsider what is deemed helpful to patients and how to understand the outcome of cases that are difficult, brief, and often abortive. There must be an ongoing exploration of the external challenges imposed on the analytic relationship as well as the actual change or lack of change that emerges within the atmosphere of the analytic method.

Wallerstein (2001) points out that:

> all over the psychoanalytic world – in Europe and in America (and I assume also in Latin America) equally – the complacent certainties about the distinct enough compartmentalization of psychoanalysis and of the psychoanalytic psychotherapies no longer exist.
>
> (p. xvi)

Throughout the book, I have used clinical material to show how pointless the debate about those certainties is when one is actually working with a patient. Clinical experience should shape theoretical assumptions. The question isn't "Is it proper psychoanalysis or just psychoanalytically informed therapy?" The question, for the sake of the patient and the course of their treatment, should be, "How is this individual expressing his unconscious conflicts, and how are his intra-psychic world and object-related phantasies manifesting within the analytic relationship?"

My idea is in line with Caper's (2001) simple yet eloquent statement that "The goal of clinical psychoanalysis is psychological development and . . . that psychoanalysts try to reach this goal by making interpretations" (p. 99). I think his definition would include patients who attend less frequently, don't use the couch, and terminate after a short period of time. Granted, these difficult and often confusing cases often show only partial psychological development or merely achieve a temporary stabilization. However, this is still a benefit to the patient and should be considered a success, especially within less than optimal circumstances.

What I am talking about is the practice of psychoanalysis under difficult and trying limitations. It is not brief psychotherapy and it is not psychoanalytic psychotherapy, because those are terms to define treatments that are meant to be something different than psychoanalysis from the start. Under less than optimal conditions, the outcome of psychoanalytic treatment may be similar in appearance to brief psychotherapy or psychoanalytic psychotherapy, but the method and approach are different.

Variations in outcome

I think there are variations or different levels that occur when dealing with atypical and erratic treatments. Some of these cases are just so brief and so scattered that it is safe to say no change was possible. These vexing situations are familiar to all clinicians. The psychoanalytic method is applied, but there is no real chance for benefit due to severe acting out, pathological defense systems, and external roadblocks.

Then, there are cases in which the contact is very short and overall there is no evidence of change. However, the patient may be able to use the analyst and the analytic process as a way-station, a temporary resting place in their internal storm. They achieve a respite and a touch of support, but are unable to bridge this into an ongoing therapeutic relationship.

An example of this was my patient Alan. Alan came to see me after engaging his employee assistance program. The health benefit offered company workers three free visits with a mental health professional.

Case material

Alan

Alan was a nervous looking twenty-five-year-old man who started off by saying, "Why are you looking at me that way?" He followed up with "How will you help me?" said in an anxious and demanding tone. Alan told me he was afraid people might be wrongly thinking he was a homosexual, so Alan wanted me to stop these plaguing thoughts. He reported other obsessive and paranoid ideas about how women were thinking he was looking at their breasts and how he found himself acting like certain movie stars.

Alan still lived at home with his parents. The family was very strict Catholic, and Alan attended church several times a week. He had never had a girlfriend but confessed to watching pornography on his computer. While he felt it was a sin, he masturbated and then consoled himself with the idea that it was not as bad as having sex before marriage.

In the countertransference, I felt Alan degraded me and saw me as a waiter who should hurry up and bring him his order. He would look impatiently at his watch and he would ask me, "What are you going to do for me and how are you going to fix this?" I interpreted that he was anxious about his desires for sex, about his wish for a girlfriend, about his interest in other men, and about his need to be in control of things. I said he felt controlled at home by trying to be a good son and a good Christian. But he felt a conflict about these things and it came out in how he was controlling me. I suggested he was struggling with feelings of lust, anger, guilt, and fear. When I told Alan these things, he relaxed and was not as paranoid or demanding.

However, when Alan's three free sessions were up, he did not want to continue. He could afford to pay me, but he didn't want to. Alan said he didn't think it was worth it and he could do just as well on his own. I interpreted that he felt anxious about starting a relationship with me where he was committed and had to give. I said this must make him feel dependent and not in control, similar to how he must feel about his home life, his sex life, and his mental life. Alan said he thought I might be a homosexual and he wanted me to promise never to call him at home, so his parents wouldn't know he was seeing me. I reminded him that he had refused to give me his phone number or any other personal information, but that his worry might tell us something. He said he just wanted his privacy.

Alan left after three visits and I didn't hear from him again until twelve months later. Since a year had elapsed, he was now eligible for three more free visits. Alan came in and started right where he left off. If he was friendly with another man, even very casually, Alan was convinced the man thought he was gay. The resulting anxiety and overtly paranoid stance left Alan socially isolated. Recently, he had been fired from his job and he thought his peculiar ways had made him undesirable to his boss. Alan said, "My worries make me act like a freak, so of course they fired me!"

Again, I engaged Alan with the analytic method. I continued to explore his phantasies and fears as well as his defenses against these deep conflicts. I interpreted the transference as best I could, and encouraged Alan to look at his interpersonal style with me.

This time, Alan told me that one month prior to seeing me the first time a year ago, he had had sex with a prostitute. This was the only time he had done so, and he felt very guilty. I suggested that his guilt, as well as the wish for more sex, had provoked some of his obsessive thinking and general panic. He felt other people were accusing him of being a dirty, perverted man. I interpreted that Alan felt so torn about his phantasies and wishes that he projected this self-judgment onto others and then felt stared at and judged. Alan seemed to relax a bit and agreed with my comment for a short while. Then, he went back to demanding an "answer" to his problem.

Alan told me he wanted to continue after the three visits, but said he wanted me to charge him a quarter of my usual rate. I said I would be glad to see him for a reduced rate due to his recent unemployment, since I knew he would never ask his family for help. But I added that he seemed uncomfortable depending on me and giving to me so he had to ask in a way that put me down. He could be back in control by bidding me down to a bargain basement price. I interpreted that giving to me and engaging in an equal relationship without that sort of power struggle must feel too close, dangerous, weak, or homosexual. Alan said, "It isn't worth it. I know what is wrong with me. I don't need you." Since he had no more free sessions, Alan said goodbye. That was the last I saw him, until perhaps next year.

Now, I don't think Alan experienced any major psychological shift in his three plus three visits with me. However, it would be wrong to dismiss his case as meaningless and non-analytic. I think he was capable of achieving insight about himself and indeed did begin to reflect on his thoughts and feelings. However, Alan used me as a source of temporary support and emotional safety. In fact, to engage with the analytic method and acknowledge being a participant in our analytic relationship was a threatening dependence that reminded him of his conflicted dependence on family and religion. Therefore, Alan was more comfortable trying to control me from a distance. When the treatment began to be more intimate, and I interpreted his attempts to make me a servant with magical advice, he fled. So, Alan benefited momentarily from the analytic process, but was unable at this time to attach himself to it long enough for any lasting change to occur. His case is of a type that is frequent in private practice settings: brief, scattered, and demanding. It has an 'almost, but not quite' feel to it in the countertransference. As it is so brief, it is difficult to use this case for research purposes. However, it seems wrong to discount this type of analyst–patient experience as worthless to study.

Barry

This next case is one in which definite change took place, within an analytic framework, but under less than optimal conditions. Usually, this means a treatment that lasts only a short period of time. In other cases, it may involve other hardships that limit the analytic envelope from developing fully. However, I am emphasizing how the essential elements of psychoanalysis – the analysis of the transference, exploration of phantasy, working through of basic psychological conflicts and their associated defenses, and a better integration of the personality – are often possible even under atypical, untraditional, and difficult circumstances.

Barry was fourteen years old, with a younger and an older brother. His parents requested I see Barry because his grades were near failing and he seemed angry, depressed and defiant. After I met with his parents, several problems emerged that immediately impacted the analytic framework, limiting and constricting the potential for me to work as a psychoanalyst. The parents had marital problems but were not interested in working on that, even when I commented on how their relational struggles might be acted out by their children. Also, both parents did not want to pay for the treatment after the ten free visits provided by their insurance plan. Finally, neither parent seemed overly interested in providing transportation for their son to make it to my office after school. These multiple obstacles to the analyst's function as a helpful container and translator of the patient's conflicts are common in private practice (Sulzberger-Wittenberg, 1970).

I began meeting with Barry on a weekly basis, although we skipped a few weeks here and there when his school schedule or family schedule interfered with our work. In the countertransference, I felt I was on a countdown clock, knowing we had only ten visits to try to make sense of this young man's life. I wondered if that was the type of pressure he might be living under as well.

When Barry had come in with his parents to the initial consultation interview, he seemed withdrawn and resistant to engaging with me. Attending the sessions by himself, he diligently rode his bicycle to my office after classes and was never late. He was genuinely interested in talking with me. Our talks included a number of topics. Barry initiated each one and I would ask for deeper associations or make interpretations based on the topic.

Barry told me he felt his math teacher didn't like him and deliberately gave him low marks on tests. In fact, Barry felt that most of his teachers didn't like him. When I explored this, it seemed Barry felt misunderstood by them. He felt they made hasty judgements about his character. Listening to the day-to-day problems he had in class, I interpreted that he was focusing on just one part of the picture. His math teacher, and sometimes other teachers, would make negative comments about Barry. However, their comments usually followed rather provocative statements or curse words from Barry. For example, Barry would say, "you bitch!" after the teacher announced a pop-quiz. Barry agreed with me, but wasn't sure of his motivation when I asked him why he related that way. Yet he seemed open to the idea that there was a reason behind his behavior, as long as I agreed that his teacher sounded "out of it" or "lousy at her job."

For several sessions, Barry brought along cassette tapes of his favorite rock music bands. Like his method of relating to teachers, Barry presented his music to me in an edgy fashion. He brought me the lyrics of his favorite punk band and said he was sick of his father telling him he was forbidden to buy them or listen to them. I glanced over the lyrics about drive-by shootings, drug use, robbery, suicide, and general mayhem. The music glorified sex, drugs, suicide as escape, guns, and getting what you want by any means necessary. While I had heard of some of the bands he liked, the music was foreign to me. So, I just kept an eye out for the themes in the music that seemed to interest Barry. I told him I could see he was interested in the rebellion and independence in the songs. I interpreted that he might feel angry and against great odds in his life, just like the song's characters. Barry said, "yeah, sometimes" and went on to tell me about the benefits of "really cranking up the volume and chilling to the beat."

I asked Barry about his relationship with his father, as the father seemed rather distant the one time I had met him. Barry said, "We get along OK. He just wants me to do everything his way. If I talk about guns, he says it is important to respect and love each other. He always wants to go hiking. He keeps telling me about nature and animals. We have to eat natural food at home. I tell him I want a chili-dog and he gives me a lecture about how many animals died to be in that chili-dog." The more we talked about Barry's experiences with his father, the more I got the picture of how Barry felt. It seemed Barry saw his father as trying to get Barry to be a clone of him, be it food, health, social beliefs, or other choices. While part of this picture was Barry's father attempting to extinguish Barry's more aggressive side, it was also an image of Barry's father turning away from Barry's own unique personality. While I had no way to know whether this was mostly Barry's phantasy, his real life experience, or a mix of both, I simply treated it as the important psychic reality Barry was currently struggling with.

Working analytically, I explored Barry's unconscious desires, his defenses against them, and how this took place in the transference. I interpreted that he wished for a closer relationship with his father, one in which his father took an interest in Barry's life. I said he was sad that his father seemed to criticize his son's interests and wanted Barry to adopt his father's beliefs instead. Barry replied, "I tell him I want to go watch the drag races and he says I am lazy and only help to destroy the environment. He wants me to learn about nature and the goddamn cycle of life." I said this must hurt his feelings and suggested that he reacts to that hurt by being provocative at school, with me, and at home.

Over the couple of sessions remaining, there seemed to be a change even though Barry continued to relate to me in the same way. Instead of provocative music, he brought in tales of minor vandalism and rule-breaking. He told me of graffiti he put on fences that involved gang references and drug references. Barry said it was "hard core" and "in your face." There were numerous stories of behaviors that were not so terrible or dangerous, but certainly designed to irritate adults. I interpreted that Barry was testing me to see if I would react like his father or if I would try and understand him. He said, "kind of." I interpreted that he was sure that I or father would not be interested in him and who he really was, so he had to rely on being the opposite of what we wanted him to be. I suggested that Barry needed to speak up for himself in a more direct way, instead of his indirect acting out. I told Barry that even if his father, I, or others couldn't give him the kind of support he needed, he might feel better letting us know how important things were to him.

So, I said things like, "I think your father doesn't get it. You want to do some fun things like go to the races with him and eat chili-dogs and share your music with him. You are doing that with me, by bringing me your tapes and your stories of all your adventures. But maybe you need to talk more about how you need and want that special time with your father. You want to be with him, doing something that shows he cares about you. You want proof that he is interested in you." Barry said, "That sure would be different." I went on to say, "You are watching me to see if I freak out and say, 'Oh my God, you are breaking the law and sneaking cigarettes and spray painting fences. Why aren't you in Boy Scouts, on a nice nature walk? Well, I think you mostly just want to see if I care and if I am interested in what you are all about. You are sad because you feel your father fails the test, over and over."

At the end of the ten visits, I called Barry's parents. I advocated his continuing treatment, but his parents refused. They said they didn't want to pay the money to continue and they felt things were better anyway. I asked them for details. Over the course of four months, Barry's grades had greatly improved, his angry outbursts had stopped, and he seemed to be participating more in family activities. I suggested this was a wonderful sign and that either more individual work or some family therapy might be helpful in maintaining these strides. Again, the parents declined. So, this was the end of Barry's treatment. In a brief time, the analytic process seemed to take hold and assist this young man on his way. While some of his improvement was probably a transference cure (me as wished for, understanding father) that went unanalyzed, I think he had begun to think more insightfully about his internal experiences and started to feel he had more choice in his life.

Chris

Chris came to me not out of choice, but as part of a work-related penalty. He was a manager at a large pharmaceutical company. He had been caught stealing several narcotic medications and a fellow employee had reported his use of drugs while at work. His company demanded he go on leave, seek therapy, attend drug recovery meetings, and submit to random urine tests.

When I began seeing Chris, he was defiant and defensive. He told me he was being forced to see me and would only come in every other week, as that was what the company stipulated and would pay for. Chris was not about to participate, be it in money, reflection, or commitment.

In the countertransference, I felt rather unsure as to whether this arrangement would last long and was doubtful about any potential for analytic engagement with Chris. He was a rather large man who was grossly obese and not exactly friendly, so I also felt a bit intimidated. However, I also felt there was something childlike about Chris. I thought it would be worthwhile to give it a try and see what emerged.

The first few months, Chris was withdrawn, quiet, and bitter. He hated coming in and told me I was in a useless field that just used people to get rich. For a while, Chris continued to use drugs at home and drank excessively, but he was no longer using narcotics and he acknowledged he shouldn't be getting high on the job.

Gradually, Chris told me about himself, but always with some sarcastic remark thrown in, often about how stereotypical and useless it was for me to be exploring his childhood experiences and making remarks about what might be going in his unconscious. While I had made some remarks about his childhood and how it might be affecting his adult life, Chris's remarks seemed to be aimed at taking the focus off him and to demean the relationship we were in.

At that point, I didn't really know much about Chris or his background. Nevertheless, I slowly began to learn about this man. Chris was raised in a troubled family where his father was an alcoholic and his mother seemed overwhelmed and unavailable. When Chris was five years old, his mother left the family. When Chris was thirty years old, two years before I met him, his mother contacted him and wanted to re-establish a connection. This troubled Chris greatly. He was furious and claimed he would never "give that bitch a chance."

In high-school and college, Chris drank excessively and used drugs. He told me he had dated various women through the years, but had never had a committed, long-term relationship. I interpreted that it might be difficult to trust anyone, after his mother had walked out on him. Chris replied, "Do you have anything better than that kind of Freudian crap?" I replied, "Maybe when you growl at me like that it means we are in an area that is tough but important." Chris said, "If that makes you feel better, fine."

This sort of hostile stance continued, but gradually Chris softened as well. He broke down several times, around the tenth visit, and said how miserable and lonely he felt. The next session he re-established his gruff ways and told me not to "make too much out of all that." Bit by bit, Chris began to contemplate himself, his life, and his early family experiences. In the transference, he acknowledged his attacks on me one day and then made more of them the next.

While I tried to get Chris to attend more often, he came in only twice a month, which was what his company was willing to pay for. Around the ninth month of treatment, which would have been the eighteenth visit, he was talking much more openly about his mother and how angry and disgusted he felt towards her. Chris started to cry. After several minutes, Chris said, "I don't know if I can count on you to be here if I fall." After several minutes of painful silence, I said, "If you trust me to be here when you fall, will I stick around to catch you or will I abandon you?" Chris replied, "Something like that, yes." He went on to tell me he had never felt anyone could be trusted. Here, at only the eighteenth visit, Chris became much more vulnerable and engaged in the analytic process.

Predictably, the next visit was more of a re-entrenchment of his defenses. He was silent most of the session and didn't reply to any of my references to the last visit. However, I felt we had established a new level of relating, at least temporarily, in which Chris was starting to reflect more on his inner experiences and his perceptions of his internal objects.

When Chris came in to his twenty-fourth visit, he related to me in a markedly open manner. He began by saying, "In the time between our sessions, I find myself thinking more about what we talk about and what we don't talk about. I really wish I could trust you and tell you how I feel and let out all the crap that I have bottled up inside me. But I am afraid of being somehow rejected, left, or completely abandoned. It feels like that is what has happened to me my whole life." I said, "Starting with your mother." Chris replied, "Yes. From then on."

A few minutes later, I commented, "You are not just telling me about these things, you are showing me too. You are sitting on the edge of the couch instead of lying down on it. We know how you do that when you aren't sure about fully trusting me. At the same time, you are being more open today than ever. So, there must be a real push–pull inside of you, taking a risk but feeling very cautious." Chris said, "You are right, Doc. But how can I trust anyone when all the evidence points to it being a stupid move? I went on the first date in a long time last week. I thought it went great. We went to the beach, to dinner, and a show. We talked about lots of things. But she hasn't called me since. I left two messages and she never returned them. It is over and I have no idea why." I said, "Maybe that is how you felt with your mother leaving, she is gone and you have no idea why. That seems to color your life today." Chris replied, "I don't know why, but I have been dreaming more than usual. There was this weird one the other night."

Chris went on, "In the first part of the dream, I was walking to some place and I saw this old woman by the side of the road, lying there. She looked pathetic. I went over to see if she needed any help. I looked after her for a while and then I kept going. But then I started running and I was on this path by the edge of a cliff. I almost fell off several times and I would have died down there. Then a park ranger stopped me and told me to slow down and be careful. I thought I would be given a ticket or something, but he was nice. Then I just kept running along."

I asked Chris for associations to this dream, but he claimed it was "pretty straightforward, just weird, no hidden messages." I suggested the dream portrayed how he had been just going along in life when his mother contacted him, asking him to visit her in a convalescent home where she was recovering from a fall. He had felt very torn. On one hand he tried to help and arranged to visit her. On the other hand, he felt she was selfish and pathetic for having walked out on him when he was a helpless child. I also interpreted that this encounter with his mother left him angry, upset, and running from his feelings. His mother's return in his life left Chris on the edge of dangerous internal feelings that he felt close to falling into. Finally, I suggested that the park ranger was myself, telling him to slow down, stop using drugs, and find his way back to a safer path. Chris told me my interpretation was "interesting" but "useless" because he "didn't give a damn" about his mother and that she didn't have the power to affect him.

At the beginning of the next visit, Chris announced he would not be returning. He said his company had asked for a random urine test and Chris had refused. As per his agreement with the company, he had to submit to this testing. As a result of the refusal, Chris's company would no longer pay for treatment, leaving Chris to pay out of his own pocket. Chris said he wasn't about to "pay for something that is such a waste of time."

I interpreted that his recent outpouring of feelings with me might have led him to take this defensive reaction. He replied, "Whatever, Doc. I don't care. This is too much work and I don't want to do the work. I don't want to pay for it and I don't want to do it. Maybe later if they pay for it again, I don't know. But this is it." I said, "Maybe it is painful and makes you angry to have to come here on your own, as if you are in my control. Maybe you feel more in control when the company pays." My idea was that Chris felt vulnerable and dependent and subject to rejection if he was asking to see me and offering to pay himself. Chris responded, "I am not willing to take that on. Why? Well, it is just not worth it."

Now, Chris fell silent for ten minutes. I asked him what he was thinking and where he was emotionally. He said, "I have shut down." After ten more minutes of silence, he said, "It is too much work and I don't feel like doing it." I replied, "It seems you are rejecting us and letting yourself down by not giving yourself a chance." After a few more moments of silence, Chris said, "I don't think I can stay away from the drugs without external controls." I said, "I can continue to be your external control if you let me or want me to be." Chris replied, "It is up to me now, it is sink or swim."

This was the last time I saw Chris. A combination of external circumstances and Chris's pattern of dealing with his life came together to produce a sadly familiar experience. Chris felt alone, persecuted, and abandoned one more time. In turn, he became stubborn, rejecting, and inaccessible. This was a pathological projective identification cycle in which the object was his foe and Chris was left to fend for himself, to "sink or swim" alone in a hostile sea of dangerous objects.

Clearly, the treatment process was not a success. However, I don't think it was a complete failure either. Chris managed to use me, in a marginal and temporary manner, as a new object. I began as a familiarly untrustworthy object and ended up looking like an unreliable or not-worth-the-risk one. But along the way, I was someone he started to practice some new ways of relating with and risk a few moments of dependency and trust with.

Discussion

Was Chris's case a typical analytic situation? In many ways, it was. The average analyst in private practice sees a great number of people who fit Chris's profile. These patients never attend multiple weekly sessions, use the couch, or show great motivation. They abort the treatment after several weeks or months. Diagnostically, they often suffer severe characterlogical problems as well as drug addiction, depression, or anxiety. So, in these respects, Chris was a typical patient.

Was this an analytic case? Well, Chris certainly seemed to fit the main criteria. He developed a transference that we tried to understand and process. He discussed dreams and we explored the genetic links between his childhood and his current adult situation. We touched on core phantasies he perceived the world through, although these paranoid views also made it difficult to work through the core phantasies. I, as his analyst, made interpretations and focused on how his internal and external worlds intersected to create distorted object-relations that kept his childhood link to a rejecting mother alive.

Externally, Chris was able to stop using drugs while he attended his sessions, and he started to ponder the disappointing and dysfunctional pattern he had with women. So, it seems that this brief, chaotic treatment was indeed an analytic situation that provided some temporary help and relief to someone in desperate need. Perhaps Chris's experience left him more amenable to seeking future help as well.

Conclusion

Chris and the other cases I have presented are meant to remind analysts of the important and helpful profession they practice. If the goal of psychoanalytic work is to assist the patient toward internal integration, the analyst must be willing to stretch the process to the needs of the patient, not try to fit the patient into rigid theoretical criteria. When being flexible in this manner, the analyst is able to be more realistic about who his patients are, what to expect, and how to accept what occurs. In this way, we can provide realistic assistance within a psychoanalytic framework to where the patient currently is positioned, internally, externally, and interpersonally.

A more realistic and elastic approach to the psychoanalytic method in private practice settings is beneficial to both patient and analyst.

Part IV

Clinical perspectives on theoretical and training paradigms

Chapter 12

A day in the life of a psychoanalyst[1]

In the 2002 newsletter of the American Psychoanalytic Association, Erik Gann discusses the findings of surveys that examined the nature of psychoanalytic practice in the United States over a period of twenty-five years. He points out that in terms of numbers, the average psychoanalyst sees very few analytic cases in which the patient comes three to four times a week, uses the couch, and works on moderate to medium range neurotic disorders.

Gann (2002) states, "Most psychoanalysts spend most of their professional time engaged in work other than clinical psychoanalysis" (p. 37). The valuable point he makes is that a rigid view of what it means to be an analyst, and what it means to practice psychoanalysis, is detrimental to the analyst, the patient, and the profession at large. He states, "We must reconsider in a genuinely creative way what a psychoanalyst is and does. In the process, we will redefine our own internal ethos, ambitions, and consensus about what is valuable and what should be valued in our field" (p. 38).

In following Gann's recommendations, the profession, at least in the United States, has been trying different tacks. Annual conferences, workshops and panels have explored these issues and debated possible solutions. A "makeover" has been suggested for our public profile. Outreach programs have been tried in an effort to educate the community about psychoanalysis. New brochures and media packages have been created to dispel the public's negative caricature of the profession. Psychoanalytic training programs have tried to "freshen up" their curriculum to better appeal to today's potential candidates. These and many other efforts are being made to salvage us from declining numbers of new analysts and new patients.

I believe there is an additional way to view this issue and another way to approach its solution. Most of the whole direction being taken is to bolster

1 Published as "A day in the life of a psychoanalyst", Parts 1 & 2 in *Psychodynamic Practice*, forthcoming in 2005. www.tandf.co.uk

the image of the psychoanalyst as someone to go to when one is ready for psychoanalysis. In other words, all the efforts are still trying to define the psychoanalyst as someone who sees patients four times a week on the couch. However good a light is put on this, we are still offering a skewed picture to the public of what psychoanalysis is all about and what these people called psychoanalysts actually do. My point is that for the public's honest appraisal of us as a resource in a time of need, we must present ourselves for what we really are. Eric Gann is pointing in the right direction.

Trying to emphasize how different we are from other mental health professionals by underscoring the number of times we see a patient per week or by use of the couch only fosters the public's rigid and suspicious view of us. Instead, we can educate the public on how we provide what many other professionals do, only in a highly specialized manner. It is extremely rare for a psychoanalyst to write about his work with families or couples, and that sort of article almost never makes it into a psychoanalytic journal. Yet many psychoanalysts treat families or couples. The same applies to short-term work with individuals seen only once a week. However, all these cases are approached in a very specialized manner, utilizing the psychoanalytic perspective.

The reality of the contemporary psychoanalyst is that he or she does a bit of everything, but does it in a different way from other mental health practitioners. Rather than trying to show the public how narrow our focus is, we can illustrate how wide our abilities are, within the perspective unique to our training.

Due to the specialized training an analyst undergoes, we are not only sensitized to many of the dynamics other mental health workers look for, but much more so and at a deeper level. The trained analyst is constantly looking for the unconscious meaning of the patient's activities and words, always exploring the defenses and coping patterns, refocusing back to the transference, and persistently investigating the nature of a patient's intrapsychic world and its particular cast of objects in relation. This focus is ongoing whether the frequency is once or five times a week, and whether the patient is an individual, a couple, or a family. We have a special procedure to offer that is applicable to the real, everyday world of people's lives and their needs.

What I actually do

My typical Monday involves meeting with eight to ten patients. I will present the first five cases of one random Monday, which will be enough clinical material to give the reader the opportunity to take an insider's look at what actually takes place in my private psychoanalytic practice. This is of course surrounded by the nuts and bolts of daily life and the circumstances of the mental health field. So, while my day does include a commute, phone calls to insurance companies, paperwork, meals on the go, writing articles to submit to journals, and brief but meaningful phone conversations with my wife, these activities are not unique to being a psychoanalyst. What I think about and what I do when I am with my patients are what should illuminate the special and different aspects of psychoanalytic work.

Case 1

This is a couple in their thirties. They have lived together for five years in a close but volatile relationship. He is prone to fits of anger and she appears somewhat aloof or distant. During the first few sessions, it became clear that they are in a long-standing conflict that has now come to a crossroads. In the past, he felt she demanded too much from him, so he feels compromised each time he "gives in." Now, he says, the stakes are too high to negotiate. Two months ago, they engaged in protected sex, but the method failed and she became pregnant. She wants the child but he says unless she gets an abortion, he will leave her for good. She refuses to have an abortion for religious reasons.

In the countertransference, I immediately share the couple's tension and realize I am a part of the triangle of enormous conflict, potential abandonment, loss of life and love, and seemingly impossible standoffs. This type of countertransference reaction is common in work with couples, especially when the couple's relationship no longer functions as a protective shell of containment (Morgan, 2001) for each individual. This lack of a holding and translating function becomes a job for the analyst as the unmodified projections and phantasies leak out of the couple's relationship structure and pull the analyst into the conflict. When not caught off-guard, I use these countertransference feelings and phantasies to interpret the couple's tensions, fears, and anxieties.

As a rule of thumb, couples employ the same general dynamics to deal with a crisis in the relationship as they do to deal with their own individual, internal troubles. By and large, a couple does not show up in the analyst's office until some internal or external problem has exhausted their mutual ability to function as a containing capsule for the relationship, regardless of how unhealthy that particular capsule might be.

So, this couple came to me in a period when their normal ways of object-relatedness had gone out of balance. During the course of several weeks, seeing them twice a week, I was able to interpret their particular way of looking to me for help, containment, and understanding as a part of their dynamic pattern. I told them that the way they listened to me and waited for feedback showed a mutual desire for union and a mutual fear of loss. I interpreted that they both were looking to me for resolution and prevention of loss. This seemed to bring about a certain calm, a reduction of anxiety and a willingness to explore.

The time came when an abortion was medically out of the question and the mother to be let it be known, again, that she was resolute in keeping the child. He was shocked, angry, and confused, but seemed willing to continue talking about it.

Over the next month, I was able to use the now strengthened circle of containment, partly fortified by their use of me as the Oedipal third – a figure of authority and safety – to learn about their individual dynamics. This is usually slow going in couples work, as what is most present is the object-relations as it pertains to the couple's conflict. However, this is a porthole view into the larger internal perspective of the two individuals. There are three levels of involvement in analytic couples work: each individual's psychic world as well as the third they co-create.

What emerged was the husband's childhood history of being savagely beaten by his father throughout his upbringing. His mother devoted herself to taking care of my patient, but never was able to stop the father's brutality. My patient was frightened at the vision of having his own child, only to treat it in the same cruel fashion. He refused to put himself and the child into such a horrible replica. His pregnant girlfriend seemed to put aside all her needs to tend to his angry outbursts or to try to accommodate his needs in order to prevent his rageful attacks. Thus, she became martyr-like as his mother had been and took both the roles of victim wife and loving mother, to the detriment of her own life.

Exploring these feelings, relational compromises, and their internal entrenchments lessened the couple's anxieties and their own individual tension. They seemed more comfortable with each other. We began a period of reflection and exploration compared to the beginning treatment phase of alarm and crisis. At this time, it is unclear what the outcome of treatment will be. However, their relationship is now more manageable and they are starting to communicate honestly with each other. There is some movement in discussing how they will be co-parents of their first child. Integral to all this change and progress is the slow and careful examination of their own individual psychology. In undertaking this examination in front of each other, they are learning to support and respect each other's inner world. This leads to a rebuilding of the couple's mutual containment and emotional nourishment. As each person comes to a better understanding, resolution, and integration of their own internal object-relations, they can better see, manage, and creatively improve their external and interpersonal object-relations.

Case 2

My next patient is a middle-aged gay man who entered into a four times a week psychoanalysis, on the couch, almost two years ago. He found out that his lover of ten years had been cheating on him for at least half the time they had been together. His reaction was shock and anguish, followed by deep depression. While now greatly improved, he was still depressed, hopeless, and cried a great deal when telling me how he believed no one would ever love him again. Currently, he is taking two antidepressant medications.

Initially, my patient told me his story of betrayal as if it had come as a complete surprise. However, over time, I noticed numerous situations where anyone should have been suspicious. It appeared, on the surface, that my patient was very naive. However, the sharpness of my countertransference, the way I began to feel annoyed at the untrustworthy boyfriend, led me to interpret this naivety as a system of denial, reversal, and projection. Therefore, I interpreted that he either ignored the clues altogether or blamed himself for them if he couldn't help but notice, and put them into me to hold, through internal phantasies and subtle interpersonal communications.

My patient's patterns of self-blame were strong and he resisted perceiving his reality in any other way. We would make progress with him realizing how he sacrificed and attacked himself to avoid being disappointed and angry with his objects. Then he would retreat back into being convinced that he didn't deserve to be loved and was lucky to have had such a good man in his life. This form of blame, self-deception, and projection is part of the conflict between the life and death instincts (Segal, 1997). Instead of seeking love and using perception to locate life-promoting object-related experiences, the ego blocks and chokes off the perceptive self and the clarity between self and object. Meaning, differences, and relational details are fought against and destroyed, eliminating all useful self–object experiences or phantasies.

The more I listened to this self-accusation and disfigurement of personal reality, the more I began to sense a fundamental anxiety in my patient. I would contain this panic and his attempts to disbelieve his relational experience, only to find myself becoming impatient with him, being enraged at his boyfriend's betrayal, and then suddenly caught with the idea that he/we would be left alone with nothing if we/I were to act on those feelings. So, I tried to manage and learn from these uncomfortable countertransference phantasies and gradually struck a balance between containment and interpretation (Lafarge, 2000). Bit by bit, I would utilize some of these feelings and thoughts to interpret just what he was experiencing. I told my patient that he was letting me in on a terrible dilemma. He felt like honoring his feelings, confronting his objects on their betrayal, and demanding honesty and caring. But he felt sure that this would lead to some sort of abandonment and a hopeless state without resolution.

This line of gradual but persistent interpretation brought about a series of associations. My patient told me about his experience of growing up with an alcoholic mother and a father who was usually away with his mistress.

This marital betrayal went on for many years and, as my patient grew up, he began to see many clues. Yet his mother remained in denial about it until my patient's father announced he was leaving the family when my patient was a teen. This left my patient to care for his depressed and alcoholic mother.

These memories were very helpful to explore as they shed light on the nature of my patient's transference and extra-transference perceptions. As a child, he remembers being in the middle of his parents, trying to help "broker deals" between them, as he puts it. This meant he was the go-between for their communication, or lack of it. Also, he would try to quiet the fights and tension that seemed to be always going on. He was the supportive listener for his mother, giving her an emotional shoulder to cry on. Not only did my patient not have his parents as helpful guides and supportive anchors in life, but he actually had to provide that service for them.

Recently, the transference has been more accessible to explore, revealing helpful clues to how my patient feels stuck, alone, and helpless. I noticed a pattern in which my patient would tell me, in great detail, about the art exhibits he visited and the lectures he attended. It was usually very captivating. I felt like I was on a private guided tour, being given all sorts of interesting background and colorful details that let me imagine each event as if I had been there myself. Again, my countertransference was helpful. After a while, I started to feel guilty about just sitting back and enjoying the guided tours. Sometimes, it started to feel like the analysis was more of a casual chat about art and current affairs. I found myself giving my patient opinions on various exhibits he brought up that I had actually attended as well. I would give my thumbs up or down on the event. This brought on guilt. Self-analysis helped me see that my guilt was the outcome of feeling that the situation was one-sided. I was becoming emotionally involved in talking about these events, but my patient, who had actually had the real-life experience of being there, seemed one-dimensional and flat about it. In other words, he held back his own emotional energy and let me take the stage instead. I was excited and contributing my feelings about the topics and my patient remained carefully reserved and intellectual about them.

When I interpreted these matters, my patient seemed less anxious and less stiff. He related several important points to me. Growing up, he was careful never to interject his own feelings or thoughts into day-to-day family life. It was more important to try to give his mother a chance to express herself, so he extinguished his own personality. He also felt party to his father's secret affairs and helped to keep them in the shadows by not asking his mother why his father was always away and unavailable.

Regarding his transference feelings, my patient said he thought he could be taking a risk by including himself in our relationship. Over time, he was able to articulate this transference phantasy in which I would be bored, "put off," or in disagreement with his true feelings about life. He told me he carefully let me take the lead and then followed in a safe manner that wasn't going to trouble me or upset our relationship. I began to understand that my patient suffered with a persecutory sense of guilt in which he feared not only a loss of the object's love but a more severe and serious damage to the object. This would be caused by his self-expression and his acknowledgment of less than ideal feelings toward the object. Therefore, he not only felt it to be dangerous to share his feelings with me, whether they were about me or other matters, but also thought it was dangerous to disagree with my self-expression. In addition, these feelings and fears were part of a primitive phantasy of loss (Waska, 2002) in which the idealized object, needed for survival and cohesion, was experienced as vanished without hope of returning and in its place came an attacking or overwhelmingly needy object.

The resulting feelings are impending annihilation and internal emptiness. These concepts were expressed vividly by my patient when he made statements like, "I worry that if I don't manage it and handle it like I explained, we could end up in a sudden moment of awkward difference and you would tell me to leave and not come back, ever. Sometimes, I feel like I pull the strings, but they could snap at any moment and it would all be over. I see you as the only friend I have, the only one I can turn to, but that is like glass, ready to shatter and cut at anytime. I felt that way with my parents, especially my mother. I had to keep her propped up and go to bat for her, but I felt like there were too many times she disappeared from my life emotionally, and I was floating alone over hot coals. And my father left me, in a literal way."

Now that the treatment is approaching its second year, there is more movement to report, but still many problems. There are moments of hope, when my patient feels there might be someone in the world who would want him and would love him. There is the idea that he can be himself with me, without bringing on some type of horrible crisis, conflict, or injury. Now, he tells me what he really thinks of art exhibits, unless he thinks it could dramatically conflict with my opinions.

On one hand, he is able to mourn his relationship with the old boyfriend and acknowledge his outrage at being betrayed. Yet he still wonders if there was a point at which he could have provided his lover with more, so as to "make it worth his while." My patient is less depressed, but still relies on medication to help him sleep and maintain his motivation to work.

There is an overall psychological clarity growing regarding his family. He is letting himself see the role he played of a sacrificial lamb, peacemaker, and punch-bag to keep his parents together. And he is starting to understand the devastating results of all of this on his adult life. The hardest work continues to be facing the phantasies and feelings he has about what changing those entrenched patterns might do to his objects, and consequently to himself.

Case 3

This was a difficult case in terms of my countertransference and how I struggled to maintain my analytic focus. My patient was a fifty-year-old vice-president of a bank. He used his company's health plan to secure ten free visits to a mental health professional. In the first session, I was struck with how this man seemed kind, gentle, and honest on one level, but cold and narcissistic on another. Even though he was obviously in a great deal of emotional pain, he made it clear he thought he just needed a quick tune-up and he would be fine. Also, even though he made a great deal of money, he made it clear he would not continue past the free sessions if it meant paying out of his own pocket. He refused to come in more than once a week, so I agreed to meet him once a week, sitting up, face to face. From the very start, I was left feeling controlled, devalued, and without too much confidence. I tried to remember these feelings as we went along, to see if perhaps they were aspects of my patient he needed to lodge in me.

I met with this patient in my capacity as a psychoanalyst. For me, this means I approached this case from a Kleinian–Freudian perspective. Clinically, this translates to an emphasis on the interpretive process, a focus on the transference as well as the countertransference climate, a valuing of the here-and-now and moment-to-moment developments in the analytic relationship, an understanding of the patient's phantasy life, and the search for the unconscious meaning and experience of external reality situations (Schafer, 2002).

So, regardless of his diagnosis, the setting, or the frequency of visits, I still operated as a psychoanalyst. With this patient's particular dynamics, this meant I was only able to utilize certain parts of my analytic toolbox and others were rendered useless.

Currently in the middle of his third divorce, my patient told me he felt abandoned, lonely, and lost. Like his last two wives, his current mate was considerably younger than him. From his description, each wife was extremely beautiful, but prone to spending his money recklessly. None of them ever worked. Listening to his story, I thought he had probably married three "trophy wives" who in turn used him as a "trophy wallet".

My patient emphasized how great the sex was in his marriage; now that he was living by himself in an apartment, he felt lonely and longed for good sex. However, he told me this was no longer an issue because he had met a new woman and they had been seeing each other for about a month. The sex was wonderful and they were talking about moving in together and even discussed marriage. I interpreted that he seemed to feel so empty and without an internal sense of balance that he had to find someone quickly to replace his wife. Also, I interpreted that there was an interesting pattern that might teach us something if we examined it, because, from his description, he seemed to be diving into a carbon copy of his last three marriages.

In the next session, my patient didn't mention this new relationship, so I asked about it. He said it was over; he had broken it off because she seemed to "want too much too fast." I said I thought he might have taken what I said and acted on it. He replied, "No, I thought about it myself and felt she wasn't right. I've been thinking about it for a while." Here, I felt as though he couldn't give me credit for my interpretation and had to make it into his own idea. The tone he used to say "she wasn't right" also struck me as cold and distant.

I had encountered this feeling in our first visit as well. When we went over the details of his insurance plan, I had informed him he would have to pay after the tenth visit. He had replied, "I wouldn't do that. I have enough bills with paying my wives off. Besides, I don't think I will need more than that." Between "paying my wives off" sounding like a back-alley criminal affair and "I don't think I will need more" feeling like something said to a waiter grinding pepper on a customer's salad, I had a hard time liking this patient.

This type of negative countertransference drove me to ask him about his family upbringing. I thought to myself that surely there must be a reason this man treats his three wives and his analyst in this particular manner. I tried to bring this up in the form of interpretations about his ambivalence to trust me, need me, or depend on me. Also, I interpreted that he must be looking for people, including me, to provide emotional and mental understanding and comfort, but these objects seem not to be what he hopes them to be or they somehow change from what he thought they were in the beginning. These ideas elicited some reflection on how he felt let down and betrayed, but it seemed to go nowhere. So I sought refuge in the historical realm. This was my escape from the uncomfortable here-and-now and was also a search for the compassion I had a hard time finding in the current atmosphere.

My patient was raised in a very well-to-do family. He spent much of his time at society parties or engaged in sports. When I asked about his relationship to his parents, he said, "They gave me everything!" When I asked if there was a closeness or connection between him and either parent, he said, "No. There wasn't that. I think my mother just needed me for security. The way she was affectionate with me felt like it was for her benefit, not mine. And, my father was too busy to really be involved in parenting. But they both loved me and took good care of me."

Had my patient stayed in treatment for a length of time and been more motivated to learn about himself rather than simply to easy his psychological pain, I believe we could have utilized his childhood background in a more therapeutic manner. As it was, this early into the work, I was trying to understand him and trying to cope with some negative countertransference feelings to his cold and cutting narcissism. So, at this point I used my patient's history for two purposes: helping him and helping myself.

First, I made interpretations about how he might have difficulty making solid emotional connections with others due to the lack of these as a child. I also emphasized the angry, lonely, and empty feelings he might have had experiencing his mother as selfish and his father as too busy. This helped deepen the moment. At the same time, I was using this historical data to find some compassion for my patient that had been lacking in the transference–countertransference relationship. I believe this is common to many difficult treatments, where the analyst moves in the direction of the historical for multiple reasons, some therapeutic and some self-directed.

During the sixth session, my patient looked at me with an expression of innocence and confusion. He said, "I feel great. So, I am not sure why I am still coming. I think I have solved my problems." When I asked for clarification, he said he felt less depressed and hopeless. He had also begun visiting his wife whom he was divorcing. They had been out for lunch and spent time together on several evenings. This was under the idea of discussing financial details of the divorce, but clearly there was a sexual direction to the meetings.

I said, "I wonder if one way you feel better is that you have started to explore some of your feelings and ways of coping. Seeing things a bit more clearly is always helpful. Also, spending time with me, working together may feel soothing and gives you a sense of direction. And being back with your wife a few times may take away some of the emptiness." This was my gentle way of introducing the idea that he was feeling better by using his wife and his analyst as soothing objects, rather than having actually worked through his deeper anxieties and painful feelings. He agreed with my comments. I continued, "Maybe just feeling better isn't the right time to stop. This might be the time to look a bit closer while the smoke has cleared." He said he saw my point and would continue until he ran out of free sessions. Knowing how much he made at his job made me feel I wasn't important enough for him to spend money on, but I thought that if I brought it up we would get into a debate about actual dollars and cents rather than the deeper issues. So, I left it alone and tried to examine my own feelings more closely.

At the eighth session, my patient told me we couldn't meet on that day of the week anymore, since he had to meet with his lawyers every week to iron out all the divorce details. When I explored other possible times, he said he had business meetings, prescheduled workouts at the gym, and traveling for work. It had to be within a two-hour period on Fridays. I told him I might be able to do that in the future, but nothing was available right now. He said that was fine, to give him a call. That is where we now stand.

Knowing we would meet again only for two sessions before he would stop altogether, due to the end of his free benefits, left me scattered, irritated, and slightly sad. Again, I think this was part of a projective identification process in which this patient induced into me many of the difficult and lingering conflicts of his family and his current internal world. This isn't the first time I have dealt with this type of case, and surely it won't be the last. I struggle to learn from it so as to better understand and help the next patient who presents me with similar dynamics.

As a psychoanalyst in private practice, this is not an unusual case to work with. Is it psychoanalysis? If by that we mean, was it a treatment conducted four times a week on the couch over a period of time, the answer is of course "no". Is the treatment of a patient in psychoanalysis different than this patient's treatment? In many ways yes, but there are similarities. Many of the central components of psychoanalysis, as a method of psychological treatment, were employed, such as exploration of the transference–countertransference, the examination of defenses, the attempted understanding of central anxieties, my belief in an unconscious motivation that I conveyed via interpretation, the exploration of his historical development and its influence on his adult life, and the importance of defining key object-relational patterns, both internally and interpersonally. If an analyst makes the effort of bringing these elements to the treatment, then it should qualify as a psychoanalytic treatment (Aisenstein, 2001).

In a very brief period, my patient's core personality makeup began to show in the transference–countertransference relationship. I made interpretations, both to myself and to the patient, about these phantasies and dynamics. While momentary insight did occur, no psychic change occurred. But I began to understand what prevented such integration, and conveyed some of that to the patient. So, what I did in eight visits is modest at best and a drop in the bucket of what would have needed to happen. However, the analytic method guided my work.

Case 4

My next patient, in his late thirties, has been in psychoanalysis for nine years, coming four times a week, using the analytic couch. Over the course of this treatment, I have also seen this man with his girlfriend in couples therapy for a period of time when they were in a relational crisis. Currently, my patient has decided to terminate his treatment in three months, giving us time to explore his feelings about it and review our work. He brought up the idea of termination over a year ago and we began to discuss his ideas and feelings about it, along with all the other issues already on the table. Over the past year, he has continued to use the analytic couch, but has reduced his frequency to twice a week, due to financial hardship. With a new, successful career, his work schedule has made this turn into more of a once-a-week appointment for the past six months. Of course, we have talked about how this change is a safe way to gradually end our time together, weaning himself off a secure and pleasurable experience.

In the course of our work, this patient has made great strides. When beginning his psychoanalysis, he felt unable to achieve much in life and frequently sabotaged himself. This was traced to a painful loss of his father in an angry and drawn-out divorce when he was five. He hated his father for leaving him but was frightened to have such strong destructive feelings. His mother remarried shortly after to a man my patient disrespected, but felt obliged to be nice to out of deference to his mother. When my patient's stepfather was killed in a car accident a year later, my patient felt somehow responsible and developed tics, obsessive rituals, and panic attacks. These symptoms followed him into adulthood.

In his treatment, we were able to work through these symptoms and alleviate most of them. What remained was a self-sabotage pattern that protected him from a fear of success. He replicated his conflicts with his father and stepfather in his career by feeling competitive and aggressive with job offers and peers in the running for those new positions, then becoming afraid of his eager desires and canceling them out in some self-destructive manner. Bit by bit, we worked through these phantasies and feelings, but it was slow going at times because the transference was cloaked with the same internal vision.

Sometimes my patient felt a desire to show off in front of me and at times considered himself superior. These feelings touched off tremendous guilt and he would create a standstill in the treatment to avoid an imagined confrontation or worse. This self-imposed devaluation led to envy and resentment of my emotional freedom, which in turn created more guilt, anger, and a stalled-out course of treatment.

His relationships with women were difficult as well. He alternated between wanting perfection in his mate, and feeling guilty about that desire and trying to settle for whatever he could get as a compromise. This led to a series of failed relationships, breakups, and situations where he was used and discarded.

By the time we were discussing termination, many of these chronic problems had been cleared up. His symptoms of panic and ritualized behaviors had ceased. He had married a woman he respected and adored and they were able to communicate in a very healthy way with each other. Allowing himself to strive and compete led to several very successful promotions in a new career that he enjoyed and openly expressed pride in.

As we near the time of termination, several core issues come around again for one more round of working through. This is common in the end phase of treatment and shows that we can never expect total resolution of any internal set of dynamics, only a constant reintegration and new understanding.

My patient is once again speaking of his grief and anger over not having an intact family to visit, relate to, and count on. This also represents a piece of the transference, in that he has mixed feelings about leaving. He is sad that he will not see me anymore and feels that a critical aspect of his life will be gone. This makes him anxious and lost. But he feels happy to be leaving our relationship to become a "mature, independent adult who can make it in the world," as he puts it. This desire brings about guilt and worry that I might be lonely without him or angry that he is leaving. So we continue to talk about these conflicts which are remnants of much more intense psychological dilemmas he felt as a child and later was crippled by as an adult.

In the countertransference, I feel proud of our long work together and the many achievements our collaboration brought about. I will miss him and the unique relationship we forged. In some sense, I wish he would remain in treatment a while longer, to smooth off some of the remaining sharp edges of his core issues. However, just as my patient is working through his trepidation over termination, I must do the same. Neither one of us will ever be completely finished with his own internal and interpersonal struggles, but we can accept the jigsaw puzzle of what makes us special and continue to strive toward a gradual improvement, integration, and pleasure of our lives. This is the lesson this patient and I shared.

Case 5

My next patient is a forty-year-old man who came into treatment suffering from depressive feelings over being dumped by his girlfriend. He told me this had never happened before. All of his adult life, he had dated countless women and established a very sexual relationship with each one, but never was more than a casual friend to any one of them. As soon as he found a better-looking woman willing to have uncommitted sex with him, he would drop the last one. Being dropped by someone else left him shocked, empty, and depressed.

My patient said he thought he ought to "slow down" and take a look at his life. He wondered if there might be a better way to go about things. When he said he would immediately abstain from sex or dating while he started to explore things in treatment, I suggested he not make such a big step so fast, as it was comparable to the way he acted with women: fast changes and burned bridges. So, I was pointing out that he was already relating to me in a similar fashion as he did with others. My impression of him was of someone who made big changes very quickly, but then changed those decisions soon after. In other words, I pictured him wanting all of the object immediately, but being unable to hold on to it for very long.

So, we began a two-year analytic process that he ultimately left with some benefits, but he still recycled the old self–object relational pattern that brought him in to see me.

When my patient was three years old, his mother, a drug addict, gave him up for adoption. His father had already left the family when he was two. A series of foster homes left my patient with a sense of distrust, bitterness, and emptiness. In all his adult relationships, we could see the pattern of him desperately trying to find a good mother figure whom he controlled with sex. This let him feel loved and without fear of abandonment. Each new relationship felt powerful and fulfilling, but quickly faded, like a drug. Then, he would find the next woman and begin again.

During the course of two years of analytic treatment, twice a week on the couch, we had made a fair amount of progress. My patient was no longer depressed and he now had consistently dated one woman for six months. This relationship gave him a great deal of anxiety, but he also felt stable and loved. He cheated on her several times, but felt remorseful and we could trace the behavior to fears and phantasies of abandonment or persecution. So, he had been able to finally settle down into a relationship that was healthy, honest, and a true sharing of two lives.

However, in the transference, there was an edge of resentment and tension. Bit by bit, I discovered that he blamed me for this new life. He felt somewhat obligated to please me by going along with what he pictured I wanted for him. In addition, he told me he "intellectually" realized he was doing the right thing by sticking with his girlfriend and that it was "the healthy thing to do," but he said he felt, on an emotional level, that it was "like a life sentence to endure." Yet my patient also told me, "I finally have a full feeling inside my gut and heart and can communicate my real self." So, along with this major positive shift in his life, he felt I had done something to him, making him choose this new path.

I had wondered if this tension might make my patient abort the treatment, so he could flee his imagined persecution. When I asked about this, he said he had thought about stopping, but if he did it would be for financial reasons. He had struggled with considerable debt before seeing me, and paying for treatment often left him with nothing at the end of the month. However, I thought his idea of stopping was based more on escaping this chronic tension he felt about being trapped in an obligatory relationship.

While we had discussed the transference meanings of this tension for several months, it persisted. We explored how he felt I was taking away his chance to find the ideal woman who could give him the best sex and mother him at the same time. We examined how he split off the anxiety from being with his girlfriend and placed it onto our relationship. We looked at how he didn't want to please me so he rebelled, just as he had at his foster parents, and how he wanted me to see the negative aspects of his girlfriend and step in to save him just as he wished someone had intervened with his abusive foster parents. Also, we discussed how he felt out of control and at the mercy of a new abandonment, equal in pain to losing his mother. We talked about all these things as well as other transference complications, but were unable to work through them enough to prevent what happened next.

In this Monday session, my patient came in and announced it would be his last visit. I asked why, feeling like I had known it was coming but it was still so abrupt. He said he had "gotten enough out of therapy for now," "couldn't afford it anymore," and "wasn't learning much or getting much out of it anymore." When I asked for details, he repeated the main ideas without going into it much more. Based on our discussions over the previous few months and my countertransference in the moment, I interpreted that he was going to drop me instead of his girlfriend. I said I thought he still felt the same strong conflicts about committing to one person, loving and trusting them in the face of abandonment and hurt. I commented that he struggled with those feelings in our relationship and with his girlfriend. Now, he felt there was a positive reason to take that kind of risk and had made that gamble by staying in treatment up to now and with his girlfriend. I interpreted that his fears and doubts were so strong now that he couldn't maintain both relationships, both risks, for much longer, so he was going to let me go.

My patient said that while he still wondered about the benefits of any long-term relationship, he had no plans to leave his girlfriend and he felt very content most of the time. But he said he just needed to "move on" from our relationship. When I suggested that he give us some time, a few more visits to talk about it a bit, he said no. He had made his mind up. So, to the best of my understanding, he had to "let me go" like he had let all his girlfriends go in the past and like his mother and father had let him go. My patient said he might call me "down the road" when he was better off financially and see about restarting his treatment. I said I would certainly welcome him back. Thus, we ended the session and the course of our analytic work together.

The psychoanalytic approach helped this man to a considerable degree, yet it is a work in progress. I believe this is a fairly typical outcome in private practice, when one is engaged with difficult patients struggling with chronic personality disturbances. Overall, the treatment was successful in helping this man to understand himself better, learn new ways of thinking and living, and in enabling him to build a more productive and fulfilling life. Clearly, he still uses his old methods of coping and certain primary defenses to react to core self–object phantasies. This was demonstrated in the transference acting out termination. However, much had changed for him internally and externally. This change hopefully provided my patient with a new route on the inner map of relational experiences, leaving him with more intra-psychic and interpersonal choices than he had before we first met.

Discussion

The public perception of who a psychoanalyst is and what they actually do does not match the reality of day-to-day practice. This leaves the public with a one-dimensional and often negative idea of the analyst as someone who probably will not be helpful to them in their search for psychological assistance. This poor image of the analyst is part of the general decline of our field.

Unfortunately, the psychoanalytic community has done little, until recently, to try to dispel these images and in fact may be helping to foster them by being removed or distant on the issue. In addition, in our professional organizations, conferences, and literature, there is an endless debate about what constitutes true psychoanalysis, which often makes things more confused. While important from a theoretical and teaching perspective, the decades-long debate over what makes a treatment truly analytic seldom includes the actual clinical activities of the average analyst.

Kernberg (1999) states that the objective of psychoanalysis is structural change and the integration of unconscious conflict, the objective of psychoanalytic psychotherapy is "partial" reorganization of psychic structure in the context of symptomatic change, and the objective of supportive psychotherapy is symptomatic improvement with a reinforcement of adaptive defenses (p. 1078). He goes on to say that the mental health provider makes these differentiations based on technical approach. In other words, one would offer a certain technical stance according to what type of patient is presented. Kernberg expresses his distinction between psychoanalysis and psychoanalytic psychotherapy by stating that, "In my view neither the frequency of sessions nor the use of the couch is a conceptually significant defining feature of psychoanalysis" (p. 1080).

He goes on to note that technical neutrality, free association, the interpretation of the transference, confrontation, and clarification are all the major elements of both approaches. However, he thinks the severity of pathology will dictate the ratio and depth of each of these components. While valuable from a theoretical stance, I think Kernberg's distinctions often break down in the clinical setting because in most cases the treatment would fluctuate between the two modalities at any given time.

While Kernberg makes this same point, most of his case examples do not adequately portray the great shifts and sways that occur in a treatment process over time, in which the therapeutic experience covers the ground from supportive counseling at times to more 'classic' psychoanalysis at other times. Indeed, I believe most cases of psychoanalysis log much of their treatment time in a area that would be classified by Kernberg as psychoanalytic psychotherapy. Because of political and personal climates, most cases presented in journals, books, and conferences focus on the moments of treatment that could be easily and clearly defined as psychoanalytic, but this creates a false picture of the overall treatment experiences that most patients and most analysts have.

So, it is only at the end of most treatments that the analyst can confidently summarize the case as one of psychoanalysis or of psychoanalytic psychotherapy. Sometimes we can tell how a treatment will proceed at the very start and we see how we will need to utilize one aspect of technique over another. But this is rare. Most of the time, we have to apply our analytic approach to the individual before us and match our technique to the unique situation that unfolds. Only later can we see it in total.

Specifically, I think Kernberg is correct in how he defines these differences in treatment modality. However, he makes it sound like we quickly assess the patient to be a certain type of neurotic, personality disorder, or psychotic and then very cleanly apply the correct mode of treatment. This creates a somewhat pejorative stance for the reader and may contribute to the professional and public negativity and confusion about our true role and identity.

In real life day-to-day clinical practice, the psychoanalyst approaches the patient with all of these psychoanalytic tools from the beginning. As the transference–countertransference relationship becomes known and the patient's self–object dynamics unfold, the analyst naturally moves in one direction or another, slowly applying more of one technique and less of another. So, the way one understands a treatment as truly analytic or not is really the result of an organic, intra-psychic and interpersonal movement between the two parties that defines itself over time.

The cases I have presented in this chapter are examples of this. In each case, I could not predict how the treatment would proceed or end. In some stretches of each case, I was applying a 'pure' psychoanalytic procedure. At other times, in the same case, it became more of what Kernberg defines as a psychoanalytic psychotherapy. This acceptance of analytic flow, a transference–countertransference rhythm, is important to our theoretical considerations. But it also is something that can be conveyed in our public image. We are not strict or rigid in our approach to patients; we listen to them in a way that matches their needs.

This chapter shows that the trained psychoanalyst is helping people in a variety of settings, but doing it with the skills of a psychoanalyst. This is what the public needs to know and this is what our profession needs to become less conflicted about.

Chapter 13

How we work and why it matters[1]

In 2003, a component society of the International Psychoanalytic Association gave a conference on psychoanalysis, its ailing status in the world, and possible paths toward revitalization. In the conference brochure it is stated: "Recent studies have shown that analysts associated with the American Psychoanalytic Association see an average of 1.5 analytic patients per week. [The speakers] will discuss the irony of practitioners spending tremendous amounts of time, energy, and money to train to do something they scarcely practice."

As a graduate of another IPA institute, I would certainly agree with the part about time, energy, and money. Over the course of a five-year training, I spent four to five hours a week in my own psychoanalysis, four to six hours a week in classes, and three hours a week in supervision. The analysis and supervision cost $600 a week and the classes were $4,000 a year, for a total expense of $30,000 a year. Upon graduation, I had logged roughly 3,000 hours and $150,000 in expenses. This was, of course, all after I had graduated from a PhD program in psychology, put in 3,000 clinical hours for an internship, and taken the state licensing test. Now in my fourth year of being a certified psychoanalyst, I typically see one or two analytic patients per week, as defined by someone who is on the couch four to five times a week.

While in agreement with the conference's point about such an expenditure of resources, I want to present a different voice from the conference and the many articles and newsletter columns that share such pessimism. I believe that most of those arguments and much of the despair that analysts are experiencing are the result of a widespread, entrenched view of what we think psychoanalysis has to be. The decades-old debate of what makes a treatment psychoanalysis versus psychotherapy or counseling misses many points. It is usually more of a political fight than a practical or theoretical

1 Previously published in 2004 as "How psychoanalysts really work and why it matters", *Issues in Psychoanalytic Psychology*, 26(1): 5–19.

discussion. When it is said we have spent so much time, energy, and money to practice something we seldom do, the argument is being made that all that training is only good for the 1.5 people we see each week who come four to five times and use the couch. The argument follows that this training is wasted on all the other patients we see. I think the profession needs to realize something else that is much more important. We, as trained analysts, do what no one else does, with all our patients.

My $150,000, 3,000-hour training in psychoanalytic theory and technique is not something I use with only two patients per week. As a result of that training, I approach and work with every patient I see in a different manner than before I began my training. I meet with them as a psychoanalyst and work with them from a psychoanalytic perspective. If the public realizes this, they would see us as much more of a resource instead of what we unfortunately promote, a caricature of Freud with his cigar and austere attitude. The public will only see us as an asset in their time of need if we see ourselves that way first.

As I did in the last chapter, I will present case material from my work on an average day in my private practice. Many of these patients could be seen as needing supportive therapy, and some might call my work with them psychoanalytic psychotherapy. However, this would be using theoretical concepts and classifications as well as hand counts of sessions per week to avoid examining the actual clinical experience between analyst and patient. These patients are being treated by someone trained as a psychoanalyst, so they are receiving a different type and level of care than a patient would with another mental health worker.

Just as a patient in a reasonably successful psychoanalysis will no longer relate to themselves, their internal objects, or the external world in quite the same way, so too for the analyst. With a reasonably successful training, the psychoanalyst will not relate to any patient in quite the same way as they did prior to their training.

The usual emphasis is that we are being trained for the sole purpose of seeing someone who is mildly neurotic and to meet with them five times a week, on the couch, without any major deviations from a pure analytic framework. I think the training institutes, the psychoanalytic profession, and the general public (our prospective patients) would all benefit from a new emphasis.

All this requires a significant shift in thinking and practice on the part of our training institutes. Fundamental ways of structuring the teaching and learning process would have to be re-evaluated to better parallel the realities of clinical work. As it stands, there is a considerable void between how we are taught and what we learn to do versus how our actual careers as analysts tend to unfold. For example, many of my patients, for a wide variety of both external and psychological reasons, are unable to commit to more than one or two sessions a week. These patients are automatically considered by the psychoanalytic training institute as psychotherapy cases and not important to the training process. Since the majority of all candidates, and indeed most certified analysts practicing in the field, have a caseload made up of these patients, it seems like a better idea to train candidates on how to treat them from a psychoanalytic perspective than to ignore them. Indeed, when more of a focus is put on these cases in supervision, many of them have better outcomes and the patients sometimes find a way and a motivation to come in more often.

Another example is the cruel system of having a control case go from the beginning of supervision to a preset mark of two or three years, or a certain number of hours. If a candidate's control case terminates or reduces frequency before that set time, the case does not count toward any graduation requirement. It is brushed aside and the candidate is expected to bring a new case to supervision that meets the requirements of frequency and analyzability. This does several things. It breeds resentment in candidates for the supervisor and the institute, leaving them feeling controlled and cheated. Also, it makes the candidates focus on issues of frequency rather than the actual clinical matters at hand. Finally, it leads to the candidates' anxiety over not losing their control case contaminating the countertransference, which creates certain manipulative or perverse countertransference dynamics of trying to make sure one doesn't lose their prize control case.

In my personal experience, between three supervisors, I had five cases that were discarded. One prematurely terminated. It would have been helpful to understand, from a psychoanalytic perspective, how that occurred. In the other cases, which I had been working on for six months, nine months, and one year with my supervisors, the patients reduced their frequency because of a combination of acting out, financial problems, and scheduling difficulties. When I kept seeing them at the reduced frequency, the same psychoanalytic elements were present: the transference, dream analysis, defensive strategies, countertransference, genetic reconstruction, the interpretive process, and the working through of complex self-and-object phantasies. But I could no longer look to my supervisor for help or insight. We never talked about these patients again, because they had gone from four times a week to three, or from twice a week to once, with my case in the psychoanalytic psychotherapy training track. I was left without credit for my work with them and I was left with the feeling that those cases were now inferior and worthless to discuss. Fortunately for me and the patients, I did my best to continue to apply all the principles of the psychoanalytic approach and by and large the cases turned out well.

Psychoanalytic training should help the analyst to understand and treat the patient from a psychoanalytic perspective. Sometimes this occurs at one frequency; sometimes another. Sometimes this occurs on the couch; sometimes not. But in all cases, the patient is given care and attention in a manner different from what any other practitioner provides. This is the message we must cultivate if the profession is to thrive and grow.

Case material

Mary

My patient is a woman in her mid-thirties who came into treatment due to feeling dissatisfied with her career in the computer industry and the desire to find out why she had never felt happy in life. Mary told me, "There has never been a moment in thirty years in which I felt a shred of meaning or joy." My patient wanted to change this but also told me she was convinced it was hopeless.

My countertransference, early in the case, was of a very sincere and bright woman who was ready to work toward understanding and change. At the same time, I could tell she did feel hopeless. I was left with the impression that we had a long, slow, and complex journey ahead.

My initial evaluation led me to believe that this patient would be helped by frequent sessions, so we began meeting four times a week, with the analytic couch. Mary was dutiful about showing up and did her best to comply with her treatment. While this meant she showed up on time and answered all my questions, it also meant she quickly established a passive and timid form of transference. This eliminated any spontaneity or free association. Instead, Mary was like a small dog, ready to take my next command. I interpreted this as an effort to please me and possibly prevent some kind of trouble. My patient responded by saying she was sure I found her boring and tiring. She tried hard to think of topics to bring up that might keep me interested, but she usually was at a loss. This left her very anxious.

In addition to exploring this transference development, I began to ask about her family, her life history, and her current circumstances. I interpreted that there was probably some reason why I needed to ask rather than her bringing it up. It was obviously not a topic she considered pleasing enough to bring to me. My patient explained that she was "a loner." Mary had never had a boyfriend in her life and couldn't imagine why any man would be remotely interested in her. She felt fat, ugly, and boring. So, there was no reason in her mind why I or any other man would ever find her interesting, attractive, or worth knowing. My patient had quite a few casual friends, mostly through work. But she always declined invitations to parties, events, or casual get-togethers because she was sure people were either taking pity on her or they hadn't yet realized how awful a person she really was. Therefore, I noted how our new relationship was the most significant attachment she had.

Mary grew up on a rural farm with her parents and four siblings. She was the youngest. The family was very poor and living conditions were basic. Her father was extremely violent in temper and ruled the family with his angry moods and violent outbursts. My patient's mother was always trying to avoid conflict and tried to do whatever it took to keep her husband from becoming angry. All the children tried to do their chores and be good to prevent their father's violence.

Every Sunday, Mary's father sent her over to the farm foreman, who managed the migrant workers and the general farm operations. He lived in a small house on the edge of the farm property and each week my patient was sent over with a schedule for the upcoming week and other related messages. Along with this paperwork, she often brought him the Sunday newspaper when her father was done with it. My patient never questioned why she was singled out to be her father's secretary in this way, but the father never asked the other siblings to make these deliveries.

Over the course of several months in her analytic treatment, Mary revealed the painful details of what happened each Sunday. From the age of eight, she was molested by this foreman when she made her delivery. She was made to undress him and perform oral sex. When I asked Mary if she had ever thought of telling her parents, she said she was sure they would have blamed her if she had, but that she never had thought of telling them. My patient remembers being very scared every Sunday and not understanding why this man was doing what he did. To this day, she has nightmares about it. In addition, as an adult, whenever she is asked to do an errand by her boss or drops off something for a male friend, she becomes convinced they will unzip their pants and force her to perform oral sex. When Mary began to tell me these events, it was the first time she had allowed herself to recall them. In doing so, she started to experience great anxiety and felt like she "was going crazy." The more she revealed, the more details she remembered. Her reaction was greater discomfort and a sense of disgust. "I can't believe I am the person I am telling you about. It is so repulsive to realize it is me. You must be horrified." I interpreted that she kept these awful memories from herself all these years by blaming herself.

By splitting and projective identification, Mary created a bad image of herself to deposit all the ugly, repulsive, angry feelings she had toward her perpetrator and her family. By concentrating on how bad she was, she didn't have to think about her other objects which she felt so much conflict about. But by using this cleansing mechanism so strongly, she succeeded in eliminating her memories as well. Relying on introjective and projective dynamics to such an extent left my patient without symbolic function as well (Steiner, 1991).

These ideas helped me gain clarity about a certain innocence or naivety my patient exhibited. Mary seemed truly unable to make a link between her neglectful and abusive childhood and the deep sense of emptiness and despair she now felt as an adult. It was not simply denial or repression. It was something more alive, more relational. The negative and aggressive feelings she had about her family and her experience in it were introjected and her shock and repulsion were projected. This led to a sad world in which she felt like the loser and the oddball compared to others and she joined in with what she felt their criticism would be of her. So, my interpretations were a combination of outlining this projective–introjective identification process as it seemed to fit with her upbringing, her adult life, and in the transference relationship to her analyst. In addition, I made educative remarks about the nature of traumatic abuse and how people tend to cope with it. This was supportive in nature, but directed at highlighting her way of erasing the symbolic links between herself and goodness and her family and badness.

These interpretations were also meant to address her profound sense of disbelief that she could be the troubled woman she was describing. Mary told me she thought I must believe she was making it all up, as it seemed too bizarre to believe. I told her I thought she was so frightened and shocked in recalling these events that she was convinced I couldn't find my way to feel compassionate for her tragic history or her empty adult life.

Theoretically, I think Mary was an example of those who struggle with primitive and chaotic object-relations that make acceptance, acknowledgment, and forgiveness very difficult. Part of this inner fragmentation is the lack of a safe or compassionate ego ideal or object to trust and find solace in.

When my patient was a teenager, she started to drink heavily and abuse drugs. For several years, she would accept money from a series of men, all twenty to thirty years older than she was, in exchange for sex. Mary said she felt superior when she did this. There was a feeling of revenge and mastery about it. I interpreted that she tried to turn the tables on the horrible experience with the foreman, wanting to feel in charge and empowered. I also interpreted that this was a valiant effort, but probably left her just as sad and just as used. Mary replied, "After the first few times, I cried myself to sleep. I felt so dirty and worthless. It was the darkest hour. After that, I just felt numb." She told me she went on to have countless abusive sexual relationships with men up until her thirties, when she stopped altogether, and she never had sex or even a date afterwards.

Over a series of several weeks, Mary began to recall more details about her traumatic abuse on the family farm. She told me about how sadistic and frightening the foreman had been and how savagely he had treated her. In each session, she was more and more overwhelmed with anxiety as she relayed these memories.

Mary became convinced that she had a heart condition because she experienced shortness of breath, tingling in her fingers, and uncontrollable racing of her heart. I told her she should definitely get a physical from her physician, but that her symptoms seemed like the results of emotional panic. She had a physical exam and was found to be in excellent health. The doctor told her she suffered from panic attacks and to seek psychological help. Nevertheless, my patient remained convinced a heart attack was imminent. Mary talked another doctor into outfitting her with a heart monitoring device that she wore day and night. When this proved her to be in fine health, she thought the device was defective.

During one session, my patient started to cry and told me she was sure she was having a heart attack. Mary was in such a state of distress that it took me a while to calm her. I used a soothing tone to repeatedly reassure her that what she was experiencing was not physical but emotional. I told her there was a reason for her alarm. For the first time in her life, Mary was allowing herself to recall, share, and work with these horrible experiences of helplessness and terror. I interpreted that she was reliving the panic she felt at the hands of the foreman. This seemed to ease her anxiety a bit, but only momentarily. These scenes were repeated several times in my office over the following weeks. At one point, Mary was so utterly overcome with panic and sure she was dying of a heart attack on the spot, she got up to run out of the room. In her frantic tears, she cried, "I am so sorry. I don't know what is wrong with me. It is too terrible. I have to stop coming here. I am sure I will die!"

In that one moment of annihilation anxiety, Mary was about to abort her treatment to save herself from this impending doom. In a very tense, moment-by-moment discussion, we managed to reach a compromise. She would remain in treatment, but only come in once or twice a week, "depending if I can handle it or not. I really think I am going crazy and I am sure I am about to have a heart attack!"

During these weeks of tension and crisis, I had gradually been noting a shift in the transference mood. I felt she had been trying harder and harder to please me, but felt unable to do so. As I was interpreting this, and exploring her feelings and phantasies, it became more evident that she had come to an idea. Mary felt she must have a specific piece of historical fact to present to me each week. In other words, she was sure that to be a good and proper patient, one must confess the worst, every time. For my patient, this meant constantly recounting horrible experiences that left her feeling more and more out of control. So, I interpreted that she was in fact reliving the sexual abuse with me in our relationship. Mary felt enormous pressure to be a good girl and deliver the goods, just as she had for her father and the foreman. So, the treatment had become like an ongoing rape. I told her all this and, due to her state of panic, assured her that this was not what I wanted, but it was very helpful for us to understand what was unfolding.

During this difficult period, and for some time afterwards, we explored the transference meanings of these anxieties. I interpreted the replay of a dominant–submissive, abusing–abused relationship in which my patient felt pressured and forced to pleasure me with memories and historical facts. I told Mary she seemed to feel a sexualized obligation, a terrible duty, to bring me tales of woe. I interpreted that she was unable, at least for now, to rely on me as someone who would respect her need to find a safe pace, gradually trust me, and feel more in control of what to share. Hearing this, my patient was able to calm down and feel more secure.

However, Mary brought out another aspect of her tension when she told me, "I have nothing to offer you, I am of no value. Why would you want to see me or spend time with me? You must dread seeing me. It must be so boring and tedious." I replied, "You believe your only value is to satisfy me in this sexual kind of way, with painful memories from the farm. While it is important for us to sort out all those difficult times, right now you think that must be the only way to interest me because the rest of you has no value. I think that must be a strong way you see yourself, that you don't believe you are worth much to me, to yourself, or to others." Mary said what we were talking about felt "right on" and thanked me for "being patient" and "tolerating" her.

Now into the second year of her analytic treatment, my patient has made some significant gains. Mary now has a few friends that she occasionally visits with. Through a better diet and a new exercise program, she has lost a great deal of weight and is feeling less loathsome about herself physically. In our analytic relationship, she is less prone to panic attacks and can now allow herself to be more reflective. Within our relationship, spontaneous associations and light humor can, some of the time, take the place of a forced sense of submissive obligation.

Finally, Mary has started to write poetry. This is an important event in light of what it means to her and its historical significance. When my patient was in high-school, she won numerous awards for her poetry and in her senior year received a prestigious university scholarship for her work. At that point, she gave up writing entirely, along with other hobbies and endeavors, as she slipped into depression and drug use. Now she has returned to this passion. This is, at this time, colored with great conflict and doubt, yet it is a new addition to her newly emerging sense of self. Overall, my patient has begun to consider her value, her self-worth.

John

John is a thirty-five-year-old tailor who came to see me for help with his hopelessness over ever finding a girlfriend and for help with understanding why he can never be more successful in his career goals. His insurance company would only cover once-a-week treatment and he could only afford to pay out of his own pocket for once-a-week sessions, so we settled into a twice-a-week course of analyst work, realizing it might be helpful to meet more often but accepting our constraints. At times, due to his financial problems or insurance problems, we met only once a week. My patient used the analytic couch, as he seemed to be someone who could benefit from its relaxing, reflective, and regressive nature. Indeed, John was prone to intellectualizing and finding ways of removing himself from his feelings, so the couch seemed to help with that, along with my consistent interpretations. He was eager to pursue his treatment but approached it as more of a medical procedure that didn't involve him.

The first few months involved a good deal of data collecting. John felt comfortable and in context telling me details about his family history, his long-term problems in finding a better job, and all the different ways he failed at finding a lasting and meaningful relationship with a woman. Slowly, I pointed out this pattern. I asked him what would happen if he ran out of facts. He said he didn't know, but that it felt strange to try and imagine. I interpreted that we would have a different kind of relationship if it wasn't all about facts and figures; it might be more about feelings. John said he could understand what I meant, on an intellectual basis, but he couldn't picture what it would be like.

I also told him he might be wary of showing me certain sides of himself, so he kept it safe for now by sticking with the facts. This transference comment made John anxious and he said, "I am doing the best I can, I am telling you everything I can think of!" I interpreted that he felt I was criticizing him now, but that he might actually be uncomfortable telling me everything he feels, as opposed to everything he thinks. John calmed down and said, "Oh. I see. I don't think I really know how to do that." I said, "That is OK. I think that one reason you are here is to learn how to do that. We can work on that."

Toward the end of the first year, John had a dream he told me about. The bringing of it and the telling of it were in themselves indicative of a more reflective, less anxious, and more relational tone in my patient. The dream consisted of John being in the hospital, dying of a heart condition. I was his doctor, who came by periodically, to administer medications and check the machines by his bedside. The content of the dream was very dry and academic. I pointed out that this was also the way John conveyed the dream. John agreed, but had no other comments.

I interpreted that John was trying to connect with me by bringing in the dream, but the sterile way he told it, as a factual event, showed how carefully he had to treat our relationship. Also, I interpreted that behind the dryness of the manifest dream content was his dying of a broken heart and wanting me to understand and heal his terrible loss. I added that the dream revealed quite an intimate and vulnerable side of John and his desires for our relationship. He was interested in my comments and agreed, but had a hard time elaborating on them immediately.

However, he showed more of these deeper feelings and phantasies by bringing in another dream a few weeks later. In this second dream, John came into my office for his session, only to find me with a prisoner on death row. I was administering a lethal injection. John thought it was odd that I was killing this person, but mostly noted how he was not getting his full time with me. Again, he didn't have much to say about the dream. There were no reactions, thoughts, or associations. When I noted how calm and neutral he was in the dream, he said, "Yes, like it didn't really matter much." I said, "What did seem to matter was you not getting the time with me that you hoped for. Also, something got in the way of us being together, a violence." John replied, "Yes. I don't know what that was about." I replied, "I think the dream could be about a lot of things, maybe we will find out over time. But one thing I wonder about now is that maybe you want more time with me, more understanding or connection, but you feel I am unavailable." John said, "Well, sometimes I think you really don't get what I am trying to say." This was a major expression of feeling on his part, letting me know how he actually felt about us.

I replied, "OK. I will try and listen closer. Please tell me what kind of things I don't get." John went on to tell me how he had a rich inner life and how he thought about many things all the time, but he kept it to himself, not sure if it had any value. I pointed out that he had been hiding that side of himself, getting rid of it with a "lethal injection." I added that now he was fighting to pump some life into his experiences and relationships.

This back and forth type of transference marked the treatment in many ways. John would cautiously show his need for me and his dependence on his inner objects, but then retreat or react against this dependence. During the second year of analytic treatment, this conflictual process emerged in a particular manner.

One day, John came in looking particularly tense and awkward. After a thick silence, he told me he had considered asking me how I was doing, but then became paralyzed with confusion. He said, "At first, it was just a casual, 'Hi, how are you?' But the more I thought about it, the more I felt it would be wrong. I say that to so many people, trying to be nice and polite, but it is just a courtesy. I worry that you might think I really mean it as something more serious when I don't, so I didn't want to mislead you." I replied, "So, you are concerned that I would get a false hope, I would start believing you really care, when you don't. I could get hurt or disappointed."

John said, "Yes. I just want to be nice, but it could be misread." I interpreted his projective maneuver, "You see me as wanting your care and concern, hoping for something real but finding out it is not there. I think this is because you hope for more closeness with me, but you get worried it would fall apart somehow. So, it is easier to picture me as the one who needs something." John agreed and said, "Yes. I notice myself wording things a certain way sometimes so I have a safety net. I don't have to take a risk here." I added, "And by making it an intellectual debate of 'should I ask him or should I not ask him?,' you can avoid the emotional questions of 'are we OK and close or are we separated'?" He replied, "Oh yes, I am good at avoiding that one!"

These dynamic themes continued into our work in the next session. For a while, we had discussed increasing the frequency of his visits. Both our schedules had made this impossible for quite some time. Now, there was a chance to add one day more per week. In the past, when we explored his feelings about meeting more often John had been in reluctant agreement, but also questioned the validity of the whole treatment process. He wondered if he was "really getting anything out of it" or "really going anywhere with it." I interpreted that the idea of meeting more often brought up his mixed feelings about being closer and being more in touch with certain emotions.

Now that we had the chance to actually schedule an additional hour, these mixed feelings and phantasies came to bear. I offered a time in which he would be seeing me once and then there would be a period of two days before the next meeting. After a brief silence, John began a massive deliberation. On one hand, he said, having the separation between the sessions seemed like a "risky thing," "too long in between," and "a feeling of being lost in the middle." On the other hand, John felt that if we could have those two sessions on consecutive days it would "be claustrophobic," "too much, too soon," and "a waste of time 'cause I won't have anything new to talk about." He went back and forth for a long time, citing the pros and cons of each plan. In the countertransference, I felt I was watching a logistical ping-pong game being played, guaranteed never to be resolved. I finally interpreted, "You are in an endless debate because there is no emotion in what you say. Behind all the back and forth, though, are many feelings that you are struggling to share. You really do want to be here and you are happy about the idea of seeing me more often. But as soon as you let that in, acknowledge that you want and need more connection with me, other feelings flood in. You get scared that connection will be too much, too overwhelming. It is like you are so hungry that you want to dive in for the whole thing but then you realize you are in the deep end ready to sink, so you panic. Maybe it will make more sense if we talk about those feelings." John replied, "I do want to be here and come in more often, but you are right. I get scared that you won't be around in between and I get worried that it will be too much and overwhelming, all at the same time!" The more we talked about it, the less anxious John was. We began meeting more often.

Several weeks later, more of these issues surfaced, but now more directly and less defended. John came into my office and gave me payment for not just that session, but the next one as well, in cash. He said, "I am paying ahead, because I want to be here now and next time too!" The way he said it and the feelings that seemed to go with the message prompted me to interpret, "I think you have two sets of feelings there. You are eager to be here and work with me. You show me how serious you are about that by declaring your intent and giving me hard cash. At the same time, you sound a bit worried, like you better make sure to reserve a spot ahead of time or you might lose it, might lose me." John replied, "Well, I do get concerned that you are bored with me or don't like me, so I guess I want to guarantee that I get what I want." Here, he began to reveal some of the internal power struggles and phantasies he had. Over time, we explored his feelings of being pushed into having to make a commitment to avoid abandonment, his desires for union with a caring object, and his avoidance of the cruelty of dependence on an ambiguous object.

Discussion

Deliberately, I presented two cases in which the frequency of visits were less than what would be considered enough to define the treatment as true psychoanalysis. It is easy to say they were simply cases of psychoanalytic psychotherapy or some variety of counseling. However, the issue is more complex. Instead of frequency as the major element of definition, let the reader ask certain questions. Was there a deep exploration of psychological dynamics? Was there an emphasis on the transference and its unfolding in the analytic relationship? Did the analyst consistently interpret the nature of the transference? Did the patient come to a new understanding of themselves that led to change, internally and externally? Was there a shift in the unconscious, rigid profiles of self and other, as well as the way they related to each other? Did anxieties and defenses become illuminated and reduced? The answer to these and similar questions is yes. These two patients have been in an analytic treatment with an analyst and they have benefited from the psychoanalytic approach. For the future of the profession, this is the message for the public to hear and for the psychoanalytic community to dust off and embrace.

Summary

Engaging the patient in a psychoanalytic exploration is the way to understand something about how that person's mind is configured. Through the transference, a diagnostic picture will emerge. In this sense you don't know whether a person is "unanalyzable" until you begin to analyze them. Rather than seeing them as having a broken mind that can't be fixed – a deficit model – I think of the patient as hard to reach or not yet reachable. Chessick (1997) has remarked:

> If one must err, in my experience it is best to err on the side of mistaking a defect for a conflict-related problem because in due time this error can be corrected; approaching a conflict-related problem as a defect by direct after-education produces a therapist–patient collusion that tends to drive the conflict out of sight and make it no longer amenable to the uncovering process.

Hopefully, an atmosphere is fostered within the analyst–patient relationship that produces a general investigation into phantasies regarding the patient's internal objects. This might or might not include dreams, reconstruction, free association, and other prized items of our trade. Bit by bit, this can shift to an emphasis upon the transference as a primary vehicle to explore the patient's internal world.

In working with patients, I take as my task the exploration, understanding, and working through of their core phantasies. I assume we all possess a mind organized by primitive phantasies that may or may not emerge fully through the transference. While I approach each person with the idea that they are a candidate for psychoanalysis (Rothstein, 1994), I also use a flexible way of working.

The patient's degree of acting out, in which the ego projects core phantasies and feelings into external circumstances and relationships, is what determines what type of treatment is taking place. Hopefully, the analyst is usually able to influence this acting out with interpretation, confrontation, and adequate containment. The analysis of the transference is often the analysis of the patient's acting out. This is a flexible approach that is mindful of theoretical ideals and their importance but is also built upon the realities of clinical practice.

In the literature we look at ideals so as to learn the optimum method. In the consulting room we deal with the ever-changing clinical situation of relating with a human being. It is always unpredictable and never as we wish it to be. We do our best to match our ideals to the realities of the relationship we have with the patient.

With feedback from peers, supervisors, teachers, supervisees, and from my own experiences as a patient, I have concluded that the profile of psychoanalytic treatment offered in the literature is a seldom reached ideal. While it is helpful and necessary to have ideals that we continuously strive toward yet never achieve, we must be clear that they are ideals. Otherwise, we are building a false and idealized effigy to which we pay homage, yet can never duplicate in our offices.

Most of the literature and much of analytic training falsely divides patients into two groups: those who are "analyzable" and those who are not. I believe there are large numbers of cases that don't fit so neatly into these two categories. These patients are not written about or explored in training programs, but we see them frequently. They are the patients who come in wanting some type of understanding about how their mind functions and the nature of their behavior, but quickly oppose the analyst and the analytic process. They usually act out a great deal and stop the treatment abruptly, either after a handful of sessions or sometimes after months or even years of turbulence. Since we usually only see them for a short period and under less than optimal circumstances, our field deems these patients as unfit for study. The anxiety they are experiencing and the persecutory conflicts they quickly project into the treatment often make it impossible for them to remain in our offices for very long.

It would be easy to say that we should modify our method or abandon the psychoanalytic method for such difficult cases. However, if questions of frequency, use of the couch, duration, termination, and the concept of neutrality are flexibly reconsidered, many of these patients are no longer as "difficult." Rather than proposing a modification in "standard" technique, I feel it is best to still define psychoanalysis as the analyzing of the transference and of the patient's anxieties and defenses by the means of interpretation. However, this can be accomplished in a more inclusive and elastic way. If we refrain from setting idealized goals and are more accepting of partial successes, both patient and analyst may benefit more from the actual process.

As psychoanalysts, we utilize the transference as the primary compass to locate and understand the patient's inner life and struggles. We believe that the way our patient reacts to the therapeutic relationship is a valuable window into who they are and therefore how we can best help them. At any given time, we take a snapshot of the transference–countertransference dynamic and assess what direction the patient seems to push or pull us both in. Much of this is within the patient's unconscious phantasy world, but this internal set of forces is usually brought to life in many different external manifestations. Enactment, role-responsiveness, acting out, and other terms have been used to describe how the patient manages to fit us into their particular vision of the world.

One area in which the study of the transference and its associated phantasies and defenses has been neglected is within the assessment of the actual treatment process. The categories of treatment thus far used by our profession are supportive therapy, psychoanalytic psychotherapy, and psychoanalysis. Infinite debates and discussions take place regarding what constitutes each category. An unfortunate fallout of these theoretical back-and-forths is that they have taken on a literal meaning when working with patients. In other words, something that is helpful to contemplate in a theoretical sense has come to be a taken-for-granted aspect of day-to-day clinical practice and training.

When a new patient comes to see us, these theoretical concepts have become transformed into a rigid and systematic way of predetermining what type of treatment the patient deserves. I think one reason for this development is an over-reliance on a scientific or medical model. While valid research and scientific scrutiny are important for the growth of our field, there are certain aspects of the psychoanalytic process that do not fit into this way of thinking.

The first few days or weeks with a new patient whom we approach with the analytic method are very different than the case of a patient who goes to the emergency clinic with a hurt foot. With an X-ray machine and certain diagnostic tests, it is possible to determine, right then and there, what the problem is and what the exact treatment ought to be. With our new analytic patient, we cannot immediately declare the complete diagnosis and the exact path of cure. Even a provisional or working diagnosis does not lead to a certain or confident choice from supportive therapy, psychoanalytic psychotherapy, and psychoanalysis. Indeed, I think that to quickly decide the patient has a certain diagnosis, and therefore needs a certain kind of psychological treatment can often show a countertransference involvement in the patient's transference phantasies.

I am advocating the use of the analytic approach to the business of selection of treatment and how and when to define what the patient's treatment should be called. Rather than decide what they need, we can, over time, determine what it is they have created with us. This would then offer us diagnostic information that we could use to develop the analytic treatment. In this model, at one point in treatment we might determine that the patient has forced us into a supportive therapy situation. We could wonder why and use this data to further the analytic exploration. At another time in treatment with the same patient, we might determine it to be more of a psychoanalysis. Again, we could wonder why the patient's transference and accompanying phantasies and defenses shifted, pushed, or rearranged the analyst–patient relationship into this new configuration. In order to use this analytic mindset, the categories of supportive therapy, psychoanalytic psychotherapy, and psychoanalysis would need not to be mostly defined by external criteria such as frequency or use of couch, but by the internal, psychological dynamics at play within the transference–countertransference climate on a moment-to-moment basis.

Clinicians know that most patients seen in their private practice are fairly disturbed, operating at a severely neurotic or borderline level. Over the years, countless analytic clinicians of many theoretical persuasions have proved that the psychoanalytic approach offers great help to these individuals. To appreciate this fact fully, the analyst must realize that many patients will prematurely abort treatment or terminate well before we feel they have reached their psychological potential. I think this is a difficult clinical reality that has to be tolerated, grieved, and accepted. One way of achieving this is to study carefully the frequent cases that seem to fail, or that only partially achieve some degree of healing.

In doing so, one starts to realize that full psychological integration is a myth and that psychoanalysis is best appreciated as a way of re-experiencing life from newer perspectives. This method of exploration, when carefully applied, extends a great deal of assistance to the troubled souls we meet with every day in our offices. How much these patients are able or willing to make use of our offering is multi-determined, but is not a sign of success or failure on our part or on their part.

With this in mind, the psychoanalyst can realistically apply their craft and know that, for the most part, it is usually helpful to most people in some very critical and valuable way.

Difficult cases that never get off the ground or seem to "crash and burn" after a period of time offer us opportunities for study. These patients will continue to come to our offices, so we need to understand them and find ways of helping them. It may be that we do the best analytic work we can while accepting that patients will abort the treatment without a marked shift in their internal or external experience.

Melanie Klein (1950) states:

> My work on early development has led me to distinguish between two forms of anxiety: persecutory anxiety, which is predominant during the first few months of life and gives rise to the "paranoid–schizoid position", and depressive anxiety, which comes to a head at about the middle of the first year and gives rise to the "depressive position" . . . before terminating an analysis I have to ask myself whether the conflicts and anxieties experienced during the first year of life have

> been sufficiently analyzed and worked through in the course of the treatment.
>
> (p. 78)

The patients examined in this book were seldom able to analyze and work through all of these conflicts and anxieties sufficiently. Indeed, it seems that particular anxieties regarding loss and persecution prevent them from attaching to the analyst and the treatment in a way that could allow for a full working through. Sooner or later, many of these patients are unable to bear the intense persecutory and/or depressive phantasies that emerge within the transference, and they flee. From my clinical work, it seems that primitive anxieties concerning loss and annihilation predominate. While these patients are usually functioning within the paranoid–schizoid position, they can fluctuate rapidly between depressive concerns and fear of attack.

Klein (1950) explained the nature of these phantasies:

> Persecutory anxiety relates mainly to dangers felt to threaten the ego; depressive anxiety relates to dangers felt to threaten the loved object, primarily through the subject's aggression. Depressive anxiety arises through synthetic processes in the ego; for as a result of growing integration, love and hatred and accordingly, the good and bad aspects of the objects came closer together in the infant's mind. Some measure of integration is also one of the preconditions for the introjection of the mother as a complete person.
>
> (p. 78)

In the paranoid–schizoid position, what is introjected is part-aspects of the mother. Due to the undeveloped nature of the infantile ego's synthetic functions, integration of the object and the good and bad parts of it are not fully possible. Therefore, these are borderline, narcissistic, or psychotic patients whose immature ego slides unpredictably and erratically between idealized union and devastating loss. Their phantasies and feelings shift from sadistic guilt and superego rigidity to intense paranoia and envy. Again, primitive loss and persecutory guilt seem to be the common elements in these patients' unstable psychic structures.

As analysts, we must focus on the task of analyzing the paranoid–schizoid and depressive anxieties that come alive in the transference. This goal is different from seeking "cure" or structural reconfiguration as evidence of successful treatment. Especially for more primitive patients, the analyst will be able to do a better job if he or she realizes that the final outcome may not be optimal. However, the valuable goal we always reach for is a gradual intra-psychic/interpersonal shift in the moment-to-moment relatedness of the analytic process.

A fundamental framework within which every psychoanalyst operates is that of integration. We work with our patients' unconscious phantasy world and their object-relations to bring about some sense of order and organization. Our interpretations are the result of what the patient gives us, verbally and interpersonally. We organize the relational data within the container of the analyst–patient relationship (Levenson, 1983). For some patients, this is disturbing and they react with fright, anger, competition, or dismissal. This type of anti-integration or anti-interpretive stance is very challenging and creates slow, difficult, or even impossible treatment situations.

At the same time, these cases do not necessarily call for any deviation in technique or giving up of psychoanalytic goals and hopes. Rather, the analyst is pressed to find a stronger conviction in the restorative powers of the analytic method and in the patient's hidden desire for change. Doubt may creep into the countertransference and problems with elements of the trade such as frequency, use of couch, and so forth can create despair regarding the utility of psychoanalysis for certain patients. However, faith in the psychoanalytic method and confidence in the patient's ability, at some level, to grow and change remains essential, especially with our more vexing and trying ones.

As mentioned above, Melanie Klein (1950) has summarized the elements necessary for a successful termination of psychoanalytic therapy. Depressive and persecutory anxieties have been reduced; the relationship between external reality and internal beliefs, hopes, or fears has been better balanced; grieving and mourning for the ideal object and the ideal self is well under way, creating an integrated sense of oneself and the world; and all aspects of love, joy, and work are more synthesized and worked through. Internal harmony and creativity is more the direction than previous states of disharmony, discontent, and repetition. All these elements are obtainable with many of our patients, or at least significantly reachable. Yet as analysts we must reconcile ourselves with the clinical reality that a fair number, if not the majority, of cases will terminate prematurely and, according to our termination criteria, unsuccessfully. We take this into account as a painful hardship of our profession, but not necessarily due to the failure of our method. Certainly, the analytic method can easily become corrupt or contaminated by countertransference issues and deeply ingrained acting out by the patient, ultimately destroying the healing process. This must be consistently searched out and worked through, not as something we can be 100 per cent rid of, but as something that will be a consistent area of learning and surprise.

Hanly (in Richards, 1997) has pointed out what most analysts know from clinical experience. The four or five times a week, on the couch, criteria for psychoanalysis have been idealized because of their position of purity in training institutes as the only way to graduate. Clinically, analysts are aware that while greater frequency often provides optimal outcome, it by no means creates, in and of itself, a truly psychoanalytic process. Therefore, the difference between psychoanalysis and so-called psychoanalytic psychotherapy is often more of a political argument within institutions, centered around external factors such as frequency and use of couch, rather than the meat and potatoes of actual psychoanalytic practice. By actual psychoanalytic practice I mean the essential elements of the transference–countertransference relationship, the interpretive process, and the exploration of phantasies, object-relational defensive systems, and unconscious world views. Fortunately, this self-destructive infighting and ivory tower posturing has gained greater attention lately (Schwartz, 2003), so perhaps the way the psychoanalytic approach actually helps people is getting more focus now than endless debates over theoretical hairsplitting. In the end, the question as to what constitutes true psychoanalytic work must include what Segal (1962) discussed as the curative factors of psychoanalysis. These would be the important role of insight in the analytic work, with all the other factors related to it. For this insight to be truly therapeutic, it must come alive within the transference, another central element. The dynamics of projection and introjection are almost always at play within the transference and the patient's unconscious phantasy life. Therefore, the element of interpretation is important in bringing insight to this phenomenon. All these aspects of analytic treatment lead to new knowledge of the self, a reintegration of the ego, a clearer view of external reality, and, therefore, growth in the personality.

In the 2003 summer newsletter of the American Psychoanalytic Association, several articles deal with the decreasing public interest in and respect for the practice of psychoanalysis (*American Psychoanalyst*, 2003). The APA's Committee on Public Information developed a list of points to relay when discussing psychoanalysis with the media or with other mental health professionals. It reads as follows. "A psychoanalyst can help you:

1 Get relief from painful emotional symptoms.
2 Feel understood as a unique individual.
3 Achieve emotional freedom.
4 Improve your personal relationships.
5 Become more productive at work.
6 Take more pleasure from life.
7 Change lifelong ways of coping that just aren't working.
8 Understand feelings and behavior that just don't make sense.
9 Gain greater control over your life.
10 Stop self-destructive patterns of behavior.
11 Understand yourself.
12 Prevent the past from interfering in the present.
13 Talk things over in a safe and private environment.
14 Unlock your creative potential."

(p. 17)

On one hand, these are important and accurate ideas to let the public know about and to reflect on as a profession. This is a list of all the ways we are very helpful and healing to our patients. On the other hand, I think the list is incomplete. We do all these things, but we do them differently than other mental health workers. Social workers, psychiatrists, and psychologists could claim rights to that list as well. But we as psychoanalysts produce those same results and more by examining the unconscious dynamics between self and object. We locate and interpret the transference whenever possible. Using these special approaches makes the results on the list more lasting, more meaningful, and more powerful. This is our unique signature. It is hard to put those achievements into words that appeal to the general public, but I think we must find a way to acknowledge our special differences from other therapists in the mental health field and how what we offer is without equal.

A related issue is how the political climate and group dynamics of most psychoanalytic institutions are very conflicted. On an intellectual level, they all agree that the public should be educated about our special expertise and the resources a psychoanalyst has to offer. Yet, on an emotional level, these same organizations seem to be very frightened and defended against any flexibility or wider view of what constitutes psychoanalytic therapy. The debate over frequency of sessions, acceptable patients, the differences between psychoanalytic psychotherapy and "true" analysis all destroy the efforts to show how we actually help people in distress.

At a conference in 2003, Otto Kernberg talked about this matter. He told the audience that several decades earlier he had been on the committee that had decided on the specific number of sessions per week that were to be deemed proper for a "true" psychoanalysis. He said he now regrets being a part of something that became so deified and rigid to the point of dismissing the actual clinical work of psychoanalysis and focusing on numbers. Also, he pointed out that these now unmoving frequency rules were only invented as a standard of training, not a standard of actual practice. This has obviously been lost in the translation. Finally, he said that most of the major organizations of psychoanalysis today resist any major change, in frequency or any other now sacred rule, out of fear of psychoanalysis being seen as no different than any other therapeutic treatment. Again, I think psychoanalysis is easily distinguished from other therapeutic modes by a close examination of clinical material and clinical outcome. The more analysts are willing to share their work publicly, the more chance we have of the public seeing us as a valuable resource and of us being reminded of that.

I have quite a few patients who tell me the following: "All the other therapy I've had was good, but it didn't get to this stuff," "These things never came up in all my other therapies, this is like a whole different level," "We have gotten to certain feelings in four months that I never touched in four years of being with my last therapist," "No one has ever talked about this as a relationship before, but I can see what you mean. Looking at how I relate to you does help to see what is going on," "Wow. I would never think of it that way. You always point out an angle that I would never have seen," and "You have helped me in ways that I couldn't imagine. I grew a lot from all my other therapy time, but this is different. I have accessed some part of myself, something deeper, that was always there but I didn't know how to get to."

Even though some of these comments were coated with a positive or idealizing transference, they still represent the honest feedback from patients who experienced the psychoanalytic method. They testify to the difference, hope, and assistance the analytic process offers.

Bibliography

Aisenstein, A. (2001), "Psychoanalytic psychotherapy does not exist", in *Psychoanalysis and Psychotherapy: The Controversies and the Future*, edited by S. Frisch, Karnac, London, pp. 19–31.

American Psychoanalyst (2003), "Talking Points about Psychoanalysis", *American Psychoanalyst*, 37(2):17.

Benveniste, D. (1998), "Moments in the life of a Latin American analyst: An interview with R. Horacio Etchegoyen", *Fort Da*, 4(2). Available online at www.fortda.org/fall_98/interview.htm

Bibring, E. (1954), "Psychoanalysis and the dynamic psychotherapies", *Journal of the American Psychoanalytic Association*, 2:745–770.

Bion, W. (1962), *Learning from Experience*, Heinemann, London.

Bion, W., Rosenfeld, H. and Segal, H. (1961), "Melanie Klein", *International Journal of Psychoanalysis*, 42:4.

Bird, B. (1972), "Transference: Universal phenomenon, hardest part of analysis", *Journal of the American Psychoanalytic Association*, 20:267–301.

Boswell, J. (2002), "The Oedipus complex", in *Kleinian Theory: A Contemporary Perspective*, edited by P. Fonagy and M. Target, Whurr Publications, London and Philadelphia, pp. 77–92.

Britton, R. (2004), "Subjectivity, objectivity, and triangular space", *Psychoanalytic Quarterly*, XXIII(1):47–61.

Campbell, R. (1989), *Psychiatric Dictionary*, Oxford University Press, Oxford.

Caper, C. (1992), "Does psychoanalysis heal? A contribution to the theory of psychoanalytic technique", *International Journal of Psychoanalysis*, 73:283–292.

Caper, R. (2001), "The goals of clinical psychoanalysis: Notes on interpretation and psychological development", *Psychoanalytic Quarterly*, LXX(1):99–116.

Chessick, R. (1997), "Psychoanalytic treatment of the borderline patient", *Journal of the American Academy of Psychoanalysis*, 25(1):104.

De Racker, G. (1961), "On the formulation of the interpretation", *International Journal of Psychoanalysis*, 42:49–54.

Earle, J.B. (1979), "An approach to the study of analyzability and analysis: The course of forty consecutive cases selected for supervised analysis", *Psychoanalytic Quarterly*, 48:198–228.

Eissler, K. (1953), "The effect of the structure of the ego on psychoanalytic technique", *Journal of the American Psychoanalytic Association*, 1:104–143.

Etchegoyen, R. (1991), *Fundamentals of Psychoanalytic Technique*, Brunner/Mazel, New York.

Freud, S. (1914), *Further Recommendations in the Teaching of Psychoanalysis: Recollection, Repetition, and Working Through*, Collected Papers, Vol. IV, Basic Books and Hogarth Press, London, 1959.

Freud, S. (1917), *Introductory Lectures*, Standard Edition, Vol. 16, Hogarth Press, London, 1957.

Friedman, R.C., Bucci, W., Christopher, C., Drucker, P. and Garrison, W.B. III (1998), "Private psychotherapy patients of psychiatrist psychoanalysts", *American Journal of Psychiatry*, 155(12):1772–1774.

Gann, E. (2002), "What the 2001 Practice Survey means to you", *American Psychoanalyst*, 36(1):37–38.

Gill, M. (1979), "The analysis of the transference", *Journal of the American Psychoanalytic Association*, 27(supplement):263–288.

Gill, M. (1984), "Psychoanalysis and psychotherapy: A revision", *International Review of Psychoanalysis*, 11:161.

Glover, E. (1955), *The Technique of Psychoanalysis*, International University Press, New York.

Grinberg, L. (1964), "Two kinds of guilt – Their relations with normal and pathological aspects of mourning", *International Journal of Psychoanalysis*, 45:366–371.

Grinberg, L. (1992), "Countertransference and projective counteridentification", *Contemporary Psychoanalysis*, 15:226–247.

Hinshelwood, R. (1991), *A Dictionary of Kleinian Thought*, Free Association Books, London.

Hunter, V. (1993), "An interview with Hanna Segal", *Psychoanalytic Review*, 80(1):1–28.

Joseph, B. (1960), "Some characteristics of the psychopathic personality", *International Journal of Psychoanalysis*, 41:526.

Joseph, B. (1982), "Addiction to near-death", *International Journal of Psychoanalysis*, 63:449.

Joseph, B. (1983), "On understanding and not understanding: Some technical issues", *International Journal of Psychoanalysis*, 64:291.

Joseph, B. (1993), "A factor militating against psychic change: Nonresonance", in *Psychic Structure and Psychic Change: Essays in Honor of Robert S. Wallerstein M.D.*, edited by M. Horowitz, O. Kernberg, and E. Weinshel, International Universities Press, Madison, CT, pp. 311–325.

Karon, B. (2003), "Abstractions, the psychoanalytic escape from psychoanalysis: Ferenczi's 'For Example' revisited", *The Psychoanalytic Review*, 90(3):363–379.

Kernberg, O. (1987), "Projection and projective identification: Developmental and clinical aspects", *Journal of the American Psychoanalytic Association*, 35:795–819.

Kernberg, O. (1988), "Object relations theory in clinical practice", *Psychoanalytic Quarterly*, 57:481–504.

Kernberg, O. (1999), "Psychoanalysis, psychoanalytic psychotherapy, and supportive psychotherapy: Contemporary controversies", *International Journal of Psychoanalysis*, 80(6):1075–1091.

Kernberg, O. (2003), Conference on *Psychoanalysis and Its Discontents*, San Francisco Psychoanalytic Institute, Berkeley, CA.

Klein, M. (1926), "The psychological principles of early analysis", in *Love, Guilt, and Reparation and Other Works 1921–1945, The Writings of Melanie Klein*, Vol. 1, Free Press, New York.

Klein, M. (1935), "A contribution to the psychogenesis of manic-depressive states", in *Envy and Gratitude and Other Works 1946–1963, The Writings of Melanie Klein*, Vol. 3, Free Press, New York.

Klein, M. (1936), "Weaning", in *Envy and Gratitude and Other Works 1946–1963, The Writings of Melanie Klein*, Vol. 3, Free Press, New York.

Klein, M. (1946), "Notes on some schizoid mechanisms", in *Envy and Gratitude and Other Works 1946–1963, The Writings of Melanie Klein*, Vol. 3, Free Press, New York, 1–24.

Klein, M. (1950), "On the criteria for the termination of a psychoanalysis, in *Envy and Gratitude and Other Works 1946–1963, The Writings of Melanie Klein*, Vol. 3, Free Press, New York.

Klein, M. (1952a), "The origins of transference", in *Envy and Gratitude and Other Works 1946–1963, The Writings of Melanie Klein*, Vol. 3, Free Press, New York.

Klein, M. (1952b), "Some theoretical conclusions regarding the emotional life of the infant", in *Envy and Gratitude and Other Works 1946–1963, The Writings of Melanie Klein*, Vol. 3, Free Press, New York.

Klein, M. (1957), "Envy and gratitude", in *Envy and Gratitude and Other Works 1946–1963, The Writings of Melanie Klein*, Vol. 3, Free Press, New York.

Kunst, J. (2002), "Lessons from MacGyver: Working psychoanalytically under less than optimal conditions", *Bulletin of the Menninger Clinic*, 66(2):145–165.

Kutter, P. (1992), *Psychoanalysis International, A Guide to Psychoanalysis Throughout the World*, Vols 1 and 2, Frommann-Holzboog, Stuttgart.

Lafarge, L. (2000), "Interpretation and containment", *International Journal of Psychoanalysis*, 81(1):67–84.

Laplanche, J. and Pontalis, J.-B. (1973), *The Language of Psychoanalysis*, W.W. Norton and Company, New York.

Levenson, E. (1983), *The Ambiguity of Change: An Inquiry into the Nature of Psychoanalytic Reality*, Basic Books, New York.

Malcolm, R. (1986), "Interpretation: The past in the present", *International Journal of Psychoanalysis*, 13:433–441.

Malcolm, R. (1995), "The three 'W's': What, where and when: The rationale of interpretation", *International Journal of Psychoanalysis*, 76:447–456.

Malin, A. and Grotstein, J. (1966), "Projective identification in the therapeutic process", *International Journal of Psychoanalysis*, 47:26–31.

Meier, S. (1989), *The Elements of Counseling*, Brooks/Cole Publishing, Pacific Grove, CA.

Moore, B. and Fine, B. (1990), *Psychoanalytic Terms and Concepts*, The American Psychoanalytic Association and Yale University Press, New Haven, CT.

Morgan, M. (2001), "First contacts: The therapist's 'couples state of mind' as a factor in the containment of couples seen for consultation", in *Brief Encounters with Couples: Some Psychoanalytic Perspectives*, edited by F. Greer, Tavistock Marital Institute, Karnac, London, pp. 17–32.

Novick, J. (1988), "The timing of termination", *International Review of Psychoanalysis*, 15:307.

Oremland, J. (1991), *Interpretation and Interaction: Psychoanalysis or Psychotherapy?* Analytic Press, Hillsdale, NJ.

O'Shaughnessy, E. (1983), "Words and working through", *International Journal of Psychoanalysis*, 64:281–289.

O'Shaughnessy, E. (1990), "Can a liar be psychoanalyzed?", *International Journal of Psychoanalysis*, 71:187–195.

Pantone, P. (1994), "Projective identification: Affective aspects", *Contemporary Psychoanalysis*, 30:604–618.

Perlow, M. (1995), *Understanding Mental Objects*, Routledge, New York.

Pick, I. (1985), "Working through in the countertransference", *International Journal of Psychoanalysis*, 66:157.

Pyles, R. (2003), "The good fight: Psychoanalysis in the age of managed care", *Journal of the American Psychoanalytic Association*, 51(supplement):23–41.

De A Pado, M. (1980), "Neurotic and psychotic transference and projective identification", *International Journal of Psychoanalysis*, 7:157–164.

Quinodoz, D. (1994), "Interpretations in projection", *International Journal of Psychoanalysis*, 75:755–761.

Quinodoz, J.-M. (1993), *The Taming of Solitude: Separation Anxiety in Psychoanalysis*, Routledge, London.

Richards, A. (1997), "The relevance of frequency of sessions to the creation of an analytic experience", *Journal of the American Psychoanalytic Association*, 45:1241–1251.

Rosenfeld, H. (1958), "Contribution to the discussion on variations in classical technique", *International Journal of Psychoanalysis*, 39:238–239.

Rosenfeld, H. (1971a), "A clinical approach to the psychoanalytic theory of the life and death instincts: An investigation into the aggressive aspects of narcissism", *International Journal of Psychoanalysis*, 52:169.

Rosenfeld, H. (1971b), "Contributions to the psychopathology of psychotic states: The importance of projective identification in the ego structure of the psychotic patient", in *Problems of Psychosis*, edited by P. Doucet and C. Laurn, Excerpta Medica, Amsterdam, pp. 115–128.

Rosenfeld, H. (1975), "Negative therapeutic reaction", in *Tactics and Technique in Psychoanalytic Psychotherapy*, edited by P. Giovacchini, Vol. 2, Jason Aronson, New York, pp. 217–228.

Rosenfeld, H. (1983), "Primitive object relations and mechanisms", *International Journal of Psychoanalysis*, 64:261–267.

Rothstein, A. (1994), "A perspective on doing a consultation and making the recommendation of analysis to a prospective analysand", *Psychoanalytic Quarterly*, 63(4):680–695.

Schafer, R. (1994), "The contemporary Kleinians of London", *Psychoanalytic Quarterly*, 63:409–432.

Schafer, R. (1997), *The Contemporary Kleinians of London*, Internaitonal Universities Press, New York.

Schafer, R. (2002), "You can get here from there", *Psychoanalytic Inquiry*, 22(1):29–42.

Schwartz, C. (2003a), "A brief discourse on psychotherapy and psychoanalysis: Historical perspectives", *Psychoanalytic Review*, 90(2):153–178.

Schwartz, C. (2003b), "A brief discussion on frequency of sessions and the impact upon psychoanalytic treatment", *Psychoanalytic Review*, 90(2):179–192.

Segal, H. (1962), "The curative factors in psychoanalysis", *International Journal of Psychoanalysis*, 18(4–5):212–217.

Segal, H. (1974), *Introduction to the Work of Melanie Klein*, Basic Books, New York.

Segal, H. (1983), "Some clinical implications of Melanie Klein's work – Emergence from narcissism", *International Journal of Psychoanalysis*, 64:269.

Segal, H. (1993), "On the clinical usefulness of the concept of the death instinct", *International Journal of Psychoanalysis*, 74:55.

Segal, H. (1997), "On the clinical usefulness of the concept of the death instinct", in *Psychoanalysis, Literature, and War: Papers 1972–1995*, Brunner-Routledge, Hove, pp. 17–26.

Smaldino, A. (1991), "Psychoanalytic approaches to addiction", in *Current Issues in Psychoanalytic Practice: Monograph of the Society for Psychoanalytic Training*, No. 3, Brunner/Mazel, New York.

Spillius, E.B. (1988), *Melanie Klein Today, Volume 2: Mainly Practice*, Routledge, New York.

Spillius, E.B. (1993), "Varieties of envious experience", *International Journal of Psychoanalysis*, 74:1199.

Spillius, E.B. (1997), "Self-envy: Therapy and the divided inner world", *International Journal of Psychoanalysis*, 78:1254.

Stein, R. (1990), "A new look at the theory of Melanie Klein", *International Journal of Psychoanalysis*, 71:49.

Steiner, J. (1987), "The interplay between pathological organizations and the paranoid–schizoid and depressive positions", *International Journal of Psychoanalysis*, 68:69–80.

Steiner, J. (1991) "A psychotic organization of the personality", *International Journal of Psychoanalysis*, 72:201–207.

Sulzberger-Wittenberg, I. (1970), *Psychoanalytic Insight and Relationships: A Kleinian Approach*, Routledge and Kegan Paul, London.

Teyber, E. (1988), *Interpersonal Process in Psychotherapy: A Guide for Clinical Training*, The Dorsey Press, Chicago.

Ursano, R. and Sonnenberg, S. (1991), *Psychodynamic Psychotherapy*, American Psychiatric Press, Washington, DC.

Vaslamatzis, G. and Rabavilas, A (2001), *The Edge of Experience: Borderline and Psychosomatic Patients in Clinical Practice*, Karnac, London.

Wallerstein, R. (2001), "Foreword", in *Psychoanalysis and Psychotherapy: The Controversies and the Future*, edited by S. Frisch, R.D. Hinshelwood, and J.M. Gauthier, Karnac, London, pp. xiii–xix.

Waska, R. (1998), "Projective identification: Some clinical considerations", *Journal of the American Academy of Psychoanalysis*, 25(3):439–454.

Waska, R. (1999), "Projective identification, countertransference, and the struggle for understanding over acting out", *Journal of Psychotherapy Practice and Research*, 8(2):155–161.

Waska, R. (2000), "The ideal patient and the realities of clinical work", *Journal of Contemporary Psychotherapy*, 30(4):381–399.

Waska, R. (2002), *Primitive Experiences of Loss: Working with the Paranoid–Schizoid Patient*, Karnac, London.

Waska, R. (2003), "A mixed bag: The realities of psychoanalytic practice", *American Journal of Psychoanalysis*, 63(1):49–67.

Waska, R. (2004), *Projective Identification: The Kleinian Interpretation*, Brunner-Routledge, Hove.

Widiger, T. and Francis, A. (1989), "Epidemiology, diagnosis, and comorbidity of borderline personality disorders", in *Review of Psychiatry*, Vol. 8, edited by R. Tasman, E. Hales, and A. Frances, American Psychiatric Press, Washington, DC, pp. 8–24.

Index

For Product Safety Concerns and Information please contact our EU representative GPSR@taylorandfrancis.com Taylor & Francis Verlag GmbH, Kaufingerstraße 24, 80331 München, Germany